WALKING UP THE RAMP

Gregory A. Humphrey

Walking up the Ramp

Gregory Allen Humphrey

Copyright 2013 by Gregory Allen Humphrey
ISBN 13.978-1491064078

All rights reserved
Self-published in the United States of America by Gregory A. Humphrey

Gregory A. Humphrey
geggolopry@charter.net
http://dekerivers.wordpress.com/

Book layout by Michael Bricknell

Cover photo: Under the 'reading oak' on the front lawn of my childhood home, where as a boy I lived the adventures of Ian Fleming's' James Bond, was a peaceful spot. The white fence served as the backdrop to Mom's brightly colored flowers. Winds from the southwest brought thunderheads in summer, and stinging blasts of snow come winter.

This book is dedicated to those who encouraged me to tell my story:

> *Mom, who in the family kitchen reminded me of my love of books, told me to write my own;*
>
> *Dad, who never failed to drive me to the library on Friday nights when I was a boy, shared the gift of story-telling;*
>
> *Uncle Bob and Aunt Evie, who while seated on the sofa in their home, gave me the confidence I needed to undertake a book project;*
>
> *And, Uncle Dale and Aunt Lorene, who over a lasagna dinner, urged me onwards.*

When it comes to writing, scores are far more artful with words, and the turn of a phrase. None, however, had kinder people to buoy the spirit when it was needed than me.

> *"A lake is the landscape's most beautiful and expressive feature. It is earth's eye; looking into which the beholder measures the depth of his own nature".*
>
> —*Henry David Thoreau*

Prologue

Three New England-blue Adirondack chairs sit peaceably out on our front lawn. One for me. One for James. And, the third is for the friend, old or yet-to-be, who walks by and cares to chat for a while. The southerly facing chairs, carefully arranged under the watchful regard of a waving American flag, overlook Lake Monona whose waters lap at the rocks along the beach roughly seventy footsteps from our front stoop. These chairs in their elegant simplicity have afforded us many hours of silent reading, calm introspection, as well as lively banter, and hearty laughter. This is the spot where eclectic neighborhood conversations erupt around coffee in the daytime, or wine served up with friends around the fire pit when the sun sets.

For me, these chairs are a special place where I can escape to read a good book with a cup of Joe, and understand that regardless of what else is going on in my life, there is always a serene and reflective part of the world to call my own. The openness and freedom that the unobstructed lake view provides me makes the problems of life drift away. For one of the women on our street, our Adirondack chairs represent renewal and springtime itself; she knows that spring has arrived when the chairs come out, the cushions are neatly arranged, and the two of us are seated upon them. For me though, these three summertime settees occupy the center of my home life and I find them to be a tonic for the soul.

The ever-present lake breezes even on the hottest of afternoons, glimmering sunshine off the water, the sailboats floating along, and the cawing of the seagulls is really a way to commune with God through Nature. The lake has many moods from the smooth-as-glass blue to the white-capped choppy feisty side that demands to be noticed. Sitting and gazing at the lake is a daily ritual, a part of replenishing the soul and living. Even when the chill of fall sets in I can still be seen wearing a warm jacket hunched to the wind while reading a book. My better half, James, has 'more sense' and knows when to give in to Mother Nature and reads inside on cold days.

Over the decades of my life, I have always had special places where I could go to relax, read, and ponder life. As a boy there was the large tree in the front yard near the flower garden. On rainy days it was either inside my room, or tucked into a chair in the living room. In my teenage years, I found solace behind the row of pine trees that framed our home, or up in the woods where the scent of humus filled the air. As a young adult while working in radio there was a place along the shores of Lake Michigan that had my name on it. Later, when in Madison, I could often be found at a wonderful coffee shop that was tucked into a bookstore. But since late 2007, the place where I feel most serene and reflective is on our front lawn, sitting in our Adirondack chairs looking out on to Lake Monona. I know this is where I belong in those times when I sit there alone; or better yet, I know I am home when, with James alongside me, I put the newspaper or book aside, and gaze off into the distance over the ever-changing hues of the lake. This is where I find peace. This is the place that allows the softest of gentle thoughts and memories to rush over me.

It is on our lawn, amidst the flowers and the still-maturing trees that I often think about my days of childhood, the uncertainties of being a young adult, the valleys and mountains of my life. It is there that I feel deeply the sense of serenity that carries me through most days. It is there that I count my blessings, smile at the memories that shine again demanding to be recalled. It is there on the lawn that I grow wistful for the faces that have passed and know are never coming back.

Out on our lawn, sitting in one of those three New England-blue Adirondack chairs, I often repeat to myself a silent prayer, the same prayer with which upon waking I start out each day:

Dear God, thank you for this day.
Thank you for my life;
Thank you for letting me be alive;
Thank you for letting me live life.
Walk with me today and plant my feet
In the path you would have me take.
Let me be a light for others.

My life is not unique in any way, or memorable for any great feat. It blends and harmonizes with countless others. Yet, there is a story to be told of my dreams as a slim kid in a rural area who desperately wanted to live life on my own terms. I am finally ready to tell that tale. To get to that point in my life, though, I first needed to beat back the many negative voices and experiences from my high school years, somehow find my own sense of purpose, and discover a new level of self-confidence. I, that slim kid from a rural area, so very much longed to be a part of the larger world that I knew existed 'out there'. I just needed to find that way to connect with it.

It was not easy making my way forward. I always felt when young that one lyric by country singer Bill Anderson seemed to fit my life: "You don't see, and you can't feel the wind that's blowing at my back, and saying 'Move boy'".

Where my peers had muscle and brawn to shove their way through the world, I needed extra doses of grit and determination to make sure my dreams came true. I required the development of a strong sense of self to succeed in the world. It took time for me to realize that it was the harshness of my high school years that allowed my adult chin never to fail to be lifted in times of adversity. I grew to have the confidence and pluck to follow my dreams and live authentically.

This book is then part of my story, and how I came to be a man I really like. It is also the story of my Mom and Dad who instilled values and lessons that weave their way into the decisions that guide me still. While it is not a history of their lives it does underscore how the values they imparted to me as a boy comfortably mix with the progressive ideals that comprise my life today. Through it all, I feel a continuing comfort in the themes from my childhood still playing out in my adult life.

I write this book to tell my story. Am I writing for my own cathartic needs? Do I write this to model to some other slender kid in some other small town facing bullying or some other seemingly insurmountable hurdle that there is reason to place hope in the future? Am I writing to show that we need not cast off the better parts of our past just to move beyond the rough times? Yes, to all of that. I will make no apologies for being nostalgic or sentimental. I will speak plainly and from the heart, as I know my journey better than any other.

More importantly, I am interested in your story too. When people ask us from time to time why we have three blue Adirondack chairs sitting out on our front lawn, I tell them: One for me. One for James. And, the third is for you, my friend. Come. Sit with us. Chat for a while. Share your story with us. Share in some peace.

Gregory A. Humphrey
July 2013

Acknowledgments

When starting this book project I had two goals in mind.

First, I wanted to write my story in a manner that was honest and respectful. After fifty years, I felt it was time to put into print some of the experiences, both good and bad, which had shaped the contours of my life.

Secondly, I wanted the final product to resemble the type of books I would either thumb through or read as a boy. I wanted that old-time style of manuscript, along with calligraphic flourishes that made books come alive once the cover was cracked.

I was greatly aided with the assistance of three people who made my journey into writing this first book far easier than it otherwise would have been.

James R. Wilson was more than an editor during this project. In addition to being my partner in life, he is my best friend as he listened endlessly to my ideas and questions over months of writing and rewriting. He kept me grounded when I was pushing up against my self-imposed deadlines.

Michael Bricknell allowed for the text to meet the 'old-fashioned' quality standard that I had envisioned for my book. "I want this to look the way you want it" was more than words, but the way he used his talents to fashion the final product. His assistance and friendship over the months has been invaluable, and deeply appreciated.

Melissa, a fellow blogger who writes *TexasTrailerParkTrash*, and also who knows the mountains and valleys of writing and publishing a book provided much needed guidance and insight into how to get my book into the hands of readers all around the globe. She is another shining example of what 'paying it forward' means, and I am most thankful for her words of encouragement.

At the end of any author's acknowledgments comes the part about any shortcomings in the book being the full ownership of the one who has the name on the cover. That would be me. I trust I have done justice to those who have been a part of my story, and that the text is spirited and meaningful for those who read it.

Gregory A. Humphrey

"Nobody will ever write a book, probably, about my mother. Well, I guess all of you would say this about your mother -- my mother was a saint."

—President Richard M. Nixon,
August 9, 1974

Table of Contents

Dedication

Prologue

Acknowledgements

Walking up the Ramp..1
    WDOR Sturgeon Bay, Wisconsin 2
    My Life as "Trevor James" 5
    Dad's Silver Timepiece 6
    Reports from Egg Harbor 8
    Sunday Morning Get Up and Go Show 10
    Charlie's passing...13
    What?! No TV? 15
    DXing and the Hobby Listener 17
    'We Shield Millions'..23
    Worthy of Admiration..27
    Politics as News 31
    Plus Ça Change...35
    Dreams Never Die 38

1,268 Square Feet..41
    Neat-Nookedness 43
    A Hearty Boiled Dinner 46
    Reading Down Main Street...49
    Monday is Wash Day 53
    The Party Line 56
    Java and Journalists 58
    Starting Out 65
    All in the Family 69
    The Old Barn 71
    Reading Nooks 75
    Tree Hugging 78
    Mail Call 80
    Leaving that Place Called HOME 82

Exit Strategy..93

Illustrations... 121

Lary (With one 'R') 139
    Making Political Moxie 141
    Door County Chair... 147
    Everyone Includes Everyone... 149
    First Days... 150
    These Women Missed the Seneca Falls Convention 153
    "Elvis has left the building!" 154
    Vice-Presidential Visit 159
    Pressing the Flesh... 164
    Ted Kennedy, Legend 167
    Supreme Court Justice Shirley Abrahamson............... 168
    The Campaign Trail 169
    Every Four Years 172
    Process (and Compensation) Matter 174
    Constituents' Best Friend.. 178
    Make Each Day Count 180

Feel that Breeze! 183
    Simmering Bean Soup 184
    Red Skies at Night 186
    Listening to the Corn Grow 189
    Cozy Indoor Days... 192
    The Fierce Intensity of Storms................................... 193
    Be Prepared!.. 195
    Small Green Suitcase.. 201
    Keeping the Home Fires Burning............................... 203
    Rules for Enjoying a Good Storm 206
    A Last-Minute Confession 207

Paying it Forward 209
    A New Job.. 209
    Finding the Right Way to Say Thank You 211
    Life-Long Learning.. 215
    They Deserve Better 221
    Pushing toward a Brighter Light................................ 225

A Shared Road.. 229
    The American Dream 233
    Meeting James... 236
    9/11 245
    The Move to Madison 247
    Familial Traditions.. 252

Groundhog's Day 253
Christmas Wonderland 255
Show me your Garden 257

Epilogue 261

Appendix 265
DXing in Hancock, Wisconsin 266
Dinner with Mom 268
Anti-Bullying, Suicide Prevention
and LGBT Youth Resources 274
Hancock Public Library 276
James' Poetry 277

Index 281

Colophon 292

About the Author 293

> *"In radio, they say, nothing happens until the announcer says it happens"*
>
> —*Ernie Harwell*

Walking up the Ramp

Elvis Presley disappeared from Graceland on August 16, 1977. He was forty-two years old. Dan Sears of Memphis radio station WMPS made the first official announcement, and his was the first station to interrupt its programming with the terrible notice. Sears had just finished up his broadcast in mid-afternoon, and was taking a commercial break before he was to end the news segment with a short stock market report. While the commercial aired, he was handed a note that stated that Elvis Presley had died. The hospital itself had called the station; Sears would be the first broadcaster to break the story.

As the day progressed in to nighttime, we would learn 'The King' had been found slumped over in his home by his girlfriend, Ginger Alden, and the paramedics had failed to revive him. Presley was officially pronounced dead at the Baptist Memorial Hospital in Memphis by physician Dr. George Nichopoulos. The cause given: erratic heartbeat, or cardiac arrhythmia.

Only five short years later, shortly before five o'clock in the evening, August 16, 1982, I felt a sort of tightness in my chest, an anxiety that had accompanied me that entire day when I went on the radio as an announcer for the first time. I parked my marine-blue Chevette in the parking lot of the small cinder block-constructed station house, got out, dusted myself off, and prepared to go inside. Upon entering the somewhat cluttered WDOR studio in Sturgeon Bay, Wisconsin that day, I went immediately to the record stacks. Rows and rows of vinyl records were all alphabetized according to the artists' names and were situated behind the console where I would sit to do my job. I scanned the collection quickly and settled on a recording by 'The King'.

I placed the record on the turntable, and spoke authoritatively to the station's listeners, my soon-to-be friends. I informed everybody listening in radioland that Elvis, 'The King', would "take us to news time at the top of the hour." The song ended. I gave the call letters for the station per the Federal Communications Commission, the FCC's requirements, and hit the button for ABC News. I breathed a sigh of relief.

So began my years in radio.

As I look back, the worst time in my broadcasting career was that first night on the job when I was left alone in the station. Already very anxious to make a great impression on the listeners, I felt so much tension and pressure. I wanted to—No; I needed to let the station owner know that he had indeed made a good choice when he hired me as the newest voice for the station.

I sat alone in the WDOR studio on that Monday evening, and my hands were full. The main studio console served both AM and FM broadcast transmissions. On the AM station, 910 on the dial, President Reagan was streaming live via satellite from the ABC network from the Oval Office about taxes and the budget. On the 93.9 FM side of the dial, adult contemporary music was normally played, but on this night, we were transmitting the Milwaukee Brewers' baseball game.

Just to the left of the main console was a huge automated machine that contained giant-sized reel-to-reel tapes that provided music for the bulk of the FM programming day. In those days, advertisements were recorded on a cartridge, akin to an eight-track tape, and were then placed in two large tape carousels, next to the music tapes. A side console on that machine allowed for the preprogrammed timing and placement of the ads each hour.

I needed to juggle placing ads into the right slots for the breaks during the game. I had to simultaneously listen to the ABC Radio network and record to audiotape the commercials from the regular newscasts, which we were not carrying due to Reagan and the Brewers game. We were still required to air those advertisements later that night.

The studio seemed overly hot as I juggled all the various parts of the job; I was fully aware that management was monitoring me, and that just about anything could go awry, given all that was taking place.

As I sweat it out in the studio, my mind turned to the dark side. When I was in broadcasting school I had read *The Camera Never Blinks*, Dan Rather's amusing account of his early career in broadcasting. One story from his days in radio encapsulated perfectly for me those feelings of dread that I was having, those tremors about how far things could go wonky when I was on the air.

The famed CBS broadcaster tells of the Sunday morning sermons that came to the station on long-play albums. One Sunday, Rather put one of these sermons on the turntable to play, and knew he had enough time to head into town for some food, and still get back before the album was concluded. After making his purchase and returning to his vehicle, he turned the car radio on and heard what must have sounded like a terrific mathematical improbability, if not impossibility.

The record had a flaw, and the needle had started skipping backwards, repeating the same phrase over and over on the air. One might think that was the worst of it, but alas no. There was more. Not just any phrase assaulted sensibilities over the airwaves emanating from that Huntsville radio station. What the faithful listeners of Texas heard that morning was nothing less than a brimstone preacher shouting, "Go to hell... Go to hell... Go to hell!"

I shuddered at the thought of something similar happening to me. What I didn't fully realize, of course, was that my turn was coming.

I knew from the weather reports throughout that August summer afternoon that severe thunderstorms for the Door Peninsula were promised. I always loved a good storm so silently in my heart I prayed for a little magic that evening. I felt deeply that any storm would only enhance the experience. I knew that a good clack or two of thunder, maybe a nice down pour, or even some lightning would help me to settle in to my task, make me more comfortable, to excel.

Indeed, my admiration for Mother Nature represents a lifelong fondness. Whatever She had thrown our way while I was growing up in central Wisconsin was just fine with me; I loved it all. Be it the summer theatrics of light displays and rhythmic booms or the blinding winter snows and biting frigid cold, I would never have offered complaint.

On that fifth anniversary of 'The King's disappearance', the forecasters were correct. My first night flying solo at the station the storm clouds gathered and lowered shortly after seven o'clock, activating the street lights earlier than usual. I could see from my console through the back door of the studio that the sky was electric. The lightning that night was spectacular, dancing across the horizon. The thunder's studio-rocking booms seemed to become more numerous, and closer... My adrenaline rushed. This was going to be my night. Clack!

Then I was off the air!

Just like that, there was no signal being transmitted from our station. Electrical power was flowing to the station but our signal was no longer being emitted from the tower. While I knew how to shut down the station at the end of a broadcasting day, having been trained in that since the previous Friday when I arrived at WDOR, I had no information whatsoever about how to turn the power on. It seems it would have been a simple task to just reverse the shut off procedures and restart our transmission. It wasn't necessarily.

I frantically sought to discover that elusive but useful piece of information, which had not been passed along to me in my training. I did not want to do anything to cause damage to the machines. Was there some other order in which the buttons had to be pushed, and the levers activated to make it all happen? As I struggled to get back on the air, I also started to comprehend a strange quirk among radio listeners.

Back home when the power went off due to a storm, we logically called the electric company, and alerted them to the problem. Who would have guessed that listeners would call a radio station to alert announcers they were off the air? Did people really think broadcasters at a studio would not know when they were no longer transmitting something over the airwaves? Grateful for the help, did I really need the extra stress of answering the phone? The five telephone lines lit up before me. Five little orange buttons on the face of the telephone blinked frenetically, and I was suddenly fielding calls from very well-intentioned people. "Yes, thank you for your call. We are indeed experiencing a bit of technical difficulty. Things should be back to normal soon. Yes. I appreciate your call. Do have a good evening. Hello. WDOR. Yes, thank you for your call..." At the same time, I was of course trying to figure what was to be done to set things back on course. I felt a nervous sweat trickle down my back.

After about 20 minutes an orange Corvette sped into the parking lot and the program director, the station owner's son, entered through the back door of the studio. He sputtered as to why we were off the air. To be very honest, I listened, and thought the interrogation to be a trick series of questions akin to seeing a person typing and asking what was taking place. Was it not obvious why I was just sitting in the studio and talking to most of our audience via the phone?

The program director seemed to imply that turning our transmitter back on was somehow an intuitive process with which everyone comes equipped. He soon discovered that what he felt was inherently evident was not at all the case. He stood behind me, drenched by the storm's rains, and pushed all the right buttons in just the right order and resumed our broadcasts. The AM station would have been on the brink of going off the air for the night, the FM station's game would have resumed as if nothing had happened, and I would have thanked graciously all those phone callers still lighting up my five phone buttons. The station owner's son, well I suspect he went home, and poured himself a well-deserved drink.

While on the air at WDOR I used a pseudonym, 'Trevor James'. I had carefully chosen the moniker as a way not only to keep separate my personal and professional lives but also as a way to fulfill a promise made to a very special someone in my life.

My nephew, Trevor, was a remarkable boy. He had a pleasant personality, and a most winning smile. He was always so pleased when someone had a little more faith in him than he had in himself. I tried always to extend that extra assurance to him. Trevor had a certain look in his big blue eyes when he wanted to join in some game or participate in another group's activity. That was perhaps the softest that I have ever experienced. It was, to say the least, irresistible. I couldn't help but encourage Trevor.

Trevor, who was eleven years my younger, knew that I intended to study at a broadcasting school. We joked about my being on the air, and he suggested that it would be fun to hear his own name on the radio someday. We laughed about it in silly ways over the months before I left home. When it came time to select my on-air name, no doubt remained as to how it would start--Trevor. The 'James' part came from my liking Sonny James, a country singer I continue to enjoy. 'Trevor James', then, was created, and my nephew was so pleased.

I very much enjoyed having the new name, and the freedom it afforded me as an on-air personality. I wanted that sense of personal detachment and distance for my work personae. That is to say I did not have an alias as a boy when I would 'play radio'. I still listen to some of the old tapes made from that small WDOR studio at the corner of 15th and Utah. They are good memories, but I realize that there are some classic moments missing from my radio days. Those early 'radio' performances, delivered live from my bedroom, were top quality. Sadly, they were never taped. They can only be played in my perfectly chronometered memory.

Indeed, I developed in those early days a system for perfect timing and pace for myself as I strove to make my own newscasts sound believable from the bedroom I occupied. It was hard work. I was my own copy editor and producer in those days. In short, I had to be a jack-of-all-trades in my early attempts at broadcast excellence.

My Dad came from that generation where his work-uniform pants had a small pocket about two inches wide and equally as deep where a watch could be slipped. Out in the back entry of our home on the top shelf alongside where his work cap would rest, he would place his pocket watch at the end of his workday.

Dad's silver-colored timepiece was not a fancy watch with any chain, though it did have a bow. There was no swing-out case to make it showy. It was just a plain utilitarian unit that told the time. (I cannot say precisely what happened to Dad's old watch. It was no longer available for me during the probate process.) While I do not have the physical object, I know that I carry the best part of that watch within me--that is to say of course the impeccable sense of timing it helped me to develop. Tick. Tock. Tick. Tock. That time piece marked out the seconds like a metronome, helping me, the 'boy broadcasting wonder', to keep accurate time for my newscasts.

The *Stevens Point Journal*, arriving six days a week in the mailbox, provided copy for my news stories, sports updates, weather forecasts, and even ad copy. A few times a week, starting around the time of the Nixon resignation, I would put together my own version of a long-form newscast. Of course, I could paint the picture of me in an idyllic setting in which to work: lying on my belly on the bed in my room, my feet kicking up behind me, a yellow legal pad and pen in hand, setting myself to the task of creating. In reality though, I worked hunched over more like Dickens' Bob Cratchit. I would pull the green faux leather hassock that my parents kept in the living room or near the telephone in the dining room in next to my bed and fashion it into a stool. Seated as comfortably as I could manage atop the little leather cube, I could read aloud my text directly from the paper, or make notes on the yellow legal pad resting on my bed. Not only was my back toward the door and all outside distractions, but since I am a lefty, you would see me turned toward the bed from that side, further obstructing my view of the rest of the house. I took to the task of reading quality material very seriously. It was a professional job. I even read from the obituaries to let my devoted listeners know of the lives of their friends and neighbors. I had to really. It was industry standard. When I was a boy, many of the local radio stations read aloud of the sad passing of this or that person in town. My newscasts were serious in every way, and exceeded local expectations.

Over time, this routine played out on my bed so often that I was really starting to get a feel for timing. Advertisers during my 'reports' benefitted from either thirty seconds or "if the merchant wanted to pay top dollar" the sixty-second version. I used Dad's pocket watch to time everything, and it paid off. Those early broadcasts from my bedroom really simplified my life when I was actually earning a paycheck, and operating behind a veritable microphone, and studio console.

Broadcasting isn't all about the ad revenue, though. It is a complicated business, and it has its own lingo, which has to be learned. As I grew older, and could be left alone on weekends, I would get out the record player, and find out precisely how much 'ramp' time there was from the first musical note of a song to the first word. Then I would use the watch to time introductions to the piece. An initial presentation might include the time of day, current outdoor temperature, and other banter until *BAM!* The moment I stopped talking, the lyrics to the song began. This process is known as "walking up the ramp". (For the sake of precision, let me make just one comment on the notion of "walking up the ramp". I have always referred to this practice of talking over the musical opening to a record as "walking up the ramp". I started out in radio with that term decades ago, and continue to speak of it that way. But, does the action have another name? Others refer to it as "hitting the post", or as Johnnie Putman who for many years worked at WGN refers to it as "kissing the post"—the post being of course the first bit of vocalization in the music. Since I have always called it "walking up the ramp" instead, I will not change how I write of it. The wording is now part of my life story.)

Even now as James and I drive along in the car, listening to the radio, I still walk up the ramp to a song I know. Without fail, a smile lights up James' face as I ad-lib my way with an oldie, and nail it perfectly. He even moans, "Ohhhhh! Listen to you!" when I fall short of my goal due to lack of practice. He laughs and we keep driving, an average of two to four minutes more, until the next song comes on the air. "If only Gregory had a money-making skill" is the way James smilingly makes mention of this strange ability to others when we talk about radio.

The listeners who would call into the studio while I was on the air were often faceless characters who provided information, and flavor for the listening audience. Let me give you an example. Were snowstorms to have occurred while I was on the air, there would have been a flurry of contact with listeners. First, there would have been the usual report from the local police about the road conditions, urging caution with the slick streets. I would have listened, and yawned as I had heard if many times before, but thought to myself that the well-intentioned law enforcement official did not provide the type of information I wanted.

Rather, I would wait for the man who called himself 'the Egg Harbor Reporter' to dial me up and give some gripping account of how a car nearly wiped out at the curve where he lived, or how many inches had stacked up on his mailbox. (The Egg Harbor Reporter performed his job earnestly. I can still hear his slow deadpan delivery of the information he called to share.)

Egg Harbor Reporter: "Hey Trevor, it is coming down mighty heavy right now."

Me: "It is snowing huge flakes here, too."

Egg Harbor Reporter: "The dog wanted to go outside but once I opened the door he only was interested in being outside for a minute. I can't blame him. I cannot even see the bird feeder up in the tree; it is blowing so hard. Have the scanner on and there are lots of slide-offs. Today is when you want to have a wrecker service." With that he would give a hearty chuckle. "Say, what happens if you cannot make it home and have to stay at the station?"

Me: "I call in the military for an airdrop of food!"

Egg Harbor Reporter: "You have any Kenny Rogers handy to play for me?"

Me: "With or without Dolly?"

Egg Harbor Reporter: "Well everything is better with Dolly."

Me: "Will do. Let me know if things get really interesting up your way."

The Egg Harbor Reporter was a clear favorite of mine, and often had a song request. I am not sure the man ever slept, as he had a reason to call and chat about the weather every chance he got, and I must say he was highly entertaining. He wasn't the only one, though. I also loved to hear from the folks on Sunday when snow piled up who had made it over the 'Brussels' Hill' in Southern Door County as they came back from church but wanted me to alert others to take another route.

Perhaps the best account of the local streets in Sturgeon Bay came from the lady who from time to time delivered a baked good from her oven to me at the station as she went to church. She would pop into the back door of the studio, thank me for the Southern gospel music I played starting at six o'clock in the morning, update me on the streets in winter, and drop off some wonderful sweet. Some people are nice to the person who delivers their morning paper, but she appreciated her local neighborhood radio announcer. She made many of my early Sunday mornings so much more satisfying.

I wish I had a way to get in touch with my 'baked good friend' today—to place an order! She often baked a tart-like crusty creation that had the four corners brought together with a fruit filled center, and then sprinkled powdered sugar over the top. Who doesn't like sweets? But the fact she drove to the station to drop them off meant that I was connecting with people over the airwaves. I was not sitting at their table, or talking with them over the backyard fence. I was communicating to them, and connecting with them on some level that mattered—and all through the radio. The key to broadcasting, I had felt as I listened to my radio friends as a teenager, was making that very real and very personal connection with people. I was able to replicate that with listeners in Door County. That meant a great deal to me.

Of all the media available, radio is the one medium that allows us to truly be close to one another. The 'intimacy of radio', as I like to call it, is felt in no greater degree by listeners than when it takes place from a small locally-owned radio station, with a local neighborhood announcer behind the microphone. While I was on the air, I always thought of myself as just a broadcaster from the neighborhood who tried to inform, entertain, and be companionable.

Farmers outside of town wanted to know when to bale the hay; parents wondered how to dress the kids for school. Fishermen hoped to discover the best time to find bites; workers cheered their favorite team to a win as they worked late-night shifts. And, everyone tuned in when there was news of an accident claiming the life of someone from the county. I was not broadcasting to the faceless masses, but to the guys I saw at the filling station. My audience was the lady at the deli who always treated me really nicely when preparing my large sandwich that I would pick up as I was on the way to the station. My listeners included the person who handed me my newspaper at the bookstore.

In fact, whenever I sat behind the microphone to begin my broadcast, I had the impression that I was talking to just one person. Yet, it is that mindset that allowed me to be effective at my job. That level of intimacy between those who were tuning in to my show, and how I felt about them in return is what permitted me to connect with people as though we were conversing together, even if I were the only one in the studio. I loved my job.

While there are no truly remarkable broadcasts that anyone will recall from my time at the station, I cherish my countless fond memories that resulted from Eddy Allen, Jr.'s decision to hire me for his broadcasting business. There are now only smiles and warm memories as I look back at those years at WDOR. My very DNA has me wired to be nostalgic. It was quite a thrill to be on the air to provide the latest winter storm updates, news headlines, and other events that people relied on as they went about their day. It was a real pleasure to gather news, write the story at a typewriter, and then report it with my 'outcue'.

When I took over the Sunday morning radio show, I was told to play inspirational music, and was offered suggestions--as if I seemed a heathen unaccustomed to religion. The selections offered to 'show me the way' included George Beverley Shea, and the Mormon Tabernacle Choir. While both of those had merit, if you resided in a poorly managed nursing home where the intent was to keep the old people in bed, then yes, those might have been just the ticket. But what would better suit the lady, previously mentioned, who from time to time delivered a baked good from her oven to me at the station on her way to church?

The proposed format I was to follow needed some sprucing up and I had a different idea about the tone of the show I wanted to create on Sunday mornings. I wanted something quite different for those hours when folks get up, start their day, and head to church. I was going to make their day start off on the up-tempo side. Just to be clear: when the broadcast day starts at 6:00 A.M., I think that there has to be a bit of verve to the music. I needed the extra 'umph' in my morning as much as the listeners. (Perhaps more so, as I am not a morning person. Not then. Certainly not now.)

My Mom was the one who had introduced me to high-spirited gospel music. Many a Sunday morning after we got television she would turn up Jimmy Swaggart as he pumped the piano (or, 'pie-anna' as she always pronounced it) and sing songs that had feeling and truth. Swaggart surely had his personal valleys, but there was no better Sunday music, it seemed to me as a boy, than that offered by his singers and band from his television program.

That first WDOR Sunday when I opened the broadcast day,

I pulled a selection of albums from the station's collection ranging from the Speer Family to the Oak Ridge Boys, from the Cathedrals to the gospel sounds of the Statler Brothers. I pulled from the shelves music from the Stamps Quartet, as well as the Blackwood Brothers. Things were going to heat up at the nursing home that day!

Many Sundays played out this way for me. I would stop at a small filling station on my way into work near the downtown bridge and get donuts. I would purchase a large coffee too, as I was never too keen on the condition of the coffee maker at the station. (The one I grew up with at home was always in very clean condition, and the one at the station was used by many, and never was in a condition such that I ever felt the strong desire to make a pot.) As a side note, the coffee maker sat in a small room with an old-fashioned pop machine. The soda machine had a lid that lifted, and the bottles slid along to one side and were able to be retrieved after depositing money. It was the type of machine I had seen in my childhood at filling stations in small towns, and was really quite homey to have at the station.

With a good dose of caffeine and "hit" of sugar in my system, I was ready to drop the needle on the first gospel song which would follow the news at the top of the hour. I had it all planned out. I would read a brief weather report which I would have ripped from the news teletype that had been printing off the satellite-feed overnight. Then the music would start.

I must say that I did a number of things during my tenure at WDOR but never did I have more feedback on anything than when it was discovered by a certain segment of the audience that Southern gospel music was not just going to be played every now and then, but almost completely on Sunday mornings during that roughly ninety minutes allotted to music. My listeners really seemed to enjoy the 'pick me up' music that got them in to the spirit as they headed to church. Others said that they just simply never heard that type of music on the radio all that often. It was welcomed all around. I don't recall that I had any detractors. The change in style seemingly upset no one.

As I rummaged through the recordings at the station, I came upon a glaring omission in the stack. Something would have to be done. There was not a single recording by the Happy Goodman Family. This group had some of the most uplifting, and spirited gospel music that had ever been recorded. They were largely considered one of the most popular, and significant gospel groups of the 1960s; so much so that in 1968 they proved the power of their genre when they won the first Grammy awarded for a gospel album by a gospel group. One of the leading voices of the group was that of Vestal Goodman who could lift the rafters off of a building when she started to sing. I knew one way or another that Vestal and her piano-playing husband, Howard, were going to be a part of Sunday mornings at the station.

How dismayed was I when I could not locate any music by them that first Sunday morning when I opened the station? The omission, it seemed to me, was unfathomable! So, off I headed that same week to Ace Records located on Main Street which was one of those (now) old-fashioned, and wonderful stores where anything on vinyl could be found, and if not in stock, it could be ordered and picked up in just a few days. I did a search of the possible selections and ordered a double-album set from a live concert, along with an album with some selections I knew contained just the type of sound I wanted. I paid for the albums with my own money, and still have the recordings, and play them at home on my turntable.

I still love the warmth of vinyl far more than the rather cold sound that seems to emanate from a CD. Even today, I follow a personal process when playing an album on my turntable. The album cover is first looked at and enjoyed, and perhaps any written material on the back of the jacket is read yet again. The album is taken from the paper sleeve that protects it, and dusted if warranted with a soft cloth and then set to play. When the needle touches the vinyl and aligns with a rotating groove, there is a soft sound. A second or two elapses before the music that is more rounded and rich sounding than that of a CD pours from the speakers, enveloping the ear as if it were a comforting blanket. Give me vinyl any day over a CD.

Back at WDOR, armed with my albums bought at Ace Records, I saw to it that Vestal Goodman hit the airwaves the following Sunday. There was no turning back. Vestal Goodman still remains one of my favorite gospel singers. At the time of great despair, the loss of a loved one, or times when I am feeling glum her musical styling, and vocals about truths unseen have always made a huge difference for me. (In 2003 at a *Homecoming Friends* concert in Champaign, Illinois, I was able to meet her, and even get a hug as she was slowly walking her way to the stage for the second half of the show which featured a sing-a-long with all the others groups. I hugged her, telling her I loved her, and in true southern style she said, "Bless you, darling.")

I never heard anything from station management about the more sprightly music, and think that on early Sunday mornings they were just glad that the transmitter was working. Probably more to the point, they loved it too. My listeners called, and wrote me notes and postcards with their strong approval. From time to time I would show up for work and posted on the bulletin board was a message of thanks and appreciation. That felt good, as the pay for any first time broadcasting job was quite limited. Part of the compensation, at least for me, was the side benefits. I felt quite rewarded by the approval of those who listened.

At the same time I ordered the Goodmans, I also purchased a live two-album concert recording of Swaggart. Fond memories of the mornings when my mother tapped her feet to the hand-clapping sounds of his music swept over me. The recording was just sitting there on the store racks. It was a bit of an impulse buy, but it too still gets spun on our home sound system. True to form, the volume goes up as the powerful notes from the piano are struck. Loud is just the way it is meant to be heard.

Being in our home makes it easy to reflect, and I think that is due to the considerable age of the house. This old Victorian almost demands that we put ourselves into another time and be conscious of the past. The same is true when it comes to the types of music towards which I gravitate. I enjoy most often the type of music that I listened to on the radio when I was growing up in Hancock.

In 2006 James and I had tickets to see a show in Wisconsin Dells. We had arrived a bit early and were glad that we did. Charlie Louvin and I were able to chat behind the Crystal Grand music theatre. Louvin took time to talk with me; he did not need to. Our short time together made an impression that lingers and stands out in my memory as if it all happened yesterday. Louvin was a great man.

Using my pen that I had brought along for him to sign my guitar, Louvin gave me his autograph and dated it with an "'06". We kept talking as he continued using that pen to provide autographs for others as they ambled along. I had asked him about the formative days when he and his brother, Ira, traveled the country.

Louvin was seventy-nine years-old at the time and had just released a new CD featuring a duet with Elvis Costello. (As an interesting side note, Louvin had also performed a number of shows with Elvis Presley in the 1950s). As we stood and chatted, Louvin smoked a few cigarettes and seemed to me to be caught up in his recollections. The longer he spoke the more nostalgic he seemed to become. It was clear he never got over the death of his brother.

Louvin spoke of how many weeks would end for the famous brothers as they made a mad dash from far-flung places to get back to "The Mother Church of Country Music", the Ryman Auditorium and their set for the Opry stage. To be a member of the Opry one had to perform twenty-six times a year, and was remunerated at fifteen dollars per appearance, a far cry from what could be made on the road. Charlie estimated that their Opry act lost them on average over fifty-thousand dollars per year. He was proud to be a part of the Opry and never complained.

The day Charlie Louvin died I sat in our living room and did what I suspect many classic country music fans around the country were doing. I played again the music of the legend I had met in the Dells. I suspect for many who lounged on a sofa that night the time spent with his albums was more a tribute to a singer than the need to relax and kick back in the early evening.

Decades ago I had placed Louvin's album on the record player of my youth and watched it spin countless times. As I listened again at the night of Louvin's death, the song lyrics flooded back, and certain notes struck deep and hard. (That is what music should do. Transport the listener somewhere else, outside of themselves.) The album *Baby, You've Got What It Takes* with Charlie Louvin and Melba Montgomery still evokes images and sounds from the days when Louvin was charting music, and being one of the anchors for the way classic country music was being recorded. He was one of the old standard bearers of a time when singers were really interested in their fans and made it to the top of the charts based on ability as opposed to slick promotional managing. I deeply respect that.

The album was one that my Mom had in her collection, having bought it about thirty-five years prior. One Saturday, a couple of years after her death, I gathered up all of Mom's albums and records and brought them home with me. They were after all more a connection between Mom and me than anyone else in the family. No one else either liked that music, or in my Dad's case with his hearing impairment had the ability to enjoy it anymore. I was very pleased to have the records in Madison with me.

Mom's old record player is one I can see in my mind. It was one of those where the speakers folded onto the top of the player and could be carried like a small suitcase. The player was never left out but always cared for meticulously. Mom folded the wires for the speakers in place and tucked it behind the sofa after each use.

The evening Charlie Louvin died, I sat and listened to the album spin. I imagined what Mom might say as *Don't Believe Me* played in surround sound. The deep sounds, piano chords and guitar licks make the song a country classic. She would have loved it. She would have enjoyed hearing it over the five speakers spread throughout the living room.

Charlie Louvin was one of those stars with true talent at showmanship, which is far different from just being a solid singer or musician with a great manager. He and his brother were two of the voices that started during the formative days of the Opry, creating music that still resonates. Almost to the end of his life Charlie Louvin was standing tall and proud on that round circle center stage at the Opry.

As the songs spun I thought about the memories music evokes for me. One singer out of Alabama with a desire to do more than pick cotton his whole life. A woman in Hancock, Wisconsin who liked music and picked up the singer's album at Tempo or Woolworth's on a Saturday shopping trip. A record player kept in pristine condition because it brought so much entertainment to the home. A kid who fell in love with the genre of music that speaks to the central components of life. And, all of this was being played over the radio airwaves.

My parents made some great decisions on my behalf when I was a child. One of the very best was not to have a television in our home during my formative years, those years when I was growing up. As a result, I learned to love to read. I consumed books of all types. All of that reading helped me to become the man I am today. I also discovered radio, and a special stage in Nashville where on Saturday nights the nation's longest running radio show is performed.

By the late 1960s, television was fast becoming omnipresent. New national traditions were being formed. If you think about it today, most everyone has seen at least one Rose Bowl Day Parade on television. Every aspect of the floats or marching bands can be seen in full color, a nice advancement over the black and white days of early television. It took a while to bring that level of technology to the rural areas, though. When it came time for an annual Christmas parade in Door County, one of the WDOR broadcasting staff provided a full color version through language for the listeners at home. The 'theatre of the mind' is always more powerful and inventive than any image that can be actually shown on television. A good book sets the stage, and tells a story in much the same way that radio does. Both allow us to use our minds to create the added aspects to the reality that the story's narrator recounts or that the radio broadcaster is announcing. Both are very personal experiences—no one will ever conjure the same images as the one's you have created for yourself. In that way, books and radio are very intimate activities, and can be proven to be the most special of media.

For all their similarities though, books and radio are not

quite the same. I make no apologies for having what many label as an old-fashioned and traditional view about radio. I was born in 1962, and I am very fortunate to be able to say that both books and radio were essential parts of my growing-up years, and that both remain a daily habit as an adult. I do also firmly believe that, more than a narrator, a radio broadcaster is a guest who is invited into someone's home or car. There is an ever-present sense of immediacy with radio, whether previously recorded or performed live. If that broadcaster is doing his or her job well, it will seem they are talking only to the person listening. There can be a bonding between an announcer and listener through radio that can be tighter and more complete than anything television can hope for, surpassing even at times the bond between book and reader.

As a youngster when my friends turned on television for entertainment, our family turned on the radio. When others wanted news and weather reports, they tuned in to a local TV channel; my parents tuned in WFHR from Wisconsin Rapids or WSPT from Stevens Point. It did not seem odd to me in the least; there was no television in our home until I was in the sixth grade.

There were times when my friends at school would talk about watching a certain show or event on TV, and I felt left out. Those feelings were never anything that lingered, and to be honest it did not occur that often. The only time I was truly embarrassed about the situation was when my fifth grade science teacher wanted everyone to watch a TV program, and come prepared to discuss it the following day. (The classroom was on the top floor of the large portion of the Hancock School where two adjoining classrooms had fire escapes that led out onto a large metal stairway. I always thought the fire prevention drills were the best when I was able to scale down the many steps of what seemed like a long descent.) I am not sure how I felt about the assignment, but when I clearly was not prepared for the class the following day the science teacher asked me why, and I told her. It seemed to me that she was purposely using her 'outdoor voice' when she informed me along with the entire class, "Well if I knew you did not have a TV you could have come and watched at my home."

I recall the looks from my fellow classmates as they turned in their seats. Some expressed quizzical facial expressions as if they thought having no television was like having no running water. Others simply sat there in disbelief. I really resented the manner in which the teacher handled the situation. She had no idea why we did not have a television, but her tone made it sound like we were poor. That tone just rubbed me the wrong way. In the intervening years since, as I have replayed this scene over in my head, I have concluded that I should have responded, "Well if I knew all you had was television at your home I would have loaned you some of our books!"

The newspaper kept my folks and me informed of what was going on in the world. Radio too was a part of our daily routine, and I still can recall rather precisely where I was when first hearing some breaking news stories over the airwaves.

For many years, tucked up on a shelf in the closet of my bedroom was a pillowcase-type sack that allowed for ease of storage for my sleeping bag. As a teenager, I used the sleeping bag as a top blanket, a comforter of sorts, when the nights were cold. As a child though, the sleeping bag allowed me to envision my own starry nights, camping inside the warm house. I must have spotted the sleeping bag in a Montgomery Ward or JC Penney Christmas catalog some previous year, and loved it. I would often find myself stuffed into my sleeping bag, lying on the gray-swirled design of the carpeted floor of our living room. The sleeping bag was obviously designed for kids who camped inside a warm house, as I was doing. With a dark blue background covered in red and white stars popping off in different directions, it was louder in design than any one would ever find in the wilderness or at some Cub Scout retreat.

I always thought it a treat to sleep in it as a kid after the Christmas holiday was over. It was almost magical to wake up with the decorated tree nearby. On the morning after Christmas in 1972, I lied there on the floor while listening to the radio I had received as a present the night before. The radio was near my head that morning upon waking, right where it should have been. The day was cloudy and gray. Mom had already pulled open the drapes in the room. I switched on my new radio. The news announcer let it be known that former President Harry Truman had died in Kansas City. He was eighty-eight years old.

Following dinner (it was called supper in those days) a bit less than a month later in 1973, I was washing my hands in the bathroom as WTMB from Tomah reported the death of former President Lyndon Johnson at his Texas ranch. It would be the same station later that year as Mom ironed clothes in the dining room when we would hear President Richard Nixon make his bold statement, "I am not a crook". That now famous quote was made in front of 400 Associated Press managing editors. It is not certain how many of those assembled for the speech believed it.

In 2012, a small group of my friends who attended broadcasting school with me gathered in Madison. We spent a great day on the Capitol Square, and then settled in at our home on the isthmus. For me at least, it was amusing to hear their sentiments about contemporary radio broadcasting since we had when younger all worked in the industry but had since moved along to other parts of life. The hours passed with ease as we reminisced, and at one point I leaned back and smiled to myself. The fact remains that twenty-nine years had elapsed, and yet there was no shortage of conversation. It dawned on me that at one time we had used our ability to talk and talk to make money.

As former radio announcers, we commiserated that the pay was pretty awful, and the hours sometimes not the best. But we all had a chance to follow a dream, and have an experience that not too many have a crack at exploring. There was something heady about having others tune us in for news and information, or to want a certain song to be played to meet an emotional need.

No one who had gathered that afternoon on our lawn pretended to be more than what we were while in the studio. We were happy to work out of small studios that were too hot in the summer and too chilly in the winter, but where we felt as though we knew our audience. We lived in the community, cared for our friends, and shared many commonalities. As such we served the community through our daily broadcasting.

One of those seated out on the lawn that day continues to be one of my longest and dearest friends. Bruce and I go back to the fall of 1981 when upon first hearing his voice I was certain I was sitting next to the future of NPR. Even today there is still that deep-toned calm, reflective, analytical feel to the stride of his comments, making the delivery of even mundane sentences a delight to hear. As I relaxed in the afternoon sun, I again wondered why he was talking to me instead of working behind a microphone speaking to the masses.

When we get together and start wandering back in time it never fails to lift the corners of my mouth, and wipe the years away. Bruce has a way of making sense of the state of radio today as compared to the hopes and ideals we both had as young broadcasters back in the early 1980s. "We started at the end of an era" Bruce mused to sum it up. They are simple words, but yet convey a major truth.

When Bruce and I were both kids, each in our separate communities (he in Stevens Point, and I a bit further south in Hancock), we each enjoyed taking our radios at night to the place where the best reception could be found. For me, the choices were somewhat limited by the fact that I had to be plugged in to an electrical outlet. Most often, I was hunkered down next to the soft glowing radio dial right in my own bedroom. We did have a radio that ran on batteries, but that was saved for special uses, such as riding out the storms in the basement when severe weather hit. In those earlier days, I could receive only AM and FM signals, but when I was a teenager, I obtained a radio which allowed me to also enjoy the shortwave radio frequencies. How liberating!

In short, Bruce and I would tune the radio dial to get stations from places about which we had only read. If boys in the 1930s lay awake at night wondering where the sound of the train whistle might take the passengers, Bruce and I were marveling at the invisible signal that transmitted sound from faraway places right to our own bedroom-based receivers.

This may sound a bit geeky by the standards of how kids amuse themselves today, but I feel confident that there is much less charm to be found in a video game than in the hisses and pops of an AM radio when trying to get WBZ from Boston on a clear night in Wisconsin. Imagine for a moment what that represents. Someone sitting in a small studio some 1200 miles of driving distance away (that's almost nineteen hours of drive time by today's standards!) was sending out a signal that could be captured and listened to even in the central part of Wisconsin! Not to mention that this was long before the advent of digital radio dials where some kid the age I was could tune to the precise station. Instead, it took real dexterity to get the dial tuned--just so. Finally. There it was. Among the cluster of other stations that also rubbed up against the signal was that elusive distant station.

I began DXing (the telegraphic word for long distance) as a young boy. I am not sure how it started, but recall that I found it fun and something I could do by myself out in the country. I could DX for hours and never get bored. Searching the heavens for radio signals was easiest at night, an optimal time for such activity. As with my foray into playing radio as a child, I engaged in DXing very seriously. I even kept a journal of my DXing finds. I told my friends at school about it, but they thought me strange regarding this matter. In fact, they were not sure that what I told them about my DXing experiences was even true.

Where did DXing begin? In the early days of radio stations were not sure how far their signals reached, and so asked listeners to send in reports of when and where the station's signal was heard. The station would then send out postcards to the listeners.

I thought often as I sat at WDOR in the heart of Door County about who was hearing my voice, and where they were located. At times the station would receive a card or letter from someone who heard the signal in places that seemed impossible. Those signals heard at distances were due to a 'skip' in the atmosphere. By the time that I was on the air, I don't think anyone in the station responded to those kinds of letters or notes any longer; I can't help but think of the missed opportunity to communicate with the listener, and learn of his/her personal story.

When Bruce and I attended broadcasting school our sound studios recreated the conditions of real radio stations from Lake Charles, Louisiana to Butte, Montana. Every school studio had access to the record library where a large selection of 45-rpms was stored in alphabetical order. Each studio had a cart machine to play commercials, and a reel-to-reel tape machine that might be used for news actualities, or advertisements. We even learned how to splice tape, and with great precision so as not to allow listeners to know. During our air shifts we had to take the record and place the needle on it, while backing it up one rotation so that when the turntable was turned on there was an instant start to the recorded sound, and no 'get up to speed' noise. College students today, with all of the automation and computer wizardry found inside of a sound studio, would think they had entered the *Twilight Zone* should they enter such an "antiquated" space as the one which Bruce and I once knew.

In fact, back when Bruce and I worked in radio automated stations were a minority in the industry. The idea that a local disc jockey could be fired so that a 'personality' sitting in a studio in New York could play to the audience via satellite was a ridiculous notion. To pretend that could happen, with the public aware of it, while the station declared it to be a sound business decision would have been considered pure insanity.

Things have changed though, and as a case in point, we can consider the reality of radio broadcasting in Madison in 2010. From 10 A.M. to 3 P.M. weekdays on WOLX 94.9, Ken Merson hosted Madison's Greatest Hits from a recording studio in Baltimore. On WCHY 105.1, San Francisco-based voice talent Will Morgan posed as a jock named Charlie. At WMAD 96.3 Star Country, local program director and midday host Tyler Reese was laid off and replaced by another Baltimore radio personality who broadcasted as Michael J.

A bell rang out when the news wire that ran continuously at WDOR indicated breaking news. Or sometimes two bells...or worse yet, three... Each time one of those bells went off, there was an adrenaline rush which ran through the entire station. The person nearest the machine ripped the copy, and ran to the studio thrusting it in front of the person on-air. The audience was there right alongside the disc jockey who would interrupt the playing of a song, and alert those listening of the information they needed to know. The news wire bells may have tolled for a tornado warning for the county; they would have sounded equally to mark the death of Marty Robbins. One would have heard them ring for any number of reasons: the explosion of the Space Shuttle Challenger; the death of Leonid Brezhnev; or the assassination of Indira Ghandi.

The intensity of the drama playing out in the news connected the person behind the microphone to the audience. There was a sense in the radio studio of a large family where information was shared with those who were listening, and the feeling of an intrinsic bond of 'we are all in this together.' The bells sounded for the memorable events.

July 20, 1983. Frank Reynolds succumbs to complications from acute hepatitis though he also had bone cancer; he was fifty-nine years old. Reynolds was someone who seemed so comfortable in his own skin as anchor on the *ABC Evening News* and later as co-anchor of the *World News Tonight*. During the Iran hostage crisis, he began the thirty-minute late-night program *America Held Hostage*, which later was renamed *Nightline*. Reynolds had a worldly perspective, and easily connected with his audience. His death came to me as a shock, and really made me quite sad. I had faithfully watched his programs right up until his last broadcast, three months before his passing. For my own WDOR audience, I prepared a several-minute tribute with cuts from his time on the air. I had plenty of material to work with as the ABC Radio Network had much to choose from thanks to the satellite feeds that came to the station. I think everyone was moved when both President Reagan and his wife, Nancy, attended the funeral. Burial was in Arlington National Cemetery, thanks to the efforts of the First Lady. Reynolds would later be posthumously awarded a Presidential Medal of Freedom.

January 28, 1986. The much-anticipated tenth mission of the Space Shuttle Challenger took off from the launching site in Florida. At 11:39 AM EST, something went very wrong with one of the O-rings to the solid-fuel rocket booster. The Challenger began to break up, and all seven crewmembers were lost. I arrived for work later in the day as the tragic news from Cape Canaveral gripped the nation. I broadcast that evening the news updates, along with the airing of President Reagan's touching words to a grieving nation. The President's planned speech that night was originally to speak to the country about the State of the Union, but instead reminded the citizenry that there are those in our lives who meet challenges with joy; that there are those who live to serve for the betterment of others; and that as the crew members of the Shuttle were pulling us in to the future with their discoveries, that we needed to continue to follow them. He concluded, "We will never forget them, nor the last time we saw them, this morning, as they prepared for their journey and waved goodbye and 'slipped the surly bonds of earth' to 'touch the face of God.'" As the President thanked us all for listening, no one had a dry eye.

Sharing these news stories with the public was what I had long wanted to do. Imparting information not yet known, and advancing the details of a story so the larger truths could be understood was part of the reason for the adrenaline rush that took place for me when the bells of the news wire sounded. I saw my job this way: there was a local, real, average, every-day run-of-the-mill man behind the microphone who knew the community, and the needs of the audience. There was a connection between those on each end of the radio signal. After all, that was the way radio always operated. More importantly, that is the way that radio best serves the public.

So much of radio has now lost that charm, that essential quality. As my friend Bruce said perfectly, "We started at the end of an era." Not only is that connection between the local broadcaster, and the audience greatly diminished, but it is sad to see so many AM stations resorting to 'trash talk'. I know there are those who contend I am politically biased when it comes to this topic. That's simply not true. My concern is not based on friend or foe, political ally or enemy. My objection is about the very nature and character of radio. It is genuinely about the quality of what is on the airwaves, the airwaves which the public owns.

When I worked in radio thirty-one years ago I had at the station several small picture frames containing images of my nephews, my parents, and a close friend. I often had one of them on the console in front of me when announcing the news or weather report. I was aiming the tone of my delivery as if I were back home chatting over the dinner table. If the truth be known, I was always the one who wanted to break the latest news and such to family; that was another reason I wanted to work in radio.

The WDOR FM signal reached as far away as Milwaukee at night, and I spoke to listeners from southeast Wisconsin from time to time on the phone. It was then that I felt a bigger responsibility to do my job in the best way I could. I was not only representing myself on the air, but also the station. More importantly, I was delivering important information, and I treated my job with respect.

Being a friendly neighborhood broadcaster now seems quaint, and probably even deadly for what too many program directors seek out when playing for ad revenues. I think if more broadcasters had a picture of their family on the studio console they would find it hard to spout some of what gets sent over the airwaves. They also might find the listening audience would respond positively to civil talk, and higher standards.

I have a not-so-secret passion, which always seems to intrigue people. My name is Gregory Humphrey, and I am a life-long fan of the Grand Ole Opry.

The Grand Ole Opry began just five years after commercial radio was born in the United States. In 1925, the National Life and Accident Insurance Company built a radio station as a public service to the local community with the hope that the new medium could advertise insurance policies. The station's call letters, WSM, stood for the company's motto: "We Shield Millions."

At 8 o'clock on November 28, 1925, the station started a program with championship fiddler Uncle Jimmy Thompson that would become the *WSM Barn Dance*. In 1927, the show was renamed the Grand Ole Opry. The show has aired continuously every weekend since it started, and holds the distinction today of being the longest running radio show in U.S. history.

Our dining room was where the family radio was placed atop the blond-colored buffet. Mom always had a variety of table linens over the large wooden piece of furniture ranging from a bright multi-colored runner which she had purchased on her honeymoon to Mexico to a far more elegant white laced crocheted article. As a boy I recall many a Saturday night when the radio would be turned just perfectly so as to capture the signal from the WSM studio. I would move the electrical cord around and use the cord's antenna-like effect to allow for better reception. Those nights in Hancock fostered a love of radio and a thrill at the sound of a fiddle.

Direct from Nashville, the Grand Ole Opry would fill the dining room. I wondered not only how the radio signal made it so far to our home, but also dreamt of what it must be like to be in the audience for the performance. It was a long dream. In 1997, as my parents celebrated their fiftieth wedding anniversary, Mom, Dad and I were set to discover how wonderful it truly is to sit in front of that world-famous stage. Even before getting to our seats, I could hear in my mind's ear the famous "Now let's go center stage as the big red curtain rises for the star of this half hour...!"

We took a Lamers' tour bus to Nashville, departing from the Elizabeth Inn in Plover, Wisconsin. I was a guest of the hotel that night, and the early morning sun glinted off the van line's metal hull as it waited in the parking lot of the inn for everyone to board. The excitement was palpable.

The first night in Nashville, I parted company with the rest of the tour group as I had secured a ticket, and a ride to the Grand Ole Opry. While the whole tour had tickets for the Saturday night show I was not about to be in Music City, and miss the Friday night Opry. I was on a solo adventure.

Upon first entering the Opry House I just stood in the back looking down at the rows of seats that curved gently in front of the large stage obscured by the famed curtain. All I could do was grin. Above the stage there was a large video screen from where just minutes before show time played a short video of the history of the Opry.

With a then darkened Opry House the live band kicked in, the WSM radio announcer, stationed behind a very large and substantive lectern at stage left, stated with clarity: "Live from the Grand Ole Opry House WSM proudly presents the Friday night Opry. And we have a great show in store for you tonight. Cracker Barrel restaurants brings you this portion of the Friday Night Opry. Now let's go center stage as the big red curtain rises for the star of this half hour; ladies and gentleman, here is Porter Wagoner!"

The curtains rose, the lights blazed. The stage lit with brightness from every angle and corner. The sequins of Wagoner's Nudie suit scintillated, the steel guitars reflected prisms, the banjos twinkled as they were plucked, and fiddles picked up speed. As the evening continued, excitement mounted as Alan Jackson decided at the last-minute to make an appearance. Thanks to a scheduling conflict many Opry fans, me included, had yet another reason to smile as Jackson walked on to the stage with his guitar.

Though Grant Turner was a voice I grew up listening to as the Opry announcer he was not the one who broadcast that evening from the stage. He does nonetheless deserve mention here, as it is his voice that still resonates in my head when thinking about Opry announcers.

Jesse Granderson "Grant" Turner, the Texas-born 'Dean of the Opry announcers', largely considered by many to be the 'Voice of the Grand Ole Opry', served on that show's announcing staff for forty-seven years. (For the sake of trivia, Turner rode an all-night bus to Nashville and auditioned for WSM, where he joined the staff on D-Day, the day the Allies invaded Europe in World War II, June 6, 1944.) In fact, Turner's pleasant conversational style is one of the reasons why I had my radio tuned so often to WSM. On the weekends, Turner would introduce the host of the half hour (or quarter-hour portion) of the Opry. In between the musical numbers he would read the colorful and nostalgic advertising scripts for the products that brought the Opry to the air.

Today most people dislike commercials on radio but Grant Turner made the ads fun and enjoyable; Turner's homey gentle readings for items such as Martha White Flour, or Goo Goo Clusters were as much a part of the show as Bill Monroe and his Bluegrass Boys. While Martha White did not sell her product in my

Walking Up the Ramp

hometown, and one couldn't find anywhere in the Stevens Point area one of those real clusters (consisting of marshmallow nougat, caramel and roasted peanut covered in silky milk chocolate), listening to all this as a teenager was the stuff of dreams. I fell in love with radio.

The trick was, of course, that Turner made his work sound effortless and easy. The fact that it came across that way is testimony to his professionalism. Anyone who has worked behind a broadcast microphone knows that it is not as easy as it looks--or sounds. But Turner was able to blend his down home sensibilities with broadcast know-how in such a way as to encourage us to invite him into our homes. Countless did every weekend.

Grant Turner was on that world-famous stage on Friday night, October, 18, 1991 doing what he loved best. When the radio show concluded, he went home. The big red curtain had unknowingly come down on his last announcing performance on WSM radio. The next evening every performer gave a nod to the podium along with a few kind words about Grant Turner. He had died at home from a heart attack.

I wrote fondly of Grant Turner on my blog, *Caffeinated Politics*, and was very pleased when his daughter, Nancy, happened to read it. She commented about taking Grant to the hospital the night be died, and about her mother, Audrey, who was never mentioned in the press over the years. "Thank you so very much for the very nice story you prepared and placed on this website. I am Grant's daughter, and I still miss him each and every day. Last week was the anniversary of his death, and it touches my heart, recalling taking him to the hospital, not knowing his heart was tearing. My own mother died fifty days later. I missed her even more than he for she was an alcoholic. They married around 1951 and I was born in '53. Not many know about her, but her name was Audrey." The headstone for Grant Turner asserts: "He Lived His Life Making Others Happy". How true that was!

When my parents and I traveled to Nashville together, I can say that it was a time of excitement and wonderment. When I woke up Saturday morning in Nashville I had one mission to complete. I was determined to make sure my parents were recognized from the stage of the Opry for their Golden Anniversary. I placed a call to the studios of WSM where Eddie Stubbs was doing a show. I knew him to be a singer, and fiddle player who once worked with Kitty Wells. He was a walking, talking music historian when it came to classic country music. He also always had perfect clarity and tone when on the air. That morning he also proved to be a pure gentleman. Stubbs answered the studio line, and I quickly got down to the reason for the call. I asked that Royce and Geneva Humphrey be honored from the stage of the Opry that evening. After taking the needed information Stubbs told me "considered it done."

That evening during the broadcast on clear channel AM 650, 'The Air Castle Of The South' the announcement was made that an anniversary couple from Hancock, Wisconsin was in the house, and with that, the Opry House crowd gave a loud hand clap as my parents were introduced. I was seated to the right of my Mom, and she looked at me, grinned, and mouthed the word "you" which was a code of sorts meaning that she did not want attention made over the matter. I had seen that word mouthed over the years by her in the same light, but that announcement from that stage during the radio show remains one of my most precious memories.

During that show we saw Grandpa Jones, Charlie Louvin, Wilma Lee Cooper, Del Reeves, and a score of others. The Opry is not just another musical venue. This is about as real and authentic of a slice of history as one can get when it comes to what early radio, and early country music represent. Inasmuch, the closer one can get to the past and experience the living stars of yesterday, the more accurate is the understanding of the time when the likes of Minnie Pearl, and Roy Acuff were taking that stage. When the Grand Ole Opry all started none of those singers and musicians knew what the future held, but were sure they wanted to be there when that big red curtain went up. For eighty-seven years that tradition has endured.

Nashville is not the only place to meet and greet the Greats. I have been fortunate not only to see many of the legends in places like Wisconsin Dells, but I have gotten to talk with some of them too. A few even added their autograph to my guitar. Over and over, those older performers leave the stage yet want to linger and meet the fans. Whereas contemporary artists are heavily managed and are more concerned with selling products, these 'old timers', as people call them, care far more about allowing fans, many far older than me, to share a memory with the singer, and take home an autograph or a snapshot. I really marvel how utterly content these stars are to stay as long as fans keep talking. It is as if these performances are not over until everyone has a personal memory to take home.

A few years ago, I again had the chance to see Little Jimmy Dickens on stage. James was seated alongside me for his thirty-minute set in the Dells. Dickens, age ninety-three, was ever energetic, had a series of snappy one-liners, and even did a slight costume change during his performance. He still had the crowd under his control after all these years; his career in country music has been long, having started with the Opry in 1948. I think the vast majority of the current 'fifteen-minute wonders' who have success due to slick public relations and promotional staff will not be anywhere near a stage when they are in their eighties, let alone nineties as Little Jimmy is most weeks. (The older performers are truly national treasures.) In short, you can imagine my excitement when Little Jimmy, all 4'11" of him, stood next to me and agreed to sign my guitar—not a great instrument, mind you, but rather a gift I had been given as a late teen. His signature alone makes that wooden sound box worth far more than it ever will be for its musicality.

The blond-colored buffet table from my family home, the same buffet table where the five inch by nine inch radio once rested, is now in our Madison home. New memories are being created with it. For me though the best of recollections will always be the look of a radio sitting on the left hand side waiting to be turned for the best reception come Saturday night.

National Public Radio. Wisconsin Public Radio. WSM. WIND, WBBM, and WGN from Chicago. These are the radio stations whose broadcasted presences filled my childhood bedroom. The truly remarkable radio personalities impacted how I came to view the medium. Their authoritative voices and professional conduct behind the microphone influenced me.

Every weekday morning in the summer when I was out of school Earl Nightingale's five-minute program *Our Changing World* could be heard on WFHR out of Wisconsin Rapids. If memory serves me correctly it aired at 10:30 A.M. It might seem strange but I somehow link his broadcast with the patterns of sunshine that decorated the gray tile on the kitchen floor as it came in through the southern facing window during that time of morning. The window would often be raised on summer days and so the wind through the oaks in the back lawn could be heard softly murmuring. What most struck me about his show was the excellent broadcasting voice that conveyed sincerity, honesty, and authority. I never had a deep rich voice like his, but was always appreciative of those who were so blessed.

Strange as it may seem, though, I was more often drawn to those stations farther away from home. As a boy in Hancock, I tuned in to talk radio from Chicago, and bypassed the stations that were closer to me, despite their significantly stronger signals. The world, it seemed to me, was more exciting in Chicago, and let's face it--I was lucky to have grown up with civil and professional radio broadcasters such as Eddie Schwartz, Wally Phillips, Steve King and Johnnie Putnam, Clark Weber, or Dave Baum, all of whom where legends on the air. I loved it when Baum always ended his show with the tagline of "Mama, get the coffee ready, the kid's on his way", or Clark referred to himself as "Mother Weber's oldest son". As a teenager I never knew radio to be ill tempered, lewd, or boorish.

If there was ever one person I truly felt was a 'radio friend' it surely was 'Chicago Ed' Schwartz. From his days at WIND and then at WGN, he was a dynamic presence on the radio. His voice was softer than that of most who find themselves on radio, but his authority and professionalism when behind a microphone were never in doubt. The amazing connection he made with his listeners both in Chicago, and as far as the airwaves would allow him to be heard, showcased his civility and big-heart for the causes that he loved. When he promoted his food drive for hungry folks in Chicago no doubt remained that his concern was deeply ingrained. He wore his heart on his sleeve, and its gentle beat reverberated inside the radio.

I still recall an awesome snowstorm that hit Chicago, but missed central Wisconsin. As a boy I wanted the snow in my backyard, but had to content myself instead with talk from WIND. Eddie Schwartz broadcasted hour after hour about how Chicago was crippled by the snow and wind. I recall being in my bedroom and feeling as if I were there in the midst of a wild torment. As he conversed with snowplow operators, police officers, and folks trying to get off the expressways, I more fully understood the power and intimacy of radio. Eddie Schwartz was there. He was talking with real people about a veritable situation on the ground. No editor stood between Eddie and the man-on-the-streets reporters like there would have been the following day in the papers. The news was live, and immediate. And I was there with him! I listened as the snow fell and the plow trucks struggled to keep traffic moving. I was right there in my bedroom cheering on the policeman who helped stranded motorists. My bedroom was Chicago as people recounted time after time how it was the worst storm they had ever witnessed, even if it wasn't. I wished I could have been there, microphone in hand, feeding a good story to Eddie myself, but alas Hancock is a distant shore to Chicago's hustle and bustle. I suspect that there are few young people today who can comprehend what I am talking about, but they have missed something by not knowing radio in this fashion.

I think too that Eddie Schwartz and I had much in common. On the air, Schwartz talked at times about how his interest in radio started as a youngster. His grandparents had given him a portable radio as a gift. In high school, he was invited one day to watch a broadcast live, and it made him even more determined to get a job in radio. In the more than two decades that Eddie hosted late-night programming, he used his talents for the betterment of so many. 'Chicago Ed', who had been a Columbia College student along with Wheel of Fortune's Pat Sajak, was the first of his class to get the much sought after broadcasting job. Eddie's health deteriorated over the years, and after suffering bouts of renal failure, this wonderful broadcaster died in 2009 at the age of sixty-two. Reports at the time stated, "'Chicago Ed' was laid to rest under sunny skies". Let it be so.

I add to my list of favorite radio personalities the famed voice of the WGN studios from the heart of Chicago.

"Stand by for news!"

I grew up listening to Paul Harvey on WDUX Waupaca, where on weekends I recall many Saturdays spent sitting in the car with my Dad while listening to the broadcast of news and commentary as my Mom shopped. Even though I never met Harvey, I really felt as if I knew him. Harvey was like a guest in our home so often that he felt like family. Who would not have poured a cup of coffee, and had him at the table should he have knocked upon our door?

Paul Harvey captivated millions of radio listeners with his daily delivery of the news in a fashion that was uniquely his, and so readily identifiable. One never had to ask who was on the radio; his distinctive style was a give-away.

Harvey had a very firm set of values, and political points of view that often ran counter to my outlook on life and government, and yet I was one of his biggest fans. He had a warm rich voice that never missed the proper way to pronounce a word, and made each, and every syllable ring with clarity. I loved as a kid to just listen to the way he said words. I always smiled when he ended his show with a story that was aimed to lift spirits and provoke a smile. There was never a broadcast that did not end with the classic "Gooood Daaay!"

Every now and again my Dad would mimic Harvey's way of leading into a commercial by repeating 'page two'... 'page three'. Harvey not only read the news, but also wrote his own script. When the time for an ad came, he would mention his page number. It was that segue between news and advertisement that led some to chastise Harvey for his style. Perhaps it was because I was a long-time listener, and clearly knew the difference between the two but it never seemed to me to be blurring news and sponsorship in any way, and it certainly didn't degrade the quality of his program. Quite the opposite. In fact, it was a unique show that worked, and never lacked for advertisers. ABC executives have been quoted as saying Harvey brought in more than ten percent of the network's $300 million in advertising billings at the height of his career.

WDOR carried Paul Harvey twice daily, and also his famed

Rest of the Story during the news hour in the evening. I still recall the kick I got when reporting the hour of evening news, and had the chance to say "Time now for Paul Harvey's *Rest of the Story* brought to you by First National Bank of Sturgeon Bay." As a kid I never thought it would be my voice that would be the lead-in for the guy with 'the voice'.

But every broadcaster who left an imprint on me did not have to have national recognition or work in a large city.

On WFHR Wisconsin Rapids Arnie Strope really conveyed what it meant to be a local broadcaster. He might talk about a flat tire on his way to work, or what he had for breakfast and weave this and that into a narrative that made the banal life event folksy, and interesting. What most amused me about his time on the air was the *Trading Post* show. His program would air at 9:00 A.M., and Mom and I would listen to Strope as he fielded calls from folks wanting to sell firewood, or give away canning jars. We never sold or bought anything, but my Mom enjoyed the tidbits that Arnie would tell about his family, or what he did over the weekend, filling that air time as she washed dishes and Arnie waited for more phone calls.

What is strange to admit is that as a boy I had a small notebook (with a red cover) and took down a list of those items for sale or give-a-way along with the phone numbers. I would sit at the buffet table in the dining room and write down all the information like Arnie was doing. What stunned me then, and even more so now is that folks would call in days later, and ask for the phone numbers or addresses they had missed! And he had them!

Make that Arnie and I had them!

I must say that I never had to do a similar program when I worked in radio. Arnie's program was uniquely his, and he did it each weekday. Arnie was inducted in to the Wisconsin Broadcasters Hall of Fame in 1992, and folks are asking who the heck 'Trevor James' was! It is all a matter of perspective.

The radio continued to be my Mother's chore-time friend. For the rest of her life, she always found a local broadcaster to be a part of her routine when sprinkling and ironing the clothes or dusting the house. As my Dad got older and became harder of hearing, her listening to the radio was often limited to the times when he would be outside. The radio was not something he could clearly hear. The ambient noise of the radio disturbed him rather than to entertain. Of course, Mother's life would have been easier if he had agreed to get a hearing aid!

While no one else has any reason to recall much of what I ever broadcast on the air there are events that stand out for me personally because they seemed to encapsulate two of my passions: radio and politics. I even had the look for this kind of work. For many years in the brim of a fedora (the type newspaper men wore in the old black and white movies) I stashed my press passes from the days when I covered these types of stories.

On Labor Day 1984, I attended my first major political rally, and it would be the first such rally I would cover for WDOR news. I was young, eager, and so excited that I could barely contain myself. Days before the event I had completed a background check to gain press credentials which allowed me onto the risers with the national journalists and reporters. Knowing I was going to stand alongside some of the journalists for whom I had deep respect was as electrifying as the rally itself. The process was meaningful to me since it was my first major political rally with a presidential nominee.

The weather was gray, cloudy, and cool. I wore a white shirt and necktie. I traveled from Sturgeon Bay to Merrill in my light blue Chevette (the owners manual mentioned something about Zero-to-Sixty and needing to pack a lunch) and still recall the feeling that life could not be better. I was doing what I had always really wanted to do, which was to get closer to politics, and report about it. I knew then that not everyone could say they get to live what they dream, and so as I drove along I tried to take in every moment, every detail.

At underpasses along my route there were cops, and dark-tinted SUV's where security details were established. The local radio stations in the area were broadcasting special reports about the rally, and how to avoid traffic jams. An awesome electricity filled the air since it is not everyday such a small place is the epicenter of an event that draws such a political crowd.

Many political analysts were questioning whether the traditional start of the presidential fall campaign was best done in a place like Merrill. A small town is not the type of place which would typically generate the massive crowd that a campaign wants to show on the evening news. Walter Mondale and Geraldine Ferraro had started that Labor Day in New York, and encountered rainy weather. The crowd consisted of fewer people than they hoped. Sprinkles fell in Merrill too, a fact which was not lost on those who thought it an omen for the election outcome.

Once at the rally site, I climbed to stand with the rest of the press corps and was truly pleased to be about three feet from Lynn Sherr and Brit Hume, both from ABC. I smiled to myself when Sherr asked Hume how to pronounce "LaFollette". I later laughed out loud that same evening when she mispronounced it on national news. Everyone has on-air slips, and it was comforting to me to see it happen even to the professional reporters, knowing that my 'professional reporting career' was only a number of hours old at that point.

The music ramped up, and Mondale and Ferraro took to the simple outdoor platform. Each in turn gave punchy, dramatic stump speeches. A light drizzle fell, and Mondale cast aside his jacket, rolled up his sleeves and told the audience that the rain did not matter as that is what made Democrats grow. "Be it rain, hail, sleet or snow, it makes no difference as we will win in November."

I knew at once that my 'political infection' was for real. Never before had I felt so alive, or so in the moment. I thought back about the hard times of high school, and all that it had forced upon me, and that those days were truly over, and defeated. I recall looking through the drizzle at the candidates. The television press captured video; print media still photographs, and still more, like me, made written notes. I saw it all up close, and knew that I had been lifted from my personal valley. I was now living my life, and it was grand!

Geraldine Ferraro was absolutely loved by that crowd in Merrill as she spoke from the heart about her goals. There was a strong sense that the party faithful understood the deeper social significance to her being nominated to a national ticket. The applause, enthusiastic; the warmth for her, genuine. It was history in the making.

Later I recorded some interviews with potential voters. I was most interested in sharing with my listeners back in Sturgeon Bay how these Merrill rally-goers viewed the first female nominee. Overwhelmingly, each interviewee stated that Ferraro was breaking new ground, and they were glad Labor Day in Merrill was where she spent some of her time.

As exciting as the Mondale/Ferraro rally was it was nothing could compare to covering a visit by President Reagan to Oshkosh, Wisconsin. I was to report on the rally for WDOR on May 30, 1985 at the Winnebago County Courthouse. A couple of days in advance of the event, the radio station owner asked if I wanted to try for a press pass and travel to Oshkosh and report on the President's visit. Did I want to go?!! All of this was happening to me, someone who never thought life could work out like this.

The morning of the event, I feverishly tried on several shirt and tie combos before deciding on just the right look. Again in

Walking Up the Ramp   33

that Chevette that had seen better days, I traveled from Sturgeon Bay down to Oshkosh and parked at the county fairgrounds where a shuttle bus took a bunch of us reporters to the center of town where Reagan would speak. (Us reporters. I felt that kinship deeply.)

    I quickly realized that we were taking the same route as the Presidential motorcade. A reporter for the Milwaukee Journal told me to look at all the windows of the homes. They were all curtained. All the doors were shut. The Secret Service had shut down the streets and instructed the people not to be outside or near the windows for security reasons. At the intersections dump trucks and huge empty busses blocked the way. The Journal reporter saw I was a `newbie' (the never-ending grin was the tell-tale sign) and filled me in on the secrets of a Presidential visit.

    The site of the event, the County Courthouse and surrounding area, filled with tens of thousands. Up on the press risers I was lost in the power of the presidential event. Large speakers blared music from the stage with all the Republican politicians, both state and local, doing their bit at the podium. Military helicopters flew overhead and sharpshooters were seen on every rooftop in the area.

    The motorcade was but a few blocks away--traveling at a high rate of speed, I had already been told. Black limousines pulled into the square alongside the Courthouse, and from the press risers the view was terrific. I was looking slightly to my right, and the sun was behind me. The rally had been staged perfectly for the coverage to be aired nationally that evening on the major newscasts, and headlined the following morning in the newspapers.

    Hail to the Chief started an eruption from the crowd. It was as if God himself had just landed. In seconds, Reagan strides with confidence to the podium. His famous wave was offered. Applause washed over the courthouse in continuous torrents of welcome. I can still see the bounce in Reagan's step, his flawless black hair, his wave and genuine delight to be out in the crowd of citizens he loved so much. The jocular moments during his speech brought smiles and laughs from the crowd. I noted from the press assembled all around me that we too had been caught up in the moment. Ronald Reagan certainly did have an infectious quality. I had been impressed with his communication style from the years of watching news coverage, but it paled to what his live appearance felt like, or how it resonated that afternoon as he spoke to us all about tax reform.

    I was very caught up in the dynamics that were playing out around me. The national media impressed me. The long photojournalist lenses on some of the cameras surely cost more than my beat up Chevette. No other event in my radio career ever matched those minutes for me. I tried desperately to slow my mind down, and soak it all in before it was over. I dreaded slightly the arrival of the bus that was to take us back to the parking area. I realized on that return journey back to my Chevette that I still had a grin on my face. I knew instantly what my story would be for the evening news hour on radio.

The ABC network would cover the tax simplification plan about which Reagan spoke during the speech. The morning papers would detail the plan even further. No one would tell our radio audience the story first hand about what it felt like, and looked like to witness such an event the way I could.

I had felt something new, and understood that not many would ever experience it firsthand in the way I had. I could bring to my listeners through words the sights of shuttered windows, and sharpshooters on buildings, and goose bumps on my arms when he waved to the crowd. I could tell the story of how it felt to be with the national press. I could describe seeing a president in the flesh, knowing that my audience was also like me in having limited access to such moments. I could identify with what anyone of my listeners would want to know about the larger story that would not make the headlines in the morning paper.

Upon my return to the station, I threw myself into writing my news script on an old black typewriter that was located in the sales department. I recorded it. I knew that if I tried to do it live I would talk too fast, or just burst with happiness. It was the best story I ever did in those four years at the station because it was so real. It had energy and verve, a perspective different from everything else that my listeners would see or hear about the event. It was my heart talking.

I have wondered why more reporters at the local level do not allow themselves to report such a story in the manner I did. I guess on one hand it might not have been 'hard reporting', and others might have considered my report to be a 'soft-ball' for a controversial president, and his policy idea. The fact that I was a liberal Democrat makes that point pure silliness. I have always considered the media in its totality to cover politicians, and issues in a fair manner. Inasmuch I do not think every reporter has to cover an event in the same way, or stress the same points. As an adult I seek out the alternative viewpoint, and the perspective that is fresh and different from the pack.

Different from the pack. Months before I traveled to Oshkosh I had written the White House for the chance to have an on-air interview with President Reagan. It would surely surprise my political friends that I made it clear I had no desire to ask any partisan questions. Given that Reagan was a former broadcaster I wanted to talk about the way radio stations had once operated, and the moments that stood out for the former announcer. I was not surprised that I never heard back from the White House, but am quite sure the interview would have been most friendly. I suspect he may have even smiled about the chance to again tell the stories again of his days as an announcer.

My simple start in learning how to speak, and operate in a broadcasting frame of mind while in my bedroom coupled with my love of finding faraway stations on the AM dial late at night underscores a simple truth about radio. At its very best radio is a special medium where it all comes down to one person communicating to another person. Though that person receiving the transmission is not seen, or heard from for the most part, we all know what it feels like to have such a friend 'inside the radio'.

There are days when we all need a mood-lifter, and the friendly local neighborhood radio announcer may be the just the ticket with lively music and banter to make the day go smoother. We all have had the cold and flu with the associated restless nights when the darkened bedroom seems more peaceful with the lighted dial of the radio on the nightstand, and a voice that seems to connect directly. We all have images in our mind of what the announcer looks like, or what he or she is wearing. We have a sense of what they may be like when out and about, and fashion over time a whole persona around the faceless friends who are found on the radio dial.

Let me put it another way.

Over my lifetime radio has changed in so many ways. There has been a technological shift that is both stunning, and exciting. With everything going digital the days of how radio was broadcast, or how the studio functioned when I worked at WDOR seems ancient. At the same time as the technological changes have occurred there has also been a decline in the tone, and spirit in some of radio. What I find unacceptable is the harsh, acerbic, rancid, and mean tone to what passes too often as broadcasting these days. I am certain that radio can still be profitable by being companionable, professional, and something that listeners want to invite into their homes.

While I was working at that small AM/FM station we may not have been cutting edge, but we were local. Local neighborhood disc jockeys with the current weather and local fishing conditions, high school sports reports, and even the local obituaries were read on certain long-form newscasts. In the shorter newscasts we still provided the basics concerning those who had passed away along with funerary details. There is something very comforting about local radio that provides listeners with information so they can pop in to the funeral home and console a family from the other side of town. I have long lamented the passing of local radio programming of this type.

    I expect radio personalities to be like my guests in the house. I like good talk, humor, and spirited conversation with ideas that sometimes conflict with mine. What I do not want, and will not tolerate, is the most base of shock jock talk just because some radio station has an itch for a rating. I wish to be thought of as a listener that deserves respect, rather than just a notation in a ratings book. I refuse to give in to the 'lowest common denominators' when it comes to radio broadcasting. I know there is a market for the connection that listeners gravitate towards if given the choice on the dial. Large broadcasting companies are setting the rules, and that saddens me.

    Over the past couple decades I have been more interested in the standards we should want honored by those who hold broadcast licenses. I am really concerned about our airwaves becoming ever more angry places than the friendly ones I recall from my youth. The AM dial has become littered with heated political talk that makes bombast, and rancor the foundations for ratings. That style underscores what I think is often wrong with radio. Compare that crass style to the calibrated and cerebral offerings from NPR to gauge how far radio has too often been allowed to drift. This isn't to say that there are not many wonderful stations. This noticeable shift in content and tone is just particularly evident among some stations.

    I still recall as a kid the time my Mom was not pleased to hear the word "damn" used by a politician in a news actuality. She felt there was no need for cursing on the airwaves, and that it sounded bad. I mention this to show that there was a time, and it was not so long ago, when broadcasting standards were a desired thing. Listeners noticed when things ran counter to the expected norms. For the sake of full disclosure, though, I do remember at the time telling my Mom I did not think the word usage was out-of-bounds. She held to her belief that people who were educated could find word choices that did not offend, especially on the airwaves. She was right of course.

    What I could not see when younger was the turn being taken in radio broadcasting, a curve that was long and unseen due to the length of its arc. Little by little standards were lowered in radio broadcasting that now allow for someone to go on the airwaves and make lewd and completely outrageous statements. Worse yet announcers who make such statements on the radio expect to get

Walking Up the Ramp   37

away with it.

I certainly had moments on the air that I regret, but they were not planned, and seem quaint given the scope of what can pass as radio fare today. The biggest 'controversy' was due to my lack of pre-reading a piece of copy prior to news time.

Imagine this scene for a moment. So there I am on air, reporting the news, and as I move down the typed page comes a person whose last name was Stauffaucher. He was at the time the new Sturgeon Bay City Attorney, and I had not previously encountered his name. I was sitting behind the microphone, pacing my delivery just like I had done in those innocent days when I sat in my room with Dad's pocket watch. Not missing a beat, the name came off just like you can imagine it did.

The name slipped off my tongue quite naturally, and so it couldn't be stopped, but that didn't keep the little editors voice in my head from shouting. There was no disputing that I put the hard 'u' sound into the name for all the listeners across the region to hear. WHOOOPPS! The key to such an incident is, as the old underarm deodorant commercials used to recommend, 'never let them see you sweat', pretend it did not happen, and move on with the show.

As I continued the newscast I could see the lights of the phone near the console start to blink a bright orange with someone on every line desiring to talk to me. Even the long-distance lines from Algoma and Kewaunee were blinking! Good Lord! I knew as soon as the word had slipped past my lips that the mispronunciation was going to be a problem. I wasn't wrong. Naturally the general manager of the station was on one of the lines, and was irritated with me. My first thought (left unstated, of course) was about how boring his life must have been if he were always listening, and just seconds away from a phone to place such a call.

Ed Allen, Sr. later came into the studio, and told some stories of his time while working at WGN radio in Chicago, and soon we were laughing. I must say he could be a class act, and he regaled me with wonderful old stories as he had a great deal of old-fashioned broadcasting under his belt. He was a fine mentor, and I appreciated his sense of humor, usually. I have thought over time that at some level he too was laughing about my verbal gaffe. He just cautioned me to read local names more carefully as they were at times different from what I had perhaps been accustomed to in the area of the state where I was raised.

While I never did anything aimed at shocking my audience, I admit and am proud that I worked to provoke constructive thinking among our listeners. I proffered news stories that were multiple-part series on many issues that I felt needed to be highlighted. I selected diverse topics which ranged from gun control, teen suicide, AIDS, and dating services. I would research, conduct interviews, write news copy, and report them in two-minute reports in three or four part series that aired throughout the week. While the station had feedback from the listening audience no one wanted to throw their radio against a wall, nor wanted me to apologize.

I must add that at the end of the day, it is the listening public who needs to be held accountable for those who continue to broadcast most rudely on the nation's airwaves. Too few citizens step up and demand the public airwaves (which they own) be better used. Too few listeners demand that a more common-sense tone be attached to the list of responsibilities with which owners need to reckon when considering how they operate their station.

I end this chapter with a moral to a story that comes via radio. As a teenager one of my favorite radio stations was WGN where a wide variety of topics were discussed daily. The talk show hosts were always just 'real folks' who happened to have a broadcasting career. Even when working at WDOR I still wanted to be hired one day at the famed Tribune Tower in Chicago. Needless to say that did not happen, but my long-held dream of someday being heard on WGN Radio stayed with me.

It took until 2008 but finally I made it on the airwaves of WGN as part of Steve and Johnnie's *Life After Dark* radio show, which dominated Chicago late night radio. WGN can be heard in over thirty states at night, and worldwide on the internet. Steve and Johnnie are a married couple who mastered the art of conversation and how to engage a radio audience during the overnight hours. James often joked over the years that they were his 'babysitters' as I often got so quiet and relaxed when they came on the air. If you ask him, he still holds significant resentment towards the station management who decided to take them off the air!

Every Tuesday night Steve and Johnnie devoted a portion of an hour-long segment of their nearly six-hour talk show to the topic of cars. From time to time they liked to talk on-air with new car buyers about the pros and cons of their recent purchase. I had just bought my second VW Beetle in mid-January that year, and contacted them with the news. Within hours their producer, Dan Sugrue, had called me to affirm that they would be interested in doing a segment on my new car.

A couple weeks later at 2:00 A.M. my WGN dream came true.

It was a blast! For about twenty minutes I gave my views on the latest version of the VW Beetle, including the changes in exterior molding, seat design, engine performance, and over-all appeal. To be honest I am not a guy who knows much about cars in general, but I certainly had plenty of thoughts about the actual car I bought and owned.

It was also good to discover during that interview that I was not alone when it comes to naming my cars. (Steve and Johnnie name their cars too!) They laughed heartily when I mentioned my first Beetle was named "Beetle Bailey". It was then they told a story of trading in a favorite car, and how we really do become attached to the vehicles we love.

It was a real kick to be on the airwaves after a twenty-two year hiatus, and it meant the world to me that this time it was over WGN Radio! Steve and Johnnie not only made it possible, but so easy and fun.

Those who appear on the car portion of the talk show were always treated to a nice 'goodie' as a way of saying thanks, but as James knew when he looked at me that night after the broadcast, I would have done it for free. A week later a coupon arrived in the mail for two Maine lobsters from Lobster Gram. For as much as we enjoyed the lobsters, the best part was the CD of the broadcast that was included in the mailing.

As we get older, and move along in life, it is easy to forget the dreams that lifted our sails when younger. Sadly, many come to a point in life where they put aside the notion that anything is possible. Life gets packed with lists of things that must be done, or places we need to be. The obligations are many, and therefore it is easy to set aside the wish lists of our youth. We need a continual reminder of what made us smile when we had aspiring hopes, and then never forget that we are not too old to make them come true. What Steve and Johnnie remind me of with that night on WGN is that we are never to let our dreams—even the little ones—be forgotten.

> *"Home is where one starts from."*
>
> —*T.S. Eliot*

1,268 Square Feet

Festus, as the story went whenever one wanted to inject a little humor into the events surrounding my birth, was almost my given name. Mom wasn't thinking of the Roman Governor of Judea, Porcius Festus. She wasn't even envisioning the former guard in the National Football League, Festus Tierney. (Yes, I had to do a search for famous people named Festus.) Festus was the name of Marshal Matt Dillon's only full-time official deputy, Festus Haggen, from the hit CBS series *Gunsmoke*. Festus Haggen was known for his simple vocabulary, and demeanor (which hid a sharp eye and considerable native intelligence). Despite his short-comings, Festus ended up being interpreted by viewers as "lovable". At least that part sounds like me.

As others like to tell it, had I been born a girl, one name under consideration for me was Gay Lynette, or Gay for short. Why not just hang me on a cross right then? Where could such an idea have come from?

My sister had a doll named Gay Lynette that once, as I have always been reminded, had long golden curly hair. (How this doll was so special that there was any serious dialogue in the family about naming me after it had I been a girl is rather troubling on the face of it.) Perhaps there is some Freudian underpinning to the fact I decided as a small boy to wash the doll's hair in the bathtub. I have no real idea what I was thinking at the time, but am sure there was nothing malicious to my attempt to bathe the little thing. Perhaps I felt some scrubbing and washing was necessitated just like Mom did for me when I was dirty? The difference between my bath time and that which I lavished upon Gay Lynette turned out to be that when I exited the tub I left with all my hair on the top of my head.

Gay Lynette did not fare so well. By the time I was done poor ole' Gay Lynette was as bald as a cue ball, with her blond locks floating around in the tub. I was surely as shocked at the sight as Gay Lynette was! Without intending to do it I had created a whole new image for the doll. I placed the doll back where I had found it, and waited for the explosion.

There is no way to overstate how traumatic that moment was for my sister. When I was first dating James in 2000 she happened to tell that story in such a way that James had to ask just how many years—make that decades ago—had this horror occurred? It seemed to James from the unfolding narrative that if he were to go to the bathroom that the doll's curls could still be found in the filter of the tub drain!

Mom often said that I was an unplanned child, which in my early years did concern me. I worried that perhaps I was not a wanted child, which is very different. I asked my Mom to clarify her thoughts for me on occasion, and she mentioned over and again how my Grandmother Schwarz told her that someday she, my Mom, would be so glad that I was born. As I grew older, I never doubted that I was the most interesting of the siblings, and therefore never thought much about being a 'whoops baby'.

I was delivered in to the world on a Saturday night but Mom had wanted the pregnancy over with for days before that. The weather was hot and sticky, and she was mightily uncomfortable. She tried to move the labor process along by cleaning the house, and vacuuming. None of that worked, and I took my time making the arrival. I was polite about it too; I waited until after CBS's *Gunsmoke* had concluded, and then let it be known to the doctors they needed to move Mom into a delivery room at the Wild Rose Hospital. (The Wild Rose facility, established in 1941, had existed a little less than twenty years by then.) Apparently, that night's episode of *Gunsmoke* had been a powerful one if anyone had considered telling Dr. Kjentvit to write Festus on my birth certificate.

My birth came shortly after 10:00 o'clock. I am, as people call it today, 'birthday twins' with President Gerald Ford, born in 1913, and country singer Del Reeves of the 1932 vintage. History further records that day as being noteworthy for being Bastille Day, the start of the French Revolution, affectionately only known to the French themselves simply as "the 14th of July".

Most people, I suspect, never go back to the hospital where they were born long after the event, nor do they get to see a photograph showcased on a wall of the doctor who helped them into the world. I was nearly fifty years old when I happened to be back at the Wild Rose Hospital. Over the years the place had been transformed in part to a swing-bed facility for people who needed assistance transferring from a hospital setting prior to going to their home. My Dad had suffered a massive heart attack, and was recuperating in one of the rooms in the newer unit. The older section of the hospital, where I was born, was largely in disuse, and being dismantled.

When one walks into the Wild Rose Memorial Hospital there are four pictures that hang on the wall. One of them is that of Doctor Roger Kjentvit who was among the first to see my face. My Mom always had the fondest memories of the doctor, and made sure many years ago that Dr. Kjentvit's obituary, and other newspaper clippings about him were given to me.

I came home from the hospital to what I would consider as a boy to be a nice-sized house. Though we certainly did not live in a large home there was plenty of space it seemed, and if one heard my Mom tell it, more than enough rooms to keep her busy with the cleaning. If one listened a little longer to this line of conversation it seemed I was always the cause for rooms to be cleaned. However, the causal relationship is one with which I have never agreed over the years. I assert that all such claims were falsely made.

The only thing I know for a fact about which she was correct in this regard was the newspaper print that matched with my fingerprints on the white doorframes in the house. There was no need for any crime scene investigation unit to alert Mom to the fact they existed, and who had absent-mindedly as my Mom described it, "swung themselves" around into another room while messing up the frame. The little black marks matched my little blackened fingers precisely. I was caught.

Mom always had a special relationship with cleaning, in spite of the spin that she put on it for others to hear. She passed down her penchant for neat-nookedness to at least me, if not by way of DNA, at least then through behavior observations. Though cleaning, and sprucing the house was never listed as 'fun' it was almost therapeutic for my Mom. She liked to get everyone outside to play or putter about, and failing that at least in our bedrooms so she could dust the floors, shake the rugs, and clean the counters. Rumors (that perhaps James has started over time) suggest she was simply looking for peace, and quiet and this was her only means by which to achieve it. Investigation results are pending.

Mom really did have a daily morning routine to spot-shine the house, and return everything 'to zero' as James and I call such actions in our Madison home. Her routine meant that her house was so clean 'you could eat off the floors'. My Mom did not wear pearls like television's June Cleaver. She would have bested the Beaver's mom on any set of domestic chores.

Mom always kept decorating magazines around when I grew up that showcased how interiors could be arranged and how remodeling could add functionality to a room. She dreamed of a bigger house, and failing that at least a larger kitchen. Even though she never had either dream fulfilled she would always sing or hum softly while dusting and placing new doilies under glassware, or washing the windows and then making them sparkle by rubbing the panes with a scrunched up piece of newspaper.

When she vacuumed, however, she seemed the most content. The last vacuum she owned had a light at the front end that made it appear there was a headlight on the appliance. Mom at times would start laughing that this was "her car" and, while cleaning, start to laugh, and at times get so into the humor of it that she could not talk. She just had to stop and let the laugh work its way through before continuing. Since she never had a driver's license, she shared a humorous back and forth between us when those moments took place.

Mom and I connected in ways that she and my other siblings did not. I was always more in tune with my Mom's thinking, and her views than I was with Dad. I think in part this is because we spent so much time together. Mom also knew how to express emotions, and was not shy for the most part in doing so. We had great conversations, and shared stories. She was the one person I always wanted to call with the latest news and gossip, and even long after her death I would still instinctively reach for the phone when something I knew she would want to know crossed my desk. I do miss her so.

My Dad was of a generation that seemed never to know how to deal with inner feelings, or how to be introspective. As a result, the conversations I had with Mom were more expansive and rounded, while often a more guarded way of talking about things that really mattered with Dad was required of me. While we could talk about the local school board races or national politics, there was no way to have a conversation about how we felt over the things stored inside. Not that I was unavailable for such conversations, as I was. Instead those conversations never resulted as he was not wired that way.

It would only be in his last years that Dad was able to find the release that tears provide, but sadly I think this was in large part due to the fact he did not have an outlet for talking, and grieving about matters in a more productive fashion. The tears at that point were like the teapot on a stove that gets to the boiling point, and just needs to release steam. If Dad had been equipped with a whistle like more modern teapots, we would have heard the screech from afar. Dad was a part of that whole generation of men who never connected with their feelings or were able to be introspective with them, and that is sad.

Through out my whole adult life, if for whatever reason I am a bit glum, I just tidy and spruce up around our condo. I do so by spending some time vacuuming and dusting. James and I keep a home very much like my Mom did, so while there may not be lots to arrange, the end result of a good vacuuming is that I just feel better. That is a hand-me-down from Mom. She would have loved the Kirby that I use. She could have sucked the dust out of the basement at the same time as she did the upstairs with this machine. The Kirby has a head light too; Mom would have thought she were 'driving' the Lamborghini of vacuums!

When I was a baby, Mom related that she found that if the vacuum cleaner were on it would stop me from crying. The hum of the machine soothed me back to sleep. I loved that machine. As a small child, I loved to play with the old canister vacuum, and push it around the floor. It had wheels, and went everywhere I could take it. It was magical.

My Mom always wished for a larger house, and was always admiring the Walker House, now a bed and breakfast, in Hancock. The house built-in 1910 by Charles Walker had a gracious look, so big and resting on a rise not far from Main Street. Mom had wanted to live in town in her younger days of being a wife, but at some point became resigned to the fact that moving was never going to happen. Even so, there were always those drives past that house over the years when the folks decided to get off the highway and go by it after either coming back from grocery shopping, or after filling the car up at the local station. "We are so close, let's just drive by", she whispered countless times. As we drove past, she always gazed out her passenger's side window and up at the house. I could not know as a child what such a house might mean to her, but as an adult I appreciate the wonder of how that place filled her imagination.

There is no way not to see the charm in the Walker House, and the potential for long hours of reading, and drinking coffee on the porch as the evening drifts down on the small town. The joy of decorating, and finding the old charms that make a house like that speak from the past would be half the fun of living there.

As an adult my thoughts have turned to the history concerning the folks who built the Walker House, and those who have lived there. What those people from the past experienced in life, along with their hopes and fears intrigues me. Moreover, I have wondered about those who occupied my own childhood home before my parents, the newlyweds, moved in and made it home. I think older houses have that way of making one inquire about the past, and imagine what might have taken place as the decades passed. Until very recently, when James and I opted to spend a night there at the Walker House, I never once ventured inside the bed and breakfast, and am most sure the parents had never once entered through the doors either.

It was not until I was older, and living away from home for a number of years that I could start to understand that indeed there were cramped places at our family home, and reasons why my Mom wished for more counter space in the kitchen, and elbow room at the table. I could better sense why she got tense around the holidays, wondering where everyone would sit as the family grew, and there were more dishes to place at the table. The home I grew up in still remained extra special and cozy, and yet I could better understand her desire for space. She loved to have everyone around, and year after year created successful holidays, but it does amaze me, and warms my heart to know she did it all in such a small space.

Regardless of the year or season, one thing was a constant every day when I was growing up. Dinnertime was around 5:30 in the evening, and everyone was expected to be at the table. For many of my years back home, a short prayer was said before we ate. Living in the country with a large garden meant that a 'meat and potatoes' type meal could always be found on the table. It was a diet of traditional fare, with a healthy mix of all those things you could find locally. Nothing was too fancy, but it was all fresh and nutritious.

On many a late summer afternoon, Mom would slip on her garden shoes, and go to the vegetable plot and bring back a nice bunch of tomatoes, a couple cucumbers, fresh radishes, and maybe a summer squash or two. Over my years of growing up there was one certainty at the dinner table: we could guarantee that there would be a bowl of fresh cut tomatoes.

I get a charge out of people who tell me they buy one large tomato at the market, use part of it over the week, store the rest in the refrigerator, and perhaps throw the remainder away as it gets too old. At our home for dinner there might have been four or five large tomatoes cut up, with perhaps a wedge left over that would be eaten at lunch the following day. There is no way to look at tomatoes and not see in my mind the bowl at dinnertime that was a tradition handed down generation to generation. My Grandma Schwarz served them that way, and now that is a custom in our home too.

One of the traditions of fall that has always been a part of my life from the very first apartment I had on my own was to make a 'boiled dinner'. Fresh potatoes, cabbage, carrots, and any other root vegetable are placed in a large pot on the stove with a nice sized piece of beef. The best time to make this food is when it can be allowed to slow simmer all afternoon, and not only fill home with a fantastic aroma, but also the light covering of steam on the lower portion of each window pane. That, to me, is one of the classic memories of Mom's kitchen.

While I didn't tend to swap recipes with Mom as James and his Mom, Marion, used to do with some regularity, I did manage to get Mom to write out a few of my favorites. James will make these dishes for me now as the produce comes in to season. There is nothing better than a pickle salad on a hot day, or some summer squash casserole as the summer nights become autumn ones. (I have included these recipe favorites of mine in the appendix so that if you'd like to share in a dinner with Mom and me, you can.)

Just shortly before my Mom became ill in 2007, she was still reminding me that she had never had a taco when she and Dad went out to eat. I reminded her that she also had never had a piece of meat that was at its most tasty since my father demanded that beef be cooked until it was well done—or well past done as the case may be. Dad also had a fear of undercooked chicken, and was never fond of the Coloma Chicken Chew, something both my Mom and I very much enjoyed. The last year Mom and I were able to attend the event we asked if an order could be brought home for him, and the disgusted look on his face was accompanied by a dismissive hand wave. I recall the chicken was delicious that day. Mom looked about as we ate and pointed out to me the various people she recognized. It was always an event she enjoyed attending; she was an avid people-watcher.

Like Dad, I too had thought that meat had to be well done, until I attended the first Christmas Party held by the broadcasting company for which I worked. I was twenty years old before I discovered that meat's natural color at dinner isn't gray. My colleagues and I were at a nice restaurant in Sturgeon Bay, and all was going very nicely until a piece of beef was placed in front of me. The meat was medium rare. Convinced that I could still hear it mooing gently, I was mindful of all the dire warnings I had heard about eating such meat. Everyone around me seemed to be really enjoying it, though. The old adage 'when in Rome' came to mind and with that I took my first bite. Never before had I tasted such a remarkable flavor for beef, and needless to say that is still the way I prefer it today. I wish there had been some way to convince my parents to have tried some foods prepared in new and exciting ways. Medium rare beef most likely would have really pleased and excited them had they had the courage to give it a try.

The kitchen table in my early years at home had a Formica top decorated in a black and white, small jigsaw design. The table came straight out of the late 50s or early 60s. Often I would look for images in the small designs that resembled a dog, bird, or some other object. The table had been stored in the garage for years, and so when it came for the probate process I looked at the tabletop and easily spotted those images for which I once hunted when waiting for dinner to be served. I was really pleased that a cousin bought the table at auction, and felt even better when it was made known to me that it was being used to wrap presents on for the holidays, and better yet that cups of coffee were once again being enjoyed at the table. This good news genuinely warmed my heart.

Like the rest of Mom's home, her kitchen was immaculate. The memories of how Mom worked to make her kitchen sparkle and shine, with wall hangings, and glass knickknacks chosen to enhance the color of the walls is something I will never forget. She had a small basket at one time that was designed to hang from the wall. She then bought different small plastic flower arrangements of varying hues of soft greens. She always strove to find just the right color for her bouquets. One of her requests of me over time, since I was the one who always traditionally bought a cloth calendar as a holiday gift, was to make sure the colors worked with the painted walls. Mom may never have gained more space in that room, and she never stopped caring how things looked or were presented.

My Dad in later years started to find irritating the loud voices. He loved to have everyone around to share the holidays, but the grandchildren ran around the house in a much more disorderly fashion than he recalled having raised his own kids. With everyone in the small kitchen, and the noise bouncing off the walls, he often retired to his large chair in the living room. Still, for the bulk of the family holiday, the kitchen was always the best room in which to gather.

When James and I came to understand in 2007 that we were moving to an old Victorian, one of Mom's first comments was about all the space we would have to store things given how limited our apartment was on the west side of Madison. While there is lots more room in a house than in an apartment, the notion of storage space is relative. I told her that the Victorian houses hardly included any closet space. The integrity of our home remains as from the day it was built so that means we have exactly one closet, and a very small one at that. I can still see and hear Mom's response. Her face was priceless. "One closet!?" All of a sudden she decided she lived in a large home since every room in her house had at least some sort of storage area.

As a child I knew larger homes came with additional amenities that most likely were very nice, but I also was aware the most important thing in a home was to be loved, and have a strong sense of security while growing up. I felt content being raised where I was, in part because I did not have anything really to compare it too, but mainly because the foundations of a strong family existed. I always felt as a kid that we were rich, and to be honest, I truly felt we were better off than many others in the area. In later years I would apply for financial aid for broadcasting school, and learn our bottom line was not as I had thought, and was rather surprised.

That level of surprise at our actual economic state of affairs is what makes all that which happened in the 1,268 square feet we called home even more impressive. Looking back there were things that could have been newer and larger. I never saw it that way at the time, and that is due to the parenting skills, love, and attention that Mom and Dad provided.

I have seen a number of old postcard views of Hancock's Main Street. Some show a mud-filled Main Street with horses and wagons, and wooden railings where a horse could be tethered. Others have old cars parked on the streets, along with the variety of stores that once were the places locals would shop and chat with neighbors.

Main Street seemed fun to me as a kid, and perhaps no more so than when the large bright Christmas lights would be hung in numerous strands high over my head above the road. The Christmas lights were physically quite large then when compared to the modern energy-star rated LED versions preferred today. The type of bulb that the Village of Hancock employed cast a nostalgic glow and is now considered 'old-fashioned'. I put it to you though: has there been a warmer seasonal glow to be found than in those large colored lights that brightened the nights at holiday time?

The Village of Hancock was itself exciting for me when I traveled with Dad on a Friday night to the barber shop. As a kid I never recall any other night of the week when my Dad thought it OK to visit Marv, a no-frills type of barber who would talk, and move about with clippers and shears in hand. For me, being a small kid, Marv would lift a slab of wood across the arms of the barber chair which had red cushy arms rests. I would climb up on to the slab, and sit to make it easier for me 'to leave with both ears', as it was explained over and over to me. I recall always asking for some of the 'smelly stuff' to be splashed on my face and neck like I had seen happen so often to the older men, Dad included. Nothing makes you feel more in tune with everyone else than a splash of something smelly when you are only seven years old. Then it would be time for me to climb down off the slab of wood and wait as Dad had his hair clipped. It was never a long wait; Dad had little hair. He never let it get very long before it had to be trimmed.

When I was older I recall that I was allowed to roam up and down Main Street as my Dad got his haircut. I liked to look inside the windows, though at that time I never went alone into any of the shops. We had a grocery store, a bait shop, a hardware store, and even a bakery. Oh! The bakery was good. At unpredictable times my Dad would bring home dessert after he got off work. The bakery made the best crullers and apple fritters to be found anywhere. How that business was not able to survive, even in a small town, is one of life's little unexplained mysteries. Beyond the bakery was the motel and filling stations. In later years I ventured up the street, and into the local library and fed my lifetime addiction to books.

The library was a special place where Winifred Carlton and I started a friendship. Mrs. Carlton staffed the desk almost every Friday. Hancock's library then sat in a small, white framed-building that was short on space, but not on the mission it served in our hometown. (The building had at one time sat on the opposite side of the street, and served as the town's jewelry store. I only recall it as having been the library.) Today, the library is reported to have nearly 8,000 volumes.

Over the years I have come to understand how important Mrs. Carlton was to me while growing up in a rural area, as well as how much that library opened a whole world that still attracts me these many decades later. I can never stress enough when local officials think about the needs of small communities to remind them of the value that a local library provides. It is truly a gateway to the future for many who seek it out.

I was reading at a more advanced level than my peers since I did not grow up with television in my formative years. By the time I was in the fifth grade I had mowed through the *Hardy Boys* and *Nancy Drew* series, and my interests were expanding into new areas. I was not really interested anymore in the children's section. I moved on instead to the books written for adults. Mrs. Carlton reminded me several times I might be more interested in the books that were written for people my age. Each time, I told Mrs. Carlton that I was perfectly fine looking where I was. This scenario played out for several weeks until she realized I was indeed going to read whatever piqued my curiosity.

After the checking out process I always stood and talked with her about my family, things happening around the area, and school. She was wise, caring, and a mighty important person to have in our community. She clearly loved books, and placed value on her time and service that she provided to others, to people like me. She volunteered her time in that small library with a sense of duty and pride.

I may have convinced Mrs. Carlton that I was reading appropriate material. I was not as successful with everyone else. It was one of those books that I checked out under Mrs. Carlton's watchful eye, and read in my grade school years that caused a most stern looking teacher to ask the most peculiar questions of me.

"Do your parents know you are reading this book?" Questions like that from a middle school teacher, well that was as close to book censorship that ever came my way. I recall standing on the stair steps of my old Hancock schoolhouse. The teacher stopped me. She pointed at my copy of *The Throne of Saturn* by Allen Drury, and just looking at it sounded her internal alarm, though for what reason I could never understand. Other than the fact it was 600 pages, and 'kids' were not supposed to read anything more interesting than some hokey dribble that I had long since passed over provides no real explanation for her remark.

The fact is my parents encouraged me to read, as it kept me interested in all sorts of things. Perhaps as important, reading kept me quiet. I am not sure if the teacher had any idea the book was about a space adventure between the United States and the Soviet Union. I can say though that Drury made for high drama in my sixth grade mind. More importantly still, I thought to myself, "Clearly it was perfect reading for a lot of people or it would never have been published". Nonetheless, the teacher sure did look skeptical about that book as we stood on the stairs. Her disapprobation seemed to me to be misdirected, at very best. She seemed not to care that I had an almost hour ride on the bus to school in the morning, and that reading was the perfect way to spend that wasted time. Worse yet, she seemed not to care about my feelings.

I finished that book, and Allen Drury has been a writer I have long enjoyed into my adult years. Today a hard copy edition of *The Throne of Saturn* sits on a bookshelf in our home as not only a reminder of a good read, but also to underscore a long-held belief of mine. No one should try to limit or question reading material of inquisitive minds. Of course, questioning the choices of a child who likes to read seems counter-productive; I am glad I didn't let the incident deter me from my lifelong love affair with books!

Those small businesses on Main Street were places where as I grew that I shopped for small presents. Mr. Fowler, an older man who did woodworking had a store with all sorts of small items for sale. His handicrafts were made with the aide of various tools, and then painted. For Mother's Day one year I bought a large wooden butterfly. It served my Mother as a wall decoration. (When my Father dropped me off for Sunday school, Mr. Fowler's wife would often be waiting in the passenger's side of their car. She had difficulty walking by then, so she didn't get out of the car any sooner than she needed to; the church pews were so hard that she found them difficult in which to be comfortable. We would talk and share a few moments together before I would go inside to get my seat. When she was able, Mrs. Fowler often sat next to Grandma at services.) At the hardware store in time for one of my Father's birthdays, I bought Dad a new rasp and various interchangeable blades for smoothing out a wood's rough surfaces. I felt so grown up making these types of transactions all on my own as boy with money I had saved and stored in the top drawer of my dresser.

Thinking back on the memory-laden images of the slow-moving downtown streets of Hancock when I was boy reminds me that I always knew at some level that I could never live there as an adult. Even though I was not sure of anything about the world I just sensed that in spite of many wonderful aspects to be found in downtown Hancock I yearned for more. The bustle of a city always drew my attention, and presented more opportunities. I wanted a place where people shared broader thinking, more diversity, and allowed for more ideas to percolate in non-judgmental ways. As I grew older, and more aware of what made me tick I felt a stronger desire to seek out a dynamic city to call home. I recognized in my teenage years that I did not want to miss out on having a new location to live as an adult, away from the one I started out with as a child.

On family vacations I always lamented the expressways that directed traffic away from the city centers. As my Dad and Mom rejoiced in the front seats about not having to confront the maddening traffic of a busy downtown quarter, I recall looking out the back window of the car and watching the large buildings tower off in the distance, and knowing that is where all the fascinating 'things' took place. People were really 'living' in those places circumvented by the expressway. I could be too. In my teenage years I knew with certainty I was not going to engage with my siblings in what appeared to me then as a competition to see who could build a house closer to our parents. I had dreams I wanted to follow. I knew in order to be the person I wanted to be, and in order to gain the experiences I needed which would allow for my personal growth and fulfillment it required my leaving Hancock.

I stood in the dining room by the heating stove in late 1986. I was about to move to Madison and start my job at the state capitol. Mom told me she knew that of her kids I was going to be the one who would follow his dreams. Mom understood that I could never be content in a small town. She also told me that all she wanted was for me to be happy. That was her way of coming to terms with who I was, and what I wanted, and needed for my life.

If one were to take a bird's eye view photo of the one hundred acres my parents owned when I was a boy it would have a neatly painted home that had expanded on the east end to accommodate another bedroom. The lawn was always well maintained. Not far from that additional room, the unattached garage was built. To the north of the garage was a large old-fashioned typical barn that was torn down, and replaced when I was little. The old, small building that was always referred to as the 'grainery' was to the east of the barn, and at some point in my childhood it was also demolished.

At the end of the drive stood the mailbox where our copy of the *Stevens Point Journal* arrived every day. From the house, arching gently toward the northwest, one had but to walk the driveway composed of small gravel, compacted over time for a smooth surface, and there awaited a connection to the outside world. In other words, each and every day when the postman would drive by, a fresh batch of 'radio copy', stories to recount to each other, surprises about local events, and items of interest for everyone landed in the round-topped box atop a little pole.

The front yard on the other side of the drive was home to one of the best trees in the lawn. The large oak's limbs stretched out toward the sun. The big old oak, featured on the cover of this book, was even more tantalizing as a sitting spot. It was a fine old tree, which I suspect must have been planted closer to when the house was built and where I could relax and read Ian Fleming. Listening to the breeze through the leaves, I would become better acquainted with the intensely dramatic James Bond.

To the south of the 'reading oak', a large flower garden lined the limits of what was our yard. Bordered on one side with a white fence, the garden bloomed in roses, hosta, creeping phlox, daisies, red cannas, bright yellow day lilies, tiger lilies, petunias, geraniums, marigolds and other pansies. Mom tended her flower beds with the same precision and attention which she gave the interior of her home. As each flower faded in its beauty, Mom kept them deadheaded so that new growth could show off the love that went into their maintenance and care.

On the other side of the little white fence, a row of rhubarb, or pie fruit, kept us in cobblers and crisps much of the spring. The l-shaped vegetable garden bent around a large hedgerow of pine trees that my Aunt Lorene helped Dad to plant one spring well before I was born. The summer sun of Hancock bathed cornrows, beans, beets, and tons of potatoes and tomatoes. Had there been a cow or pig fenced somewhere on the property we could have made it through most winters on what we grew ourselves. And were we ever grateful to Lorene for her help with those pines, which then circled back around all the buildings and ended out at the road, not far from the mailbox and my *Stevens Point Journal*. Those pines provided us with shade in the summer months for the entire time we call that place Home.

Beyond the pines which surrounded the acre and a half where the house sat, off up past the field that had served at one time as farmland for the previous owners, were the 'north woods'. That wooded area contained a small dug out that was filled with water in the spring from melting snows. The slope of the land allowed for this area at times to have a marshy look, and a swampy smell until the heat of summer dried it up like everything else. On the south side of the property was a large expanse of woods brimming with white pine and oak.

There was a lot of simplicity to the life we lived. In Mom's basement, the old hand-wringer washing machine was still being used long after my growing-up days and in to the last years of her life, when Dad bought her a modern machine, and installed it next to a dryer. Wash day was Monday. As a boy, I would join my Mother as she worked. I sat on the wooden steps leading to the cemented basement, legs hanging down through the open-rise staircase with some paper to color on or books to look at as she did the washing. Every step of the stairs could be a desktop or a bench seat for me at that age.

The last time I was home and Mom was still there, prior to her going to the hospital but never to return, she gave me the wooden washing stick. Back when Mom still used the hand-wringer machine, she had a wooden stick roughly eighteen inches in length. With the washing stick, she would safely lift with her right hand the heavy wet clothes out of the wash tub and feed them through the wringing attachment on the back of the machine. By the time that she gave that stick to me, it was worn by time and love. I stood in the back entry as she handed it to me. She had brought it up from down stairs, and I took it. I cried passionately.

1,268 Square Feet

I knew what such a personal and warm gift like this meant about how she perceived her health, and our connections to washdays. It now has a special place in our Madison home. That little stick means the world to me.

Life in Hancock was not complicated. Dad was an organic gardener before organic was trendy. He'd be bent over in the garden with a pail, and old stick to knock the potato bugs off so as not to need to resort to the use of any pesticides. He felt there was a certain way of living and interacting not only with one's neighbors but also with the land. He felt strongly that except for the large farmers who mistreated the land to make ever-greater profits that most small farmers and landowners were cognizant about not allowing the wind to whip away the soil, or saturate the area with chemicals. He wondered why the large farmers couldn't adopt a similar philosophy, even if it meant reduced profits. Dad really did care for the land and without ever saying it, he was an environmentalist.

My parents cared deeply for the little things in life. Dad liked to tell the story of the screech owls he had helped save as a boy. I hadn't heard the story in a number of years. Not so long before he passed away, I asked him to repeat his story. It was like pulling a book off the shelf that had been read to me countless times as a child, knowing it would still bring a smile to his face.

At age ten or eleven, Royce found three screech owls in the barn that still stands at the old homestead in Coloma. Royce and his brother Robert, two years younger, became the guardians of these youngsters. The mother owl had disappeared for whatever reason. A couple of times a day, the boys' Mom supplied them with bread and milk to feed the birds. Royce always continued the story with some small waves of his hand, like the fluttering of wings, as he recounted how his cousin Hiram had told the brothers: "We shoot those things." Even though Hiram blustered about such things, Royce spoke of how the cousin could not believe how the birds would fly in and land as they did on the boys' shoulders. "They would fly into the barn and land on our shoulders for feeding. They were very friendly. Robert and I were not having any of shooting them". Royce and Robert continued feeding the young owls until they had grown a bit older; the boys then released their three friends in the orchard.

Dad was an old softie. In his adult life, he made sure every winter that the wild turkeys would have corn to eat in an area in the woods where they came to scratch and peck. He never hunted them, or wanted harm to come their way. If the icy crust of snow would prevent the turkeys from finding any food, you'd find Dad lugging a pail of corn to the woods. He did this year after year.

My Mom made holiday meals for the cats. Dad helped to

deliver her gifts on Thanksgiving and Christmas. Mom would get a skillet out and put this left-over or that one into the mix, add some milk, and warm it up. Then Dad would march it out to our field and feed some cats that he knew lived across the road. In the high snow months my Dad even made a path down to the field so one of the younger cats could walk easier to the place where he fed them. My folks taught me how to be more aware of the world that is right outside our window, and how to care about things smaller than us.

The folks out in the country where I grew up were friendly. We called each other by our first names. In those winter months when people don't get out as much, it could seem as though one were living all alone on those country roads. At other points in the year, one might get the opposite impression. People seemed to know too much. I have long contended that if you don't tell people about your life, they will invent one for you. This lack of privacy in a small town is part of growing up in a rural area.

'Ma Bell', as the phone company was once called, was perhaps the biggest gossip in town. I grew up in a time when 'party lines' connected a small group of people. The party line was an arrangement in which two or more telephone customers were connected directly to the same local loop. (Prior to World War II in the United States, party lines were the primary way residential subscribers acquired local telephone service.) Here is how it worked: in order to distinguish one line subscriber from another, operators developed different ringing cadences for the subscribers, so that if the call was for the first subscriber to the line, the ring would follow one pattern such as two short rings, if the call was for the second subscriber, the ring would sound another way, such as a short ring followed by a long one, and so on. Since all parties utilized the same line, it was possible for subscribers to listen in on other subscribers' calls.

In other words, one of the ways to find out the comings and goings of those in the area was to pick up the phone and find out if anyone was talking. Then, you had to be very still so as not to alert the other participants to the call that you are listening. One could always find out some news. Of course, any such news gleaned from another family's calls was always shared in the house, with the understanding that we act like it were the first time we heard it, if and when we heard it coming from someone from outside the house!

1,268 Square Feet

For my family at least, listening in on the neighbors' phone calls was not something that we did often. When the weather was wild outside, with the snow and wind making drifts that mounded around the house, my Mom would want me to listen in on the party line, and find out the news. She wanted to know the conditions of the roads and if people were making their way home safely. Gently and quietly, I would lift the receiver so no one could hear the click, and pick up the needed news. It might be noted that President Nixon was tapping phones in Washington at the time that I was eavesdropping on conversations in Hancock. I claim the "Everyone Else, Including the President, is Doing It" defense. The major difference between what was going on at my house, and what was happening at the White House was that our illicit deeds were not being audio taped. You could say that our calls all took place within the space of those eighteen and a half minutes of accidentally erased material! In reality, Mom and I just hoped Dad could make it home for dinner on roads that were not blocked with drifts.

Perhaps the most interesting aspect to the mid-century telephone was not when it was in use, but when the summer storms made the metal appliance ring and jangle. My parents never allowed anyone in the dining room during the massive summer storms, as it was not uncommon to have blue flashes of light to come forth from the phone as it hung on the wall as it drew the lightning. It was awesome to see, thought it made some in my family really nervous.

So while Hancock was rural, and at times even rustic it was also special. Living out in the country meant that experiencing a day and night without power at least once each winter due to an ice storm was just as common as the summer evenings when the whippoorwill birds would call.

In the summer when trees would topple over somewhere in the area and take out our electricity, big decisions had to be made. One of those concerned the ice cream in the freezer. Was the electricity going to be out so long that it would melt since in those days ice cream always came in a light cardboard box? Might we need to eat it before it melted and made a real mess? Oh, how often we failed to have faith in the speed and efficiency of the power company! With spoons we would set out to make sure Mom's freezer would not be covered with melted sweetness.

Memories of my family days are now like the yellow and faded photographs that are placed in an album or stashed in a drawer. They serve to remind me where I came from, and allow me to journey backwards with an easy smile. Like for millions of other Americans there is something about Sunday dinner that takes my memory back to the days when my parent's home was the scene of just about the perfect place that anyone could wish to be. James and I have talked about the difference between the notion of home and what is a house. A house, to our mind, is a structure designed to be a place where one can live in relative comfort. A home though is quite different. A home is a place where people share their lives, where memories are made and preserved. The old home place where I grew up now is no longer a home. All that remains now is an empty bunch of lumber and nails stitched together. After my parents' passing, and everything was sold off in auction, it was as if the spirit just left the place. My childhood "home" now is a place located in the memories I keep from those days.

For me, now that I am an adult, there is nothing quite like being outside running an errand or completing some home chore in the fall when there is a chill in the air, and the wind off Lake Monona takes the first bite of the season. Stepping into our Madison home feels so good; the warmth of the place envelops me in mighty comfort. The second thing that captures my soul when I am at home is the aroma of whatever James is preparing in our kitchen. James talks about one of his favorite authors, Proust, who at the smell of the madeleine cookie was caught up in a flow of powerful recollections. There's a term for it even, he says: it is called the Proustian mnemonic, or aide memoire. I am forever being reminded of something when I smell James' cooking. There is simply no way not to get trapped in a flood of memories that cascade about when the kitchen aromas converge, and the senses are so alive.

I used to get the same feelings when I was at home with the folks. Family Sunday afternoons in Hancock were a long-lived, and long-loved tradition in my life. Starting in 1987, and for about the next eighteen years, I drove from Madison and spent a part of most Sunday afternoons with my parents. As soon as I entered the house, I knew what was on the stove cooling. In fact, there were times on the back steps before the door opened that a strong clue as to what had been baked wafted about in the air.

My Mom had one of those classic Corning-ware glass-baking dishes that had seen more holidays, birthdays, snow days, and last-minute 'someone-just-pulled-in-the-drive-and-I have-nothing-ready-to-eat' moments. On many a weekend when I showed up, it was filled with brownies, fresh from the oven. Oddly, there was always one square missing.

Dad was quite certain that it was important to test all brownies to ensure they were fit for company. Lady Luck smiled on our family always. Over my entire lifetime, I never knew of a bad batch. Dad was unwilling to take chances though—something about liability. Thankfully for those who entered our home, there was nothing to fear since we benefitted from having a live-in brownie taste-tester.

It is a litigious world we live in, but we are safe from prosecution here in Madison as well. We also have a considerate person such as my Dad was. James, too, makes sure that there is never a batch of Halloween candy that has not been sampled, just to make sure that the kids coming to our door are getting only the best, and freshest candy that can be bought.

Family Sunday's back home, once one made it past the back door and understood that the brownies were indeed safe, had a certain rhythm to them. For me, once over the threshold I would place on the counter in the kitchen a small pile of newspaper clippings that I had found in the past week that would either amuse my Dad, or pique my Mom's interest.

Clipping from newspapers is no laughing matter. It is serious work; one should be required to get a certificate in the art. For me, it is a habit I learned from the master, my Mom. Mom's scissors were dulled over time due to the frequent attacks on newsprint. When she wasn't cleaning my fingerprint smudges off the white trim of the doors in the house, she maintained a serious pile of neatly clipped and often annotated clippings from a long list of publications. Each clipping was destined to head off to some family member through the mail. If not the US postal service, some were simply stored until the information contained therein would be relevant. Mom would then disappear to her little office, where she would dig for paper scrap, only to reappear with it to support the argument she was making. Mom would have made a very good academic. She liked to be able to sustain the factual underpinnings of whatever was being discussed in her kitchen over coffee.

Clipping and saving. Sorting and filing. Mom was a consummate news source in her own right. So much so, that when I was finally able to have access to her home during the probate process which unfolded after Dad's passing, I realized how much my Mom had kept over the years. Among the clippings James and I found a large stash of articles torn from decorating magazines--from years back. She was sweetly hoarding ideas of the different designs and possibilities for the large kitchen of which she dreamed. She had a file set aside, thick like the Sears catalogue at Christmas, brimming with the possibilities for the larger bathroom for which she had always yearned.

My mania for clipping took on a different kind of focus. In the pile of clippings that I brought home on Sundays, I principally stashed articles about old cars, or a political story about farmers and property taxes. Those were the kinds of things that were sure to either make my Dad smile, or ramp up his blood pressure. It was my way of keeping him healthy. For my Mom, my clippings might be about a road project in the western states on a highway up in the mountains where we had traveled on a family vacation, or an interesting story about the history of Chicago, a topic about which she loved to read. Her grandparents, Jacob and Bertha (Kline) Schwarz, had met there. Bertha worked for a while at a shirt factory in the city, as well as at a hotel bakery where she later met and married her husband in 1889.

Mom also had a way of cross-referencing her discoveries. In her little office space, she kept a map collection. This assortment of cartographic aides included among others a detailed map of the streets of the Windy City. Once Mom had a new story about an old neighborhood or some historic article that intrigued her from a genealogical point of view, the maps would get spread out on the dining room table. In the later years when her eyesight dimmed slightly she would have a magnifying glass to see more clearly. Age affects us all. In those later years when Mom sought the assistance of an eye piece, she would be bent straining to find a street, and alongside her I stood with my glasses off all together. I had to do it that way, otherwise I could not read the small print. We must have looked like quite the pair of investigators!

After lunch my Dad would pile up the clippings along with the crisp, unread *Chicago Tribune* I bought for them every Sunday as I drove out of Madison. Armed with his reading material, Dad would toddle off to the living room to sit in his favorite reclining chair, look out onto the road that passed in front of our home, and keep constant tabs on the weather.

The *Chicago Tribune* was a favorite for my parents. My Mom laid claim first to the lifestyle and magazine sections of the paper. She lounged in the dining room to peruse it and relax a bit. Dad would take the front section and catch up on the headlines, with Mom in his line of sight from the recliner. For me, I would continue to read my copy of the *New York Times*, and I always liked the full kitchen table style of reading. I would spread out the newspaper so that I could see what was both above and below the fold. (Here in Madison though it is in the rocking chair that James and our friend Jenny reupholstered for me some years back that I sit to read the dailies.) So with my copy of the *Times* covering the table, Mom in the dining room, and Dad in his living room lazy-boy, we would all read and relax. That's what I call one fine Sunday afternoon.

Sundays are also meant for indulging one of my other personal vices. Caffeine. Mom never failed to have tea or coffee (usually coffee) made for me. (My Grandma Schwarz got me hooked on the black elixir. I'll tell you about that in a second, but I must add that I felt so grown up when I could have a little cup of Joe just like Grandpa!) When I was older, and would come back home on weekends, the kitchen was the ideal spot to sit and converse on the week's happenings. Mom may not have had all the answers to life's concerns but she always listened and had something to add as we drank a cup of coffee. Sometimes, we would have a few cups of coffee—we were grownups, after all. More importantly perhaps, I am convinced that Mom was of the impression, as I am, that words come easier over a mug of hot java.

I love coffee. My coffee addiction began when I was at my Grandparent's home. Before the evening chores were to be done Grandpa Schwarz would come in from whatever the afternoon work was, and sit at his spot at the table near the door. Grandma might have bread and jam, some homemade sweets, and always a cup of coffee. I heard so many times from her, after requesting a little, that it would stunt my growth. I understand now in hindsight that her concern for my height was a front that she put on for the sake of appearing to do the right thing. The reality of the situation was that in time she started to give me a little bit of coffee and then fill the rest of the mug with milk. My Grandma, the enabler, slowly changed her tune, giving me up for a lost cause, I guess. Little by little the ratio of milk to coffee worked out in my favor. Within time, there was almost all coffee in the cup. I prefer my drug of choice black today. Family lore leads me to believe that this pattern of behavior was a learned one. It would seem that my Mom's grandmother, Bertha, a little itty-bitty thing of a German immigrant, would do the same for my Mom when she was little. Mom's sister, Lorene, confirms that this is also how she first got hooked on the stuff as well. Lorene further adds that she is leading her own granddaughter, Paige, slowly down that same path. She calls Paige's a "cappuccino", yet we all know that soon enough, it will be nothing but coffee in that mug.

Living next door to the small farm that my grandparents operated was a great way to grow up as a kid. The fun times that took place just over the blacktopped road from our house were numerous. Many Saturdays, I would stay with my grandparents while my Mom and Dad went shopping in the 'Points'. Grandpa would often take the small tractor off down the country lane, with me riding along, to get wood to be stored near the back door for the stove. There was a special place made just for me to sit, or so it seemed, as I hung on and made the trek back into the woods with Grandpa.

It was a pleasure to head over the road to Grandma's house to watch the big events, such as the moon landing, on her television. The astronauts would change, as would the number of the Apollo mission, but the anchor of the CBS News broadcasts, Walter Cronkite, remained ever-present and informative. I recall a Saturday morning as if it were yesterday 'Uncle Walter' explained with a plastic model of the moon buggy about how it would operate, and what precautions needed to be taken to insure its successful movements on the lunar surface. Grandma kept chips or cookies to nipple on as I sat there in rapt attention. Grandma sat with her coffee in an arm chair off to the side and behind me, while I sat on the sofa and we would watch Walter on that large console TV set. Later I would re-create the events in my backyard. The green grass at my parent's home would be the gray surface of the moon. Walter's voice of the events unfolding would echo in my head as I moved slowly to impersonate the gravity free conditions that the famed astronauts encountered.

Fresh baked cinnamon rolls smelled heavenly whenever I walked along the south side of their house to the back door. The heart of Grandma's kitchen was the big black cast iron stove. That heart beat with the warmth from burning wood that crackled and filled the air with its scent. Grandma stood alongside it in her ever-present apron; Grandpa warmed himself near it on cold days.

The stove was unlike any other I knew as a boy, and after all these years of talking about it I have never encountered anyone else my age (other than relatives) who can relate to the delight it brought while I was young. There were so many ways one could enjoy that wood stove: the smell of wood smoke that curled out of the chimney when the stove was stoked; the sound of crackling wood inside the iron burner along with the sizzling fried potatoes in a skillet on top; and, the glowing embers that could be seen on the side through the grates.

After dinner Grandma washed dishes using water heated in the stove reservoir. I would dry the dishes but not before I had drizzled a little water on the stove's hot surface and watched the drops of water skitter about and evaporate. "Just a few drops," Grandma would say. I think she always knew how much I really wanted to drip on the super-hot cook top. On cold days I can still see my Grandfather, with a cup of coffee in hand, pull the main oven door down and sit on it for warmth. I also recall poking the embers with a wooden stick from the side grate while grownups sat at the table talking over a cup of Joe.

Every summer as a child there was one week when all the grandkids who lived in various places around the country, or across the state, would visit the grandparents. With plenty of wooded land to play in, and hide from one another, one would think that there would be no reason to run through Grandpa's rows of corn. Am I right? Wrong.

Even though I still recall Grandpa telling us all not to play in the corn, and not to trample it, I think all the grandkids have fond memories of somehow 'forgetting'. Once the race was on to hide and not be found there was no better place than in the deep green rows. The rows of corn gave off that scent of new growth that comes after a hot summer day in the sun. Loud giggles and screams when one of us was finally located can still be heard if you just listen hard enough. You have to listen carefully though—when all else is quiet on that land.

My poor James finds coffee unpalatable. It is one of the few things upon which we do not agree at all. He will make tea and claim to be as pleased as I am—but coffee drinkers know he is missing out on something wonderful. His claims that the grounds themselves just smell burnt are not based in reality, I fear. He has yet to divulge though what may be the real source of his animus towards my guilty diurnal allowance. One of the simple pleasures of life is the smell of coffee as it is brewing, followed by the sound of it being poured, the steam rising into the air. The only thing that is better is the first sip.

Indeed, I love the smell of fresh ground coffee. I love to fill the coffee pot and as it brews, pull one of my favorite mugs off a kitchen shelf. You have to agree that coffee is simply more enjoyable if the mug's design and decoration are just right for the day and mood. We have a variety of mugs to fit every season and every mood. There are times when I stand for a few seconds and ponder the choice for the day. James is often reminding me that we need to slim the herd that is in the cupboard. He just doesn't understand. I will readily admit that one of my weaknesses involves new and colorful mugs. I find it difficult to get in and out of stores where fancy mugs are sold, and not find myself in possession of one.

A good cup of coffee bolsters the spirit. Some days require it just to make it through; and, as we all know, there are days when things just don't work out like they should. On the day my Dad passed away in the family home, I thought of Grandma and Grandpa and the many cups of coffee that they shared in their fifty-one years together. I recollected fondly too Mom and all the cups of coffee that we had sipped slowly. The day my Dad died was a long horrible day. In anguish we waited hour-by-hour. Had my Mom survived, she would have had the kitchen organized, and she would not have forgotten that it is the little things like a hot cup of coffee that help get people through the rough times. She was unquestionably compassionate. On the day my Father died, though, not one pot of coffee was made. Not a single one. And, I certainly wasn't in a position there to make one for us all, despite the tonic that it would have been for all those of us attending Dad in his dining room hospital bed. I've spoken before about what constitutes a "home" for me, as opposed to what a "house" represents. It is a funny thing to think about, perhaps, as a loved one lay dying, but the determined absence of a percolating pot of coffee was a real sign that 'home life' where I grew up was indeed finished.

In essence, the true nature of a good cup of coffee shared among people who love each other is that transcendental quality of fellowship. By being together and partaking in something so insignificant, but doing it as a group, we touch on the spiritual connection that exists between us. That day in April was already very difficult to cope with emotionally. So much was missing. Mom wasn't there to care for Dad as she had always done. My siblings were there, but not helpful to me in any emotional way. What was missing from the day my Dad died was some spiritual context.

My Dad's last day among us was so different from how things were allowed to be when my Mom was in the hospital four years earlier. During my Mother's final illness, I spoke several times with hospital clergy. I asked James at times to get Father Dennis Lynch to say a prayer, and to read from the *Twenty-third Psalm*. I did not feel as though I were walking through the valley, and in the shadows alone.

The August day when my Mom passed away I had the opportunity at about noon to be alone with her. As she had so often done in our home as she cleaned and washed, I sang out loud two songs for her. I did the best that I could to render *Blessed Assurance* and *How Great Thou Art* for her. Through tears, I sang softly and I held her hand.

With my Dad, it was just so different. We were all at home in the house where my parents had shared a lifetime of hopes, and dreams and it felt more impersonal than the Stevens Point hospital room where my Mom was treated to tubes and beeping machines of all sorts. No one came to lift the spirit, to share a few words from the *Bible*, to offer comfort. There simply was no spiritual context for us, Dad's loved ones, so that we could frame the situation, and understand what God's plan must have been. When I left that night to go home to Madison, I felt an uneasy emptiness spiritually that I had not felt when Mom was so sick.

"Leaving home" is a process. I went through it when I first went off to broadcasting school. I experienced it again as I left Sturgeon Bay, Wisconsin to take up residence in Madison.

"Leaving home" showed itself to me in a new light too in 1997, at the time my parents celebrated fifty years of togetherness. What do I mean?

As I prepared to leave for my home in Madison I stood in the doorway to the place where I had spent my youth and looked at my parents. They stood close to each other; dressed in their finest clothes. My father still had on one of his nattiest ties of varying colors, and my Mom sported a fashionable blazer of dark lavender, green and gray. She had taken off the corsage to preserve it. She had worn the spray of flowers during the afternoon's festivities. As the day drew to a close, and I was about to leave they each gave me a hug, and again spoke of what a wonderful day they had enjoyed with the family that had attended.

"Everyone should know what a day like this feels like" were the words my Mom spoke as she hugged me. My Dad and I embraced in one of our rare moments of this type, and smiled at Mom as he joked about "doing this every fifty years."

The fiftieth wedding anniversary for my parents was something that I had thought about, and planned for over the course of a couple of years. I knew that whatever our family planned it had to be tasteful, memorable, and refined. I wanted the party to resemble the events I had read about for other notable couples that had marked such a milestone. There could be no plastic table clothes or green stamp card tables for my parents. I wanted to mark the occasion with class and grace.

My idea was to have a party at an elegant bed and breakfast, where nice china would be used, tea cups would all match, tasty food would be served, and the atmosphere would be one of warmth and charm.

My parents had only been alerted that they should be dressed-up, and ready to go somewhere at a certain time. They had no idea where, and until my Uncle Bob showed up in his large car, they had no clue by whom they were to be escorted. The party was held in Plainfield. The plan went off without a hitch. The whole affair still ranks as one of the perfect moments in life where all the pieces came together, including the weather.

I had made recordings of music from the 1940s that played softly in the background, photos from over the years were assembled for people to view and reminisce about as family sat about and retold stories from over the years.

When Mom passed away my folks were just shy of sixty years of marriage. After all those years my parents were still in love and devoted to each other. In a society where the term 'starter marriage' is not only used in everyday conversation, but also practiced by roughly half of those who are wed, I feel strongly that my parents made ideal role models for the relationship I have with James.

Six decades after taking their wedding vows Dad was still holding the door for my Mom, and she would continually look out the windows at home to make sure he was safe doing whatever project he had slated to be com-

1,268 Square Feet

pleted that day. With three kids, the woes of a work-a-day world, and the economic ups and downs that all confront as a married couple, my folks knew at the end of the day that which really mattered.

Regardless of the differences over this issue or that, and yes there were arguments on a raft of issues that at times did get loud, my Mom still was up to make coffee and breakfast for Dad, and every night he was back home for dinner and to sleep in their bed. We all take lots for granted in life, but I never failed to recognize the importance of the relationship my folks had, and how they nurtured it over their lifetime together.

Dad's side of the family seemed more prone to drinking and divorcing than my Mom's family. Mom would jokingly refer to her in-laws as 'the outlaws'. I recall as a boy the stories my parents would tell about those who got divorced, always repeating and stating plainly the idea that it was not right to just get up, and leave when things started to get rough. "Walking away is too easy" was a refrain I heard often as a boy from both of my parents, and the tone it was presented with made no more embroidery to the argument necessary.

Dad behaved differently in many respects from some of his relatives, and I think that was one thing that struck my Mom at the time of their courtship. Dad was a gentleman from the start, and never stopped being one.

Mom's family had a very stable foundation in most respects, was more religious, and in my mind offered a more serene example of how to live life, and raise a family. I interacted far more with my aunts, uncles and cousins from Mom's side. I never was old enough to know my father's parents, but was privileged to live across the road from my other pair of grandparents.

All families, however, have some saucy stories, and as I grew older I came to know things that made me very aware a good tale can be learned if you just wait long enough to hear it. It seemed cups of coffee Mom and I shared while sitting in the kitchen made for the perfect atmospherics to swap a few good stories about families.

When it came to creating a solid home life, structured and nurturing surroundings, and a complete sense of stability my parents did a most admirable job. I have no way to relate to the up and down world that a family in chaos experiences. I never went to bed not knowing I was loved, or wondering if home life was about to change. The only evolution in our home was my siblings leaving for their adult lives, and that I can assure all was not something to lose sleep over. Had I owned any boxes I would have given them for the cause. My Mom might have missed them, but I loved the extra space, and additional freedoms it allowed me. Being the youngest

1,268 Square Feet

does have its perks.

The story of how my parents first started knowing each other starts with my Dad, Royce, delivering milk to the Schwarz family in 1945. Mom's siblings speak of her being "smitten" by the tall lean man in the truck. Soon it was she who would run out into the yard to get the butter and greet the deliveryman. The Schwarz girls recall Royce carrying chunks of ice with tongs to the icebox. I, of course, never witnessed it, but from the stories over the years a certain image has formed in my mind of how it must have looked.

Mom had moved from Arkansas with her family into a home directly across the road from where my folks would reside their entire married life. For a few weeks right after the Schwarz's moved to Hancock they had lived in what would become our home until the one they wo[...]r the rest of their live[...]ction fingers pointed [...]s the road' when it ca[...]

My Mom [...]oung couple. Stories [...]days that continued [...] the country there wi[...] was a farmer ridding [...]t one could never be s[...]d, at times taking sor[...] As a boy I can attest [...]unting for the sour [...] the road".

Mom was [...]Hancock, where she [...]tatorian of her class [...]ithin a few miles of H[...] (Van Buskirk) Humphrey on June 30, 1902 in Coloma. He would leave home and serve in the military during World War II, and then return to work, get married, and raise a family. He returned from the War to fill a home with love, and it was in the dining room of that place that on April 11, 2011 Dad passed away.

My Mom was named Geneva, but so many called her "Genie" over the years that it seemed it might be her actual name. She was born on New Year's Eve 1928 in Ozone, Arkansas to Herman and Annabelle (Ross) Schwarz.

On December 3, 1947 Royce and Geneva were married in Westfield, Wisconsin and then started driving southwards for their honeymoon in Mexico.

One can conjure up the musical mood of those early years as my parents dated, fell in love, married, and started on the road to togetherness. Many years later my Mom often referred to one song in particular that Dad loved to hear over and over:

> *Ole buttermilk sky*
> *Don'tcha fail me when*
> *I'm needin' you most*
> *Hang a moon above her hitchin' post*
> *Hitch me to the one I love*
> *You can if you try, don't tell me no lie*
> *Will you be mellow and bright tonight*
> *Ole buttermilk sky?*

    Hoagy Carmichael's "Ole Buttermilk Sky" was the style of music that speaks to another time, and one can see the stars and the moon in some romantic alignment as the honeymooners left Wisconsin for the their trip. That Mexican adventure was but the first of many in their life together.

    Dad was an amazing storyteller and could retell one his classics, and make it seem as if it was the first time the tale had been heard. The oral tradition, or the ability to tell such stories is fading as society changes, but when a great one is told, it is easy to recall.

    My Dad, Royce, told a delightful tale from the days when he was five years old and the family lived in the old house on land that was owned by Hiram Humphrey. (At the time Hiram, a large framed man standing 6' 3" who also had a love of telling jokes, was working for the Ford Motor Company in Milwaukee.) Being a slight boy Royce's parents were concerned about his health, and took him to see the local doctor. Upon a medical exam the doctor found a heart murmur that was taken quite seriously. To hopefully remedy the matter the doctor prescribed pills that were to be administered on a regular basis. The doctor had warned that the pills would have a terrible taste, and would need to be swallowed fast to make it all the way down. As a side note, I mention that I have never known my Dad to take many medications and can recall that my Mom would often say it was almost impossible to get him to swallow any pills. However, her frustration about his stubbornness over taking pills appears to have been a lifetime affliction of his.

    In any event, at age five Royce would put a heart pill in his hand and go out on the porch to take it alone so to get it down fast--or so he led everyone to believe was the case. In reality, Royce carefully dropped each dose in a crack in the porch. One by one, week after week, the pills went from the container, to his hand, and through the hole until out of sight. It was only after someone saw Royce drop the pill into the crack that his plan to thwart the doctor came to an end.

After all the years, Dad would always add, "I forget who 'ratted me out'", but he still recalled with a smile that there was a 'pyramid of pills' under the porch. His act of disobedience was discovered only when a plank was pulled up! As for the heart condition the doctor said that there seemed to be no change without the medication, so the pills were discontinued.

When in the mood Dad added to his story that the same doctor recommended that he walk barefoot in cow manure to assist his health. (I asked for clarification on that part of the story but all I ever got was a repeat of the doctor's ideas. I never asked, but am hoping, that my Dad also put those doctor's orders aside too.)

Imagine that it's Sunday again and Mom, Dad and I are in what seems like separate rooms each doing our own thing. We're reading and relaxing, but it's a small house. We can still talk together, and comment on this or that as we read.

Sunday's at home were days of routine. At some point my Dad comes to the kitchen, and his voice is slightly higher due to a degree of disbelief as he asks me, "Do you know what they are selling a used [insert model and year] car for in Chicago?" Being almost illiterate on such matters I would listen and be amused that he seemed interested in such things. My Dad always was more in to cars, and related matters than I ever will be.

When it came to sports Dad and I were on the same page. We did not know very much about what was taking place on the sports pages. On football Sundays I would at some point try to find the scores of certain games that were being played. I would turn the TV on to get the score and see if the Bears had won, and the Packers had lost. We never watched football at home, but I still wanted to know the scores. It is nice to know who wins or loses so that I can sound like I participate in that part of the American experience. To be honest I really do not care, and never have.

As per her usual, on this and every other Sunday, Mom is puttering about in the kitchen. My Mom was a wonderful cook though she would always be the first one to say otherwise. People always loved to be at her table. Simply put she was too humble about her abilities in the kitchen.

Every Sunday for dinner there would be one constant item--a large bowl of mashed potatoes. One of my favorite meals from childhood was ground hamburger and cream of mushroom soup over potatoes. I hasten to add that my 'comfort food' was not representative of my Mom's cooking skills, as she excelled far beyond Campbell's soup in the kitchen.

Ours was a very 'meat and potatoes-type' family. The roaster filled with a piece of beef, chicken, or pork surrounded with potatoes and carrots is just about as good as it comes for Sunday dinner. Mom never disappointed in the kitchen.

Some of Mom's dishes were very simple, and others took a certain amount of experience to get to turn out right. I must say there was one baked good that she made particularly well: angel cookies (a recipe for which I have included in the appendix). Angel cookies were not complicated or hard to make, in fact they are very 'basic', and yet remain the perfect holiday treat. No Christmas season was complete without several batches. After leaving home I would call Mom and ask if she had done any baking as of yet for the holiday. I always seemed to call before the cookies were made, but soon thereafter they were always in the cupboard where they had been placed since I was in the third grade. Mom's Angel Cookies are simply put grand little gems of sugar and love that still make for smiles all these decades later.

Without doubt, and by everyone's definition, Mom was the ultimate maker of chocolate fudge. I have yet to find any to compare, and James who is a most remarkable cook has not yet been able to recreate the recipe. Mom made a batch of fudge for everyone's birthday. If you were a part of Mom's family, you got fudge. James was very moved, and appreciative of finding that he too was 'in the family' when early in our relationship he had his own plate of fudge to enjoy come the end of April.

Defining who is 'in the family' and who is clearly not is subjective work. Mom clearly believed that if James was an important part of my life, then he deserved such recognition. Dad had made it known in his own way in late 2000 that James was now a part of the family as well. As an act of kindness, this too was very touching. We all waited to take a place at the holiday table. Dad placed his hand on James' arm and gently led him to the place he would occupy at our table. James was seated right next to Dad. By way of these small gestures, my parents let us know that they were welcoming and affirming about our relationship. In return, we shared our unwavering respect.

Our shared routine Sunday of coffee, conversation, and papers ended when Mom became very aware that she was sick in the summer of 2007. She passed away shortly thereafter. I am comforted knowing that I can still go back home through memory to those Sundays when Dad reclined in his easy chair while Mom filed her nails while seated on the chair next to the window and her little bookshelf in the dining room. I am transported back to the table where my Mom folded her laundry, or still see her in the yard on bended knee, her gardening gloves on, as she pulls rogue weeds out from between her hens and chicks and the creeping phlox. For me, it is this continuation of traditions and memories that then work themselves into the fabric of our current life that makes James and me rich. We are, in fact, creating new pages for the Sunday papers Mom, Dad, and I used to read. Mom and Dad aren't here any longer, but the routine Sundays of home are firmly a part of the lifetime of memories being created everyday.

In the early 1970s what my family always referred to as the 'old barn' was torn down. Anyone with a good arm could have thrown a snowball from the front door of the house and made a white impression on the old wood. My family never used the barn for farming purposes, and over time both the age, and the unsightliness of the barn took its toll on my parents.

As a boy the old structure was not welcoming to me at all. It was dark inside, and large cobwebs stretched from all corners. I have often thought back and wondered if there had been a kid my age to explore it with, would my impressions been different? I suspect they might have been. After all, my grandparent's barn on the other side of the country road in Hancock was old, but in it I found wonderful places to hide and play. The difference of course was that Grandpa's barn was a place of life, and action. Milk cows were fed and milked there, and I recall a radio played at times when my Grandfather worked inside. There was a whole different world of activity going on in that barn from the one on my side of the road.

I often feel very sad when old buildings are torn down. It always feels like a part of where we come from has just been demolished. That said, I was pleased when my parents decided to raze their old barn. First of all a brand new building without cobwebs would take its place, and secondly, there would be lots of 'action' happening just outside our home during construction.

I liked it best as a youngster when things were 'happening'. When the new road was constructed and all the heavy machinery rumbled in front of our home for days on end I was quite certain there was no better time to be alive as a boy. That certain exhaust smell from the engines was great to experience! Mom, however, was not pleased to have that smell "throughout the house". I feigned having no idea about what she was talking.

When my grandparents baled hay in the field nearest to our home it allowed me a front row seat. I was, as always, delighted with something 'going on'. I am not certain that she would have agreed, but I always thought my Grandma had a perfect place to sit as she rode on the baler. She needed to make sure the twine was not getting bundled together in the machine's inner workings. Grandma would have her head covered with a huge kerchief to keep the dust off, and Grandpa would fill a wagon with bales. I know that I thought at the time those bales were the heaviest objects imaginable. They were so big next to the seven or eight year-old me.

My Dad worked at his job with Waushara County with a man named 'Pinkie' who came over and helped with the building project. Over and over I had heard the story of how Pinkie would not take any money for helping bring down the old barn, nor would he take any for assisting my Dad with the new one going up. Pinkie only wanted the old wood and carted it off in his truck. My Dad was happy to have the help, and not have the debris left behind. In the end, as Dad always reminded those who heard the story, he made sure that Pinkie was paid, even though it was hard to make sure the money got into the pockets of Pinkie. The money transfer finally did take place, though Pinkie refused over and over to accept it.

In any event, the new building went up--a building that was soon to be always known as "the barn", which would always remain separate from the "old barn" when telling stories. A new barn. What would my needs be for such a structure? I first thought of the need to have a workbench. Every boy needs a good workbench to tinker on the latest project, and store the 'essentials'—those things that were not allowed under penalty of death, or so it seemed, to be placed in one's bedroom. The 'essentials' certainly could never have been stored in one's bedroom closet or under the bed, for example. They might as well have been contraband. Granted, I really did not have at the time lots of projects I was tinkering with, and so I am not exactly sure why I felt the need to have a workbench, but it was nonetheless a desire that required action. Where after all was I to put my 'essentials'?

With scraps of left over this and that from the work that was taking place I started to fashion my bench. The only thing I recall about Pinky directly is how he leaned over one day and showed me how to take old nails and straighten them out with a hammer to re-use them on my creation. I cannot say for sure exactly how it must have looked as I worked on taking the bended kinks out of my nails, but given my age and my total lack of carpentry skills, it must have been a sight. I do recall that at some point Dad told me that he would help me build a workbench—but not until after the building was completed. I must have looked a bit pathetic with my lack of any real skills for Dad to feel the need to take on yet another building project! I sure was grateful for the help.

With the rough pinewood that was left over from the barn building, my Dad and I made what I knew was the best workbench ever. Hands down, it was pretty spectacular. On the back of the bench, where one might hang tools he placed two supports and finished it off with clapboard siding. The workbench had a nice wide work surface, and a shelf underneath for adequate storage of 'essentials'. When it was finished, we placed it in the west end of the new building in a little area that was always my space. Being the youngest of the three kids I had the luxury of not having to compete with others for a place in the barn. By the time I was in my teen years, the other two were out of my hair. Divine Providence, really.

The bench never did see much real work. It was used more for a place to store my belongings, as opposed to doing woodwork or car repair. Truth is, I never had any real skills with those tasks, and even less desire to know anything about them. In my world, the bench was more of a place to fill a bird feeder, than successfully make one. I knew my limitations, and I readily accepted them. Not being frustrated over the workings of the internal combustion engine or fiddle-faddling with carpentry DIY, do-it-yourself, projects allowed me to pursue my real interests. Because of the gentle use that the workbench actually received, today there is not a ding or an oil spot on it. It has always served its function for storage admirably.

For nearly four decades it sat in the same spot storing some of my things. In 2010 I brought it to Madison where it now sits in our basement and has a new role to serve, and one that fits my life. It was born a worker's bench, but it grew to a potter's bench, and it is getting much more use that way. Within twenty-four hours of it being here, a large plant was re-potted on top of it, and seed catalogs now call it home. (I can also let you in on a little secret. My desire to keep the work surface spotless and in the condition in which it sat all those years back in the barn is strong. James put a weather sealant on it and a sheet of Plexiglas helps to protect it from spills and worse.) Like everything else in life, the bench has changed, and adapted to the place and time in which it finds itself. What a good little workbench!

Given his difficulties with walking in the final years of his life, Dad would never have been able to make it down into our basement to see the placement of the bench. What upsets me more is that my Dad never saw our Madison home, despite repeated invitations to come. Dad would have loved the house, and all the original woodwork including the floors, and large detailed framed windows looking out to the lake. He would have loved the fact the house was constructed from white pine like that which dominated in the woods back home. He would have remarked with fondness that the home has stood sturdy from the winds since constructed with square nails in 1892.

Years after James and I had moved to the isthmus Dad was still asking in a not-too-sure tone, "So you live near the lake?" It was sad in so many ways. Since he did not drive long distances any longer, he would have needed a ride to get here, and yet no one made sure he was able to visit our home. It was a clear case of being 'so close, yet so far away'. In short, it all amounted to a series of denied experiences, which he tried to rationalize away for me in an attempt to preserve family unity. It still hurts.

James and I didn't want to let him never see the place we call home. We compiled a series of photos, and put them in to an album so he could see the house inside and out. Dad remarked later on the phone that he really enjoyed the pictures, as it allowed him a better sense of where we lived. "I can feel the breeze off the lake," he said while referring to some of the pictures. The fact is that he should have been able to feel the breeze for real and in person.

We inherited the condo from a friend, Henry X. Dudek, in 2007. Like any other new homeowners we wanted to fix and transform the place before we had visitors. We had spent many happy hours herewith Henry over the years, and could not emotionally bring ourselves to live in Henry's space as others likely would have. We needed to make it ours. We needed our home to represent who we are as a couple, and not serve as a shrine to our benefactor and friend.

We worked hard to put our colors on the walls and infuse our tastes into the space before showing it to others. There is no way to describe how painting every room, getting someone to do the ceilings while James used spackling on countless feet of cracked wall space drained us of energy. It took three months of non-stop work to make the house our home.

James and I are among those who have few skills, as we like to put it. James at least came from a carpentry family, his Dad being a contractor of many decades. We spent hours helping Henry's Personal Representative distribute his belongings among friends and family, followed by feverishly working to make Henry's home into a place that we could call our home. We just couldn't get it all done in time. We just couldn't get it all done before Mom slipped away once her colon cancer was diagnosed. She got to see pictures of the outside of the home, but she too was never to visit or see the inside. She was amazed at the location of the house, and saw the potential for how things could be arranged. Her situation was very different from Dad's. She didn't have the time left to make a trip to our home.

I know Dad would be pleased to see the workbench has a new location to rest on the Madison isthmus. I am sure he knew the day James and I moved it away from Hancock that it will always be a treasured memory.

As I mentioned before, Dad and I always had a different kind of relationship than the one I shared with Mom. The differences manifested themselves in the little things. My Dad and I never went fishing, hunting, or threw many baseballs or lots of the other stuff one sees in the movies. Dad and I never once watched any sporting event on TV. Never can I recall throwing a football with him. All of that doesn't matter. There were countless times…and I mean countless times when Dad had me sit in his lap while he read to me. It isn't that we didn't spend quality time together. The things we did do together made an impression on me. I think it is for that reason that my silly little bench to store undetermined 'essentials' is a lifetime keepsake. That is the reason that books too have played such an important role in my life.

If Mom's impact on me was felt strongly in the kitchen as we talked and offered ideas for this and that, Dad's great presence in my life came in the form of creating within me a love of reading. While Dad was never a big reader, or a 'bookish' type of man, he nonetheless was always comfortable with providing reading material, and books as a way to spend time, and open new horizons. There is no way that a kid who had the type of personality or curiosities that I had can ever say thanks enough for how he proved to be a great parent in this regard.

Over and over, the story of *Little Raccoon* was presented with Dad's voice making great vocal intonations as the pages turned. *Little Raccoon* was a wonderful thirty-five cent book from the Rand McNally Junior Elf book collection. On the front cover, a little raccoon holding a dandelion blower in his paw represented for me summer fun. Thinking back on that book, which I have along with all the others from my youth, makes me wonder how my Dad did not go crazy reading them to me for the umpteenth time.

Dad often read to me in a chair in the dining room. It was in that same room on the dining table where a neat stack of *Stevens Point Journal* newspapers would be placed. Many a day when I came home from school, I would grab the newspaper to read my favorite cartoon, *Buz Sawyer*. Buz was an adventurer of high-daring action against such villains as pirates or hijackers. Week after week the story would grow, and the tension would mount. I asked myself every week, how would it all end? Without fail every Friday there would be a breath-taking-cliff hanger-not-to-be-resolved-until-Monday's carton panels would be printed.

One *Buz Sawyer* strip still stands out for me. In this particular episode, Buz Sawyer jumps from a plane with a parachute that will not open! For a ten-year old boy in the early seventies that was high drama. *Buz Sawyer* was always a cartoon, and never became more (or less) than what I came to love each day as a boy. There were no spin-off movies or television programming. He was just always a guy who won every bad situation week in, and week out in the local newspaper.

What I still find amazing is that in three or four squares, five days a week, a whole story and real interest could build so that I was left wondering how everything would turn out on Monday. It was Roy Crane, the creator of *Buz Sawyer*, who helped me understand the power of cartooning. Now as an adult I think the craft can convey a stronger message, when done properly, than long-form essays. Political cartoons are proof of that fact.

Following the *Buz Sawyer* must-read, I would grab the large atlas that Mom stored on the back bookcase and lay out on the floor next to the spread out newspaper. That is when I would look for places written about in the paper. I had no way of knowing where they were. Cairo to Cincinnati, it made no difference as I loved to locate the places in the newspaper, and then work my way through why it had made the news. Did it equal the fun my friends had who went home to afternoon television? Hard to say, but I think it was, and it all resulted from the wise decision to have a daily newspaper.

I have never been without a newspaper, and find the current cutbacks for the newspaper industry quite concerning. I hope never to see a day when the daily read does not land with a thud on my stoop. As a nation we will lose much more than just that special time of the day when we curl up with it. We are in fact going to suffer tremendously for the loss of accountability that the newspapers provide to insure that our government has journalistic oversight, a loss of a daily record of events that makes for historical documentation, and a sense of commonality that allows us to have some overall reference point as a nation.

I started to become politically aware during the final months of Richard Nixon's time in office. It is safe to say that without the intrepid newspaper reporting of Carl Bernstein and Bob Woodward while working at the famed *Washington Post*, the sins of Watergate along with the other tales of deception might never have been uncovered. While some might have applauded that lack of illumination concerning our leaders, most will agree with me that the newspaper played not only a dramatic role, but an essential one, in making sure our leaders were held accountable for their actions.

Where will the reporters be found in order to hold our state and national leaders accountable when the newspapers fold up and shut down? I can only assume that a politician would snicker if a blogger showed up to investigate a legislative scandal. On the other hand with pen and notepad in hand a reporter from the daily newspaper in Madison sends a message when she enters a room with a question, and a barrel of ink behind her. I think there is a real level of concern about the need to monitor government, and policies. It cannot be done on the cheap, or by amateurs. After all, while many like to grouse about the press, let us not forget they are professionals, and do much to keep us free and safe.

When I mentioned recently to an aunt that without newspapers her genealogy research would be much more difficult, it only took a second for her face to register the realization of what the end of newspapers means for all sorts of historical fact checking. If you want to know what the first-hand feel of the Civil War was like go back in the archives of the *New York Times*, and feel the first impressions. They are much different than later versions of the events as they were written at the moment of anguish and uncertainty. There is a truth to the tone of the writing that is priceless. God help us if we ever lose that first writing of history. After all, that is what a newspaper, when all is said and done, is all about.

When I was a boy 'Uncle' Walter Cronkite was the anchor at CBS. Most Americans watched Cronkite in order to be informed about the news of the day. No matter where we lived, or what we thought, we had a point of reference as a nation when discussing the news. Cronkite would say that he had given the nation the headlines, but for the rest of the story viewers needed to pick up their morning newspaper.

To some extent the front pages of the *New York Times*, *Washington Post*, or *Los Angeles Times* can make the same type of claim as helping with our point of reference as a nation. These papers often set the topics for discussion on radio, or by the pundits on the evening cable news shows. I think it important that as a nation we have some points of commonality in viewing the issues of the day. For much of our history the role of newspapers has played that key role.

Books were never strangers in our home, and getting new ones to read, even at an early age, was something that was encouraged by my parents. On the kitchen counter, several times during a school year, coins would be laid out so as to buy some books from the *Weekly Reader*. The books might range in prices from thirty-five cents up to eighty-five cents. I would get up in the morning for school, and there would be some coins so I could make a selection or two, and get some books. What I find remarkable to this day is that child-like feeling of merriment as a kid over the joy of the books arriving in the classroom is very similar to how I feel when bringing home a purchase from Barnes and Noble as an adult. That lifetime feeling of joy over buying books started with some coins from my Dad's pocket in my school days.

Especially since I have been out on my own, I have sought to find that special spot, a nook really, which I would call my reading spot. I have needed that special place as a refuge from the trials of adult life: work, friends, 'frenemies' (friendly enemies, as they are known today). A reading spot, that place where you sneak away to avoid the world, requires peace, tranquility, functionality, and needs to speak to me as being uniquely mine. I found my first such nook out in the front yard of my parents' home. Beneath the large towering oak tree of the front yard shade was abundant, and I found the softest grass upon which to sit long hours. Except in the fall when the acorns dotted the lawn, one couldn't ask for a more perfect place to sit, and read.

There were other spots on the farm where I could escape with a good book. I loved to sprawl out in the dining room in front of the screen door (which was never used for anything but for fresh air) as the late afternoon sun washed over me as I read. I loved to curl up on the davenport (the term my Mom used for the sofa). It was warm there in the winter. Or, if it were really cold I would find a space out of the way of the foot traffic, and sit directly in front of the stove.

Certain books are in fact linked in my memory to places where I read them around the home. I indulged in *Nancy Drew* in the rather stiff looking but fashionable brocaded green chair. When I was in my twenties, a lawn chair on a Sunday afternoon in the back of the house is where I started my first John Grisham novel. The memoir of Richard Nixon—I was seated behind the pine row at home while enjoying the pleasant breezes. Books and memories: I loved our home, and I loved to read.

I can't stress enough the importance of trees, not only for reading nooks, but also for giving us the connectedness that we need and should foster with our surroundings. Trees also, when allowed, willingly participate in the rituals of our lives. In some ancient cultures even festivals were dedicated to their honor.

Before purchasing a VW Beetle, with a miniscule trunk, I

used to drive home to Hancock to cut a Christmas tree for my apartment in Madison. It was an annual ritual made special because my Dad assisted in making the simple wooden stand that allowed for the tree to stand upright. My trees at that time were always smaller than what was required for the store-bought stands. There was a reason for that.

As a boy I loved to walk in the woods populated with white pines and oaks. After I got to a certain age, I would take the axe along and chop on this dead branch, or even take down a very small spindly tree here and there. When I grew to be a teenager, there was one tall white pine that I would wail on with the axe. All the tensions of youth were unleashed on that tree. At the end of my teen years I had discovered there was far more tree than angst. When I left home it was still standing, but with a very haggard look. Since then, the 'wailing tree' has come down with age, and others have grown up in its place.

I had narrowed my stress-releasing axing to a single tree thanks to some thoughtful words from my Dad. I was just a boy when he told me that one just never knows when a tree would be needed to hide under in the rain. He looked as though he were sheltering his face from raindrops as he spoke. One can never foresee, he added, the need to climb up one in order to get away from a wild animal. Dad imitated the noise of a bear and its growl. I discovered then that trees were my friends, and I should respect them.

I have forever loved trees. They need the same sort of protection that Dad encouraged me to give the trees at home. I am unable to recreate the sounds of the forest as Dad could do, so in the recent past have used my 'voice' in a different way to make sure that Madison protects its trees too. I worked, through my blog, to impassion others to join in the cause of saving trees at the time of street construction. Huge trees on city terraces were being harmed. Working with my alderperson we now have a city ordinance to help in the fight, I am proud to say.

All trees have value according to Dad. Some small trees seemed to me to lack that postcard quality of rounded beauty we as a culture value most at the holidays. One side of so many little trees on our property seemed to be deformed. They did not get enough light, or were too close to other trees in the woods. Dad would comment about the misshapen trees, "They all want to be a Christmas tree!" As I got older, that message seemed ever more important to me. When it came time to chop down my own trees for Christmas, I always sought out a nice tree, but one that was not perfect. My friends would smile, and gently chide me about the 'Charlie Brown' tree. Yet, decorated in all the lights and glass ornaments the tree was always perfect, just as it was for Charles

Schulz's Charlie Brown, and his friends.

    Each season for years and years, I took my Dad's axe to the woods, and dragged my tree through the snow to our 'barn' where Dad would eye it up, and then reach for some wood pieces in the pile near the back of the building. He would measure a bit then take the wood, and place it over the side of a wooden potato crate, and cut for perfect dimensions. He would hammer and fashion the pieces together so the small trunk of the tree would fit without slipping out. As he worked, I would look out the door of the barn, and see my Mom at the kitchen window. She carefully watched our progress, ensuring that we didn't do anything foolish, or hurt ourselves. Steam collected on the windowpanes from something wonderful cooking on the stove for dinner.

    Days after I had the tree back in Madison my Dad would phone to inquire as to how it was standing. I always answered that it was up, and decorated without a single problem. Vendors do not put less-than-perfect Christmas trees on the lots in the city, but I can say with all honesty that my little trees could stand in competition with any of them, if the competition were about conveying life's lessons on love.

    I never asked Dad about how or why he came up with his philosophy about Christmas trees. It just fit him, and never seemed to need an explanation. It means we all are needed in life, and all fit in somewhere. And with a little help from someone can be that which we dream.

One of the things I loved to do as a kid was walk to the mailbox at the end of the driveway and pick up whatever the postal service had brought us. There was almost a military precision when I was young as to when the delivery would be made. We often waited, and almost watched at times for the local mail carrier to make the rounds, but were rarely to know a time when it did not arrive shortly before noon.

    It was so much easier on some days to know when the delivery had arrived. When we had the flag up on the box to alert the driver of mail to be picked also meant when the flag was down, the mail had arrived. Otherwise I could make repeated trips back and forth to see if the mail had been left when particularly anxious for a certain mailing.

    For a kid on some days out in the country getting mail was as exciting as it got. There was a period of time that I was writing to ranger stations all over the country asking for information on wildfires and prevention of such disasters. There had been a wildfire in the west I had read about in the daily paper that had caught my attention. It seemed so adventuresome to be a fire fighter in the rugged regions of the nation. I wrote letters to the rangers to find out more details.

Large envelopes with all sorts of Smokey Bear promotional materials made for day after day of mail addressed directly to me. Nothing would compare to that volume of personal mail until I started signing up to Elvis Presley fan club listings. While the national government sent everything in sterile brown envelopes, Elvis fans mailed their content in a unique style, fit for a 'King'.

The folks never paved the driveway with cement or tar, but the gravel surface had worked over time. Even with melting snow in the spring months drainage was never really a problem. Living in sand country meant the soil was dry far more often than wet.

At the end of the drive it was always the custom to look both ways, even in the country. Or should I say, especially in the country. There were so many instances of vehicles winding it up down our straight road, zipping along so fast that it drew the ire of Mom and Dad alike. How many times had I had been told since childhood of the dangers that presented itself on our stretch of road.

In all, the stretch of County KK from intersection to intersection on which our home was located is about a mile long. It is as straight heading north as it is south. It is a perfect place to pick up speed and really sail. Many a time as a boy the car that seemed 'way up there at the far end' could pass me by in seconds. Looking both ways was a lesson so engrained that I never deviated from it even as an adult.

A friendly series of rocks about the size of dinner plates lined the drive at home. Each time the lawn was mowed, the rocks, which numbered over seventy, were moved, and then replaced for the perfect manicured look. (That batch of rocks, along with some others from home now surrounds our sizable rose garden in Madison, and since one of the women who lives on our block thought the rose patch was heart-shaped recommended that the rocks be arranged in that design.) The rocks, placed by my Mom who liked their natural appeal, were like a welcoming committee for our guests. They were also like stalwart friends. The last time I made that walk to the mailbox was when my Dad was ill, and I was visiting at home. My friends, Mom's rocks, were there to greet me on that last journey down the drive to pick up the mail for Dad. I was glad they were there.

That last time when I reached into the mailbox I pulled out a packet of envelopes and advertisements that were all wrapped around the folds of a daily newspaper, *The Milwaukee Journal Sen-*

tinel, a newspaper that I subscribed to for the benefit of my parents.

That last day when I picked up the mail I looked around the home and it was still the same house, but it had changed dramatically from the home I knew. It then seemed smaller, much smaller. Things were still relatively neat, but not maintained anywhere to the degree of cleanliness or things properly placed as when my Mom was in charge. Now dust bunnies lived in corners or under appliances. While the fresh wallpaper of the living room that Mom had hung only a couple of years earlier still had a warm cozy feel, and the windows still looked out upon the same trees which I loved as a boy, there was no longer the real warm feeling of home to be experienced.

I had, in my heart and mind, been saying good-bye to my Dad and home for some time over the last years. As I sat with Dad in those final visits I realized that there was a real transformation taking place within the home. Our home as I had known it all my life was slipping away; slowly, all that was left of the place where I learned my core values, where my parents showered us kids with love, all that was slipping away so in time all that would be left was the house. With the soon-to-occur passing of my Father, the life of the family would slip out of that home.

The kitchen that seemed to hold everyone on the holidays felt so much tighter when only a handful of us were present. Mom no longer scurried around the kitchen doing this or that while telling everyone present "just keep talking, I can hear you." Her absence made home far less complete. The former master of the kitchen was gone. That which was once the center of her home was now an echo of what once had been. It was times like that I was most glad that those driveway rocks also pointed me back to the highway leading to Madison.

During those last visits with Dad, I realized that it had been nearly four years since I sat in the chair at the table where so many Sundays were spent reading the paper. It had been a long while since the three of us had gathered there to chat. All the other visits with Dad since my Mom passed away had all led us to the living room where James and I sat talking to Dad while watching vehicles pass on the road. The last visits were now spent in the kitchen which was void of that warmth that used to fill it so completely.

I reminded my Dad about the Sundays he would come into the kitchen, and put his finger to his lips to hush me as he lifted a candy box lid for a piece or two of chocolate. His cat-like attempts to sneak candy were a long-standing routine as my Mom had thought he was eating too many sweets. My father and I come from the other point of view. There is no such thing as too much chocolate.

There we were, Dad and me, in Mom's kitchen where every one of my nieces and nephews first tasted chocolate frosting thanks to Uncle Greg. I had thought it important to introduce them to something to which no doubt their parents would say no. Not one of the tikes refused to smile but rather had an added twinkle in their eyes following their small-sized first sampling. They were too young to realize it, but I worked hard to be the best uncle they would ever know.

One of them, however, nearly undid the taste testing, and blew my plans. When after visiting in the kitchen for the chocolate treat the youngster waddled, as kids learning to walk are known to do, back to the living room where everyone was assembled. There the child demanded I again make a trip to the kitchen. With outstretched arm in the direction of the kitchen, the demand for more frosting would not relent. I had to give in, and then do some more creative goofing around to move the little mind away from thinking about sugar.

In later years Mom compromised with Dad over his sweet tooth. She allowed him to consume dark chocolate. She had clipped some article from a magazine, which proved conclusively that in moderation dark chocolate was indeed acceptable. Mother's rules could be very tight—and in retrospect rather amusing.

That afternoon while we sat in the kitchen I reminded my Dad about his sneaking candy as I pushed a box of chocolates I had bought him closer to his side of the table. "Nothing tastes good anymore", he told me. Folks who know me are aware I have a tendency to not stop when there is every good reason to keep proceeding. So I moved the box closer to his reach. I finally got him to eat one. But I could see that things were different. There was no more glint in his eye at the taste of what he so long loved.

Dad was seated on the side of the table I always sat as a child, and I now was on the side from where my parents once ate. I was windswept with a level of awkwardness that was emotionally very powerful. It had to be that way to accommodate my Dad's wheelchair. I understood that, but it made the whole scene one that will always leave a lump in my throat.

That moment shared at the reversed table was not the first time that I nearly broke down and cried as the frailties of Dad's life mounted. I was nearing the time when I was to lose my last parent, and as such I had become very introspective, even more so than I had been for the bulk of my life.

We hear talk about the 'cycle of life' all the time. Smiles are shared when hearing the news of friends who bring babies home from the hospital. Morning newspapers are read to see if any names are recognized on the obituary page. We plan for graduations, and weddings, and then as we get older time is marked by the vacations we took or the moves we made. The 'cycle of life' is something we live, and for the most part something upon which we do not reflect. We are too busy living life. Living. That is how it is supposed to be.

There comes a time in life when all the individual pieces from the 'cycle of life' converge in powerful and meaningful ways. For me, one of the hardest moments to deal with emotionally came while visiting Dad at the Wild Rose Hospital following a Christmas Eve heart attack.

The place was a 'swing-bed' unit. The old portion of the hospital where I was born was shut down, and leveled. But as I walked around that day I thought about this place where I took my first breath. I also considered how as a boy many elementary school teachers had told me I was too loud. It was in this very place where I gave my first shout.

I was not a kid anymore. As I looked into the restroom mirror and smiled at the gray hair that seemed to be winning the battle over the darker hair that had once been in residence at my temples, I comprehended more fully that nothing ever stays the same.

The moment when James and I walked to my Dad's room it struck me that this man who had always been big and strong now sat in a wheelchair looking very weak, and seemingly defeated. I weighed more than my Dad did, and that fact hit hard.

Our eyes locked as I entered the room and he started to cry. No words. Just tears. His eyes screamed, "Help me!" I am not shy with my emotions, and cried with him and gave him a hug. Honesty without words. Power.

My arm was around his shoulder. My mind raced back to something I had not thought about for many, many years. When I was a young boy I often would wake up late at night when it was dark outside. I would not be able to breathe correctly. I was hoarse and frightened. Back then we called what I had 'the croup'. My parents would hear me trying to yell, and the house awakened.

My Dad would pick me up in his arms and carry me to the bathroom where hot water had already been drawn in the sink basin. My Mom would go to the kitchen and concoct some strange tasting liquid that was bitter and sweet all at the same time. I have no idea as I write this what kitchen ingredients she used. With a towel draped over my head my Dad would hold me on his lap so the steam could help my breathing. My Mom was there with a spoon to get as much of the mixture down my throat as she could.

There was no way for me, or anyone that day at the swing-

1,268 Square Feet

bed unit, to work the magic Dad did when I had the croup. As the roles reversed in life, and my Dad became needy and reliant, life had shifted. It felt akin to major tectonic plate shifts on the earth's surface.

Dad ate only a small portion of his food as we talked about all sorts of topics he was sure to find interesting. He looked at a pile of pictures we had brought, and asked again about the ducks James and I had rescued that summer at a Madison beach. When he was tired and needing to lay down nurses lifted him back into bed, and placed a cover over him.

As I stood by his bed he looked up and said, "Read me a bedtime story".

My face must have failed me, and my voice was lost. James then filled in the conversation, as he is often my voice when I am unable to speak. My Dad was saying in so many words that he knew the 'cycle of life' was moving along, and coming full circle.

Not long after my Dad returned home he was placed on hospice as doctors had found an aneurysm upon which they could not operate given his advanced age, and heart situation. He recognized the situation, and that the end was near. In spite of all of that he offered light moments, and flashes of the past to me across the kitchen table as a way to lighten the load...for each of us.

From the time he lifted a cup of milk, and winked at me across the table, to the comment he made about someone sleeping in his favorite large chair ("they can sell it now, I do not want it anymore") there were snippets of the past smiles and shared humor from over the years. With so many under foot in the house, or as he termed it over those weeks "communal living" there was not any real alone time for us. He offered me smiles about 'the orders' others were giving, and I rolled my eyes in agreement as we at times carried on a non-verbal conversation.

As I left that day I knew that coming down our country road there would be a visitor that no one could see 'way up there at the far end'. There would be no announcement of its arrival. The doctors said it would just happen.

The last time I visited with my Dad prior to his death was in March. I reminded him of something he had told me as a teenager about life, when he used his time plowing snow to make a point. We looked out from the living room windows as a mighty fog rolled around our home. It was then I passed the same wisdom back to Dad that he had imparted to me.

Many years prior Dad had used an analogy of a snow truck driver, when referring about how to live life. As he spoke he held his hands as if on a steering wheel. In those earlier years he would bounce around as if in a jostling truck. Telling me how to handle the rough times of life, he said, "Hold on tight to the wheel, drop the blade, and go straight down the road."

On April 11, 2011 death arrived for my Dad at our family home. James and I were there for much of the day, but when I had said my goodbye to Dad, told him I loved him, and heard him say "I love you too, Greg" I was able to take one last look and leave.

There was no way I wanted to be with my siblings at the time my Dad breathed his last breath. I had been at my Mom's bedside and held her hand as her heart raced, and her breathing became increasingly shallower. I held her head, and stroked her cheek as the end came. Then I took a comb and made her hair look pretty, as much as can be done given all that had happened. Family dynamics had changed over the years and that made me feel as though my Dad had been taken away from me even before he had drawn his last breath. For all of those reasons, I was able to leave at the time that I did.

I knew there was going to be a separate viewing time for James and me, as I had requested that from the funeral home. I knew I would sit on the opposite side of the church from the immediate family, and that I was not going to attend the funeral luncheon afterward.

Instead of joining my siblings with any flowers I made my own simple bouquet from the white pines in the woods behind our home. The simple flowers and dried remains proved to be quite perfect when they were all gathered in a ribbon. I placed them inside the coffin. Dad took them with him when we buried him next to Mom at the Hancock Cemetery. Soft snowflakes continued to fall that day as we lowered him to his final resting place.

James and I both thought of Dad and his plow truck that morning. The road from Plover where we had spent the night at the Elizabeth Inn was lightly covered in snow. Dad must have been thinking that his own passing had come too soon. There was still plenty of work left to be done.

When I moved to Madison, my Mom was concerned about the large city. It was many years later during one of our Sunday afternoon conversations in that same room where Dad passed away, after hearing stories about my friends, that she remarked how glad she was my friends did not smoke, and all were decent people. That may seem quaint, but she said it with sincerity. What she was offering for advice and hope in my adult years was the same things I had been instilled with many years before. She never had anything to worry about.

The values and simplicity with which my folks raised me at home are the ones I now use as my guide as an adult. There is no way for someone to meet me and not get a sense of who my parents were at the same time.

When I mow the lawn and it is trimmed and looking perfect I often take time to sit in a chair outside and take in the world around me. It is then when I feel the presence of my Dad. He would understand the desire to have it look just right. Then, much like I did as a boy back home, I sit there and read outside.

It is inside our Madison home, in the piano room (or pie-ana as my Mom would pronounce it with still a touch of her southern upbringing coming through) where I feel most often the presence of my Mom. There, the sun shines through the large windows, and dances off the hardwood floors, casting a golden hue on the surroundings. She would have loved the look and color of the room, the view to the flowers outside, and the fact that everything is neat and orderly. Then, much like I did as a boy back home, I sit on the little stool, my 'sitting post' as Mom used to call it, and dial-up an old family friend or an aunt and chat, secretly wishing that Mom could be listening in like on that party line we had when I was a kid.

Newspapers. Coffee. Sitting post. Laughter and Joy. These are the things that I am talking about when I say a house may be sold, but not the home. While Mom always wanted a larger house to live in, there is no way she could have created a more loving environment for us in which to grow up. We had a wonderful home.

When someone passed away, especially if the loved one in question is the last of a pair, a strange process called probate begins. Mom used to tell me how probate often brings out the very worst in people. She may not have been wrong, but one thing was clear to me when both my Mom and Dad had passed away. Their estate had to be divided, and I was more interested in memories than 'stuff'.

I made a list of the items that I wanted from the home place, and when it was scrutinized by my lawyer, she noted that there was more a list of yard sale items than one third of the estate to which I was entitled. I have never been a collector of items just for the sake of having something. I saw that play out with the estate of our friend, Henry Dudek, and it was ugly to witness. I wanted no part in any such drama, and never once engaged in the process in that manner.

I wanted mementoes from the home that had a story to tell, and a memory worth recalling. I wanted to honor the past, such as having an old potato crate that was turned on its side when it came time for Dad to fashion a Christmas tree stand out of wood pieces. I would seek to obtain the old aluminum pan in to which we picked apples each fall.

Such was my state of mind when James and I were finally allowed to visit the home in Hancock. The journey was emotional, and while James offered great support along the way, there is no easy way to remove items that were so long a part of someone else's life. I selected the things that had meaning to me, carefully arranged them on the old kitchen table, made a list of them, each on their own line, to give to the watchman sent to monitor us that day, and left. There is no easy way to unpack a family home and it's shared past.

A week later, when the "list" had been approved we returned to transport the carefully selected mementoes to Madison. I felt as though there was a transformation underway as the items were packed in the car. As soon as I brought them to our back porch, and James then took them into our house, the sadness of the day seemed to lift. I knew James already was thinking about how we might present, and display the items, and add another rich dimension of the past to our home. Home, after all, is something we carry deep inside of ourselves us a lifetime; for James and me our family homes reside within, and are manifest in the way we live.

In the probate process, I only took things that had memories attached to them. On the top of my list of things I didn't want to leave without were the garden shoes worn by my Mom for those fast in-and-out trips such as placing clothes on the line, or grabbing a cucumber or a few tomatoes from the garden. We never wore shoes in the house just as we don't in our Madison home. Mom's garden shoes were always placed alongside my Dad's work shoes in the back entry. I searched high and low for the shoes, and felt somehow they must have been discarded. Finally in the last minutes as James and I removed piles of boxes and everything else from a portion of the garage did I locate her garden shoes. My Dad's shoes were found off to the side. Now, both pairs sit alongside some real flowers inside our home in Madison.

Among the mementoes too was my Dad's shaving mug and shaving cream brush. I heard myself ask the ever-repetitive question of why he never allowed himself the ease of an electric shaver. These items now sit in our bathroom alongside a bottle of Avon's Wild Country cologne that James has set out to recall his Dad who lives in Maine. There is the old axe from my youth. The wood is gray from age. It now hangs on a wall in our home. Some flower vases from when I was a boy made their way here as well. They always held an array of ever-changing plastic flowers. A couple necklaces that were among Mom's favorites and a coffee mug from Chicago that brings to mind the numerous bus trips we took to sightsee in the Windy City are here now too. We placed them in the large china hutch that our friend Henry left for us.

"I can really see something this way," my Dad would say on those bus trips as he looked out at the skyscrapers while not needing to concern himself with the traffic. My Mom did not have to help with directions, and so was always smiling in the bus seat with windows that arched up high and over the top for perfect viewing.

James fashioned a wall ornament from two items that came from the parents' garage. The spade was so old that even Plainfield sand would be too tough for it to dig into, and the garden shears decades old which Mom used to trim so much grass that they are dull. Grass today would only gum the blades. None of these items are worth any money, nor are they prized by anyone else but me.

The auction of the home place resulted in the sale of the woods south of the house. The whole area has since been leveled for a large farm field. Where I had once walked, cut Christmas trees, and sat at times and read—it is all gone. Long before my Dad died I started working on the process of saying goodbye. With the family dynamics as they were, it was the only thing for me to do. By the time the probate process started I was prepared mentally and emotionally. I had in many respects already adventured on to the pathway toward healing.

Having said that, there was no way for my mind not to race backwards when for the first time I saw the trees starting to be cleared from the homestead. I again thought of Mom wanting a larger and more functional kitchen, with more space to place holiday pies. Though the nostalgia of Mom's kitchen will always remain, I understand her desire to see her space enlarged.

From my childhood there was one refrain, which I heard over and over from Mom, and it is etched on my brain. She would tell Dad repeatedly the same thing. "We will sit here our whole lives with the woods up there, pay taxes and die, and someone else will get to enjoy it."

Why my Father could not recognize Mom's desire to have her new kitchen remains one of those unanswered questions. Why the rather simple desire of Mom to have a larger kitchen—furnished in part from the large track of family pine–could never be realized astonishes me even today. Having watched way more HGTV than is good for me I am aware of the relative ease of expanding a room, and the ways her wishes could have been incorporated into the layout of the house. I also know that the price for such a project was not terribly elevated, and in fact would have been quite feasible for our family.

Simply put, Dad had the money to make it happen. Based on the sizable amounts he left in his accounts upon his passing, her unfulfilled kitchen-dream seems very unfair. While Dad was one of the most decent, and giving of people I have ever known, this one decision left undone–one that would have so greatly assisted her–leaves me troubled. Such simple dreams have no reason not to become a reality.

The second image that flew through my mind as I looked at the trees coming down, and the rugged machinery rip out a stump in the woods was that of Dad standing in a hospital hallway in August 2007. Dad was not one to physically touch others, so it was telling that he placed his hand on the arm of the doctor while saying, "I will sell my land and woods to pay you, just get Genie better." All the money in the world was not going to matter a damn at that time as Mom's cancer was far too advanced. Dad, however, was sincere about his words. He would have moved heaven and earth for a chance for more time with Mom. What I find hard to process, however, is how using the money to make Mom's life easier when it could have impacted her was not possible, but finding all the sources of money he owned for an impossible mission was something he would have undertaken.

Some of this thinking was due, with no doubt, to the Depression that had gripped and scarred so many during their childhood. My Dad was no different even though he had the ability to laugh about how strange others who had come out of the Depression could sometimes act. More than once after visiting with his one of his relatives Dad would tell stories of how there would be a pile of perfectly ripened tomatoes from their large garden on the table. Instead of being allowed to eat the freshest ones, Dad saw the over-ripe and less favorable ones being served. Time and again he was able to smile over such events as he related them to us, but then was not able to adjust his own view when it came to the simple wish of the kitchen expansion.

My Mom never got her kitchen, and she was right that others would benefit from the woods. She lived, paid taxes and died, and someone else is enjoying the land now. She never got that kitchen, and that pains me.

Each morning as I walk into our Madison kitchen one of the first things I see is a framed picture that hangs on the wall surrounding the chimney once used for the cook stove over a hundred years ago. There is no way to miss the picture as it greets everyone who enters from the hallway. The picture is one that for me brings a flood of warm memories, smiles, and at times tears. It speaks of where I came from, and who I turned out to be.

It was Christmas 2000, and James had just started coming to our home for weekends and holidays earlier that year. As a lover of the camera he was taking photos of everyone, and late in the day thought the shoes in the entrance where family coming into the home would take them off before entering was a special way to recall the day. One could tell at a glance by the shoes assembled who was present on that day. In a real and unique way, it was a family portrait. I had the photo printed, and took it with me on a subsequent visit. I recall that Mom laughed at the snapshot and thought it really different, in that special type of way, and instructed my Dad to come over and see it.

The number of shoes present in pairs meant a holiday was underway; the photo was a multi-dimensional moment in time. I saw the faces of those who had worn the shoes, carrying the baking rolls or desserts, taking off their coats, and coming into the kitchen where the stove would be on and the heat from it a welcoming comfort.

For Christmas 2007 James had the picture enlarged and framed for me. When the time came to hang it, there was no doubt where it should be placed. James got out the hammer and hung the framed memory in the heart of our home, the kitchen.

The entrance way back home, as with any room there, evokes days gone by, irrecoverable days. That door. That hinged opening my Mom would open every now and then when I was a small boy just to make sure that the snow and ice did not freeze it shut during the winter storms. It was here at the entrance that as a grade school kid my Mom gave me a super big hug upon my return from a three-day school camping trip. (And, I even think she had really missed me!) This was the place my nephew Trevor, age three, being held by Mom, decided to get sick on her shoulder and all over the floor. Not fun then, yet somehow it brought a smile, even to Mom in years to come as we reminisced about it. On Thanksgiving 1996 she cried in that doorway when she hugged me as I arrived, telling me that she was glad I was home after a rough year in which I suffered with illness. I can recall the sound she made at that door as she tried not to cry while hurriedly putting on her shoes to go across the road to my grandparents' home on the night her own Father passed away.

Over the years my parents would watch from that door as I backed out of the driveway after a visit, giving a final wave from inside, and wait until I was down the road before I saw in my rear-view mirror that she turned the yard light off. I often laughed to myself that my Dad would have wondered what was wrong with me if I had hit a deer in front of my car while looking for the yard lights to go out behind me!

I still hear the final words she said to James and me as we went through that door in late July 2007. We were leaving from our last visit with Mom at her home, my home, before she entered the hospital. I still hear those final words: "Love you both".

> *"Each of us deserves the freedom to pursue our own version of happiness. No one deserves to be bullied."*
>
> —President Barack Obama

Exit Strategy

I have thought about this chapter more than any other when writing this book. Only James and a couple very close friends have heard some of what follows. I have healed from my teenage years, and moved on from that part of life. Once I left Hancock, and attended broadcasting school, my life started moving in a positive direction. The parts that I found had not healed were processed later in my life as an adult.

I hope this chapter provides positive encouragement to someone else. My story proves that there is every reason to keep the faith, and that things do get better, even when it seems everything is dark and bleak. I want to underscore for others that there are ways to address, adapt, and be shaped by hurtful events, and still come out ahead.

I have countless notes and pages of thoughts about every part of this book. I brought them together to form the bulk of this text. I was happy with what I was writing but there was only one remaining folder on my desk that held what I had written and accumulated concerning my teenage years. On a very basic level I want this book to be honest. To accomplish that, however, meant that I then needed to include this chapter, despite my ferocious desire at times not to dredge up the upsetting past.

As I was sorting through my computer files and handwritten notes, I heard of yet another sad and troubling story. Jadin Bell, a gay and much bullied teenager from Portland, Oregon had committed suicide. He was dead. His life ended tragically on February 3, 2013. He was fifteen years old. His story reminded the nation that the people who do not seemingly conform to the social 'norms' get bullied. Sometimes, not 'fitting in' has dire consequences.

Jadin Bell's story was not unlike my own. The difference was of course that I had survived my storm. I had made it to the other side, but not without some feelings of guilt in my adult years. I had survived my storm, but like Jadin Bell, my best friend in high school did not.

There needs to be more voices added to the choir of those who stand up against bullying. If one person is somehow served by my telling this story then it was worth it. Let my voice be heard.

My voice sings in this choir of allies not for pity; I do not feel sorry for myself in any way. I only know that we must do more as a community of caring people to reach out, and prevent the bullying of kids when we see it, or know that it is taking place. More importantly, perhaps, we need to build a stronger community where such behavior isn't tolerated any longer, build an environment in which all of us can flourish, and enjoy all of our civil rights: life, liberty, and most of all, happiness.

I was in my junior year in high school. Shortly after the noon break I returned to my locker for the books needed in my next class. I was confronted with something really upsetting, and jarring upon opening the locker door. Someone had broken into my space, and smeared a banana all over my new blue sweatshirt. I had just bought the article of clothing in the fall. It was hanging there, a complete mess.

Over the course of the previous summer, I had worked at de-tasseling corn, and took great delight in having money for school clothes. I was pretty elated that year to have spending cash for new, and brightly colored shirts. Just wearing them made me feel better. Bright colors have always been able to lift, and brighten my mood.

Shortly after James and I moved in together I noted that my gray sweatshirts and other 'dreary' colored clothing items were no longer in my closet. James had noted that when I was feeling less chipper I would slip on something gray. He put a stop to it. When forced to select only from bright colors, there was less of a chance for me to stay glum. James' plan seemed to work. (He refused to relent about it too. I have no idea to this day to where my super comfy 'depression garb', as he called it, has disappeared.)

What really troubled me that afternoon in high school was not the single act of someone busting into my locker, and acting out against me. It was violating and hurtful, but that was just the latest in what was a continual barrage of bullying tactics that I suffered during my school years.

Coupled with my anger at what had taken place was also the pragmatic part of my makeup. I instantly kicked into gear, and started computing what had to be done. That is one part about being bullied of which many seem unaware. Not only is there the act itself that is damaging and harmful, but over time the culmination of such behavior forces the one being bullied to start to think in a whole new way.

There must always be an exit strategy.

I could never just go to school. I always needed to think two steps ahead, to think about my path to wherever I was headed, especially if I was not in the circle of my friends. If I was sure some of the bullies were lined along the hallway paths, or lingering by their lockers I walked around them. There were times in the early part of my freshman year I actually exited the school from one door and entered through another to avert someone wishing to punch me, or shove me inside a locker.

In addition to the way to navigate around those who were bullies, I also needed to find ways to shore up my emotional side, and not lose more of my inner self to them. While I needed to avoid more abuse from bullies in school, I also needed, as in the case of my filthy sweatshirt, to avoid the embarrassment of going home and trying to explain how something like this happened to me. I needed at all costs to my teenage pride, which is very fragile for any one at that age, to avoid admitting to my parents that I was not able to stand up to, and defeat those who tormented me. I hated being thin, and hated that I was not able to protect myself. All that I had left was at times to save a bit of my pride.

So as I held the sweatshirt, and heard the laugher from behind me I did not have revenge on my mind, as I was computing steps beyond that. I was thinking about my exit strategy from this latest situation.

I took the sweatshirt in my hand, closed my locker, and headed down the hall to the Home Economics teacher. She was, thankfully, in her classroom. I had taken one of her courses, and knew she was smart, and also someone with whom I could easily communicate.

The teacher sat alone at the end of a table as I entered her classroom. I do not recall how the conversation started or all that was said but I know it included my plea: "I can't go home like this." There was just no way I could take that sweatshirt home in its condition. I am quite certain I was less than artful with my conversation, but she was hearing more than just what I was actually saying.

That afternoon, my Home Economics teacher rose above her job. She was for me just one very amazing and wonderful human being. I will never forget her kindness, or her gentle way of making something right when really everything was wrong.

She did not make me state out loud how the situation happened. She knew, and saved me the agony of recounting the obvious. I think she knew at some level how hard it was for me to have to seek help of this kind. She just decided to act. She took the sweatshirt, told me to go to my next class, and to come back at the end of the day.

When I reappeared in her classroom shortly before the busses were to take us home for the day, she had the article of clothing cleaned and folded like I had seen it on the store shelf at the time I purchased it. She handed it to me while placing a hand on my upper arm, asking if I was all right.

What was I to say?

There are angels among us (I truly believe that), and that day for me she was one of them.

There was no way I could have taken that sweatshirt home in the shape it was, and faced my parents. There was no way I could admit that a band of high school boys from the area was making my life unbearable at school. There was no way I could start expressing to them that this abuse was taking a toll on me, and undermining and altering the way I viewed myself. There seemingly was no way to share with them that my best friend since fourth grade, Todd , was also targeted, and the words they used against us were really causing inner turmoil, and stress.

I have always heard from some that the high school years were the best, and that nothing in life ever compared. I have absolutely no way to fathom how that can be the case. My reality from those years ranks them among the very worst experiences of my life.

There is no way to hear a constant drumbeat of debasing comments, and not feel like the inner walls of your being is akin to sandstone, slowly eroding, with the debris piling up around. It is hard to express how much it hurts to walk down a school hall, and have someone come up from behind for no reason and most unexpectedly and mercilessly slug you in the arm. Having no fat on my body, and not much muscle with which to blunt the blow I can only say the arm 'burned'. Meanwhile the bully laughs as he walks up the hallway, while hurling the term "fag" back in my direction.

There is no way to overstate the disgust felt when entering a classroom, and being targeted with truly despicable words tossed about from those already seated while a teacher sits at a desk pretending to be a million miles away. There is no way to understand how it feels to be a small-framed guy, and yet urged by well-meaning peers—some really nice acquaintances—to go and clean the smile off the bully's face. They clearly understood the injustice of it, the incivility of it, and proposed a route perhaps to remedy it.

Reality is often very different though. The idea of fighting seemed to work in the movies, especially the black-and-white ones that I loved to watch after the late local news on the weekend. My ability at fighting was limited to trying to get equal time in the bathroom from my sister who seemed to think it a second bedroom. I had never been in a real scuffle in all my life up to that time, and as I write this book can still say the same. Granted, my not wishing to be hit makes the top half-dozen reasons as to why I avoid fights, but beyond that it seems a really base way to resolve an issue.

I grew up in the country. My brother was eleven years older, and our age difference meant we were never close. He quickly married after high school, and was out of the house. I was fine with that as it allowed me to claim the largest bedroom, just as I was getting to the age I needed it. The age difference, and his being a non-entity in my life meant we never bonded, and certainly were never buddies who wrestled. There were no other boys my age in the immediate area with whom I could be friends, and so I grew up without the 'rough-housing' that I knew went on at the homes of my classmates. I was not 'toughened' in the sense that many of my peers were.

On a rational level there should be no reason to think I would have needed to be anyone other than who I was while attending classes. After all, the community pays taxes so students should be able to get an education. If I came to school ready to learn that is all that should have needed concern me. And yet given the number of boorish personalities that come from families where parenting is not a refined skill meant that perhaps it would have been better if I had known how to land a punch.

My best friend, Todd, was someone I only saw at school, and chatted on the phone with at times. For all practical purposes, except for family and relatives who lived close-by I grew up in a rather solitary fashion out in the country. It is hard to understand with all that is taken for granted in today's world how it really was to grow up as I did.

I had no fighting skills in my arsenal with which to then take on a bully. Fighting, as my classmates suggested, may have made sense in some theoretical way, but it was not really in the best interest of my body. Peer pressure though is an awesome force. (As I passed my fiftieth birthday I was rather proud to know I had never once smoked a cigarette, or tried marijuana, or been in a physical fight.)

Having said that, however, does not mean that I never struck out in anger. Once in high school I was so peeved by someone who thought me an easy target that I responded. I snapped, and had the means to respond. This was an exception. A proper response was not the case in most instances when the bullying occurred.

It was in the opening days of my freshman year in high school when I was purposely tripped while entering the lunchroom

Exit Strategy

with a tray of food. I had wanted to begin high school with a fresh start, and wanted to reclaim what had already been chipped away with the constant slurs of 'sissy' and 'weakling' that had bedeviled me for years.

I was sprawled on the painted gray concrete floor in the Plainfield school cafeteria with food everywhere. As quickly as I landed the sound of laughing rose up from a group of upper classmen who thought the prank on the kid not yet weighing one hundred pounds was uproariously funny. I am sure they would have also been the type to kick the smallest puppy in the litter.

During my teen years I could get angry very quickly as puberty, and overall frustrations had combined. It was not hard to image how I instantly stood up on my feet with tray in hand and used it in a Frisbee-like fashion to sling it into the chest of one of the jerks that had a smile on his face. It made an impact, and needless to say a bit of chaos.

As one might imagine there was a phone call from the school to my parents, but there was never any serious admonishment from Mom or Dad about my action. There was the implied underlying theme from Dad about standing up for oneself. My Mom was more worried about me being safe.

What neither would ever know was the extent of the problem I was suffering, or the erosion of 'self' that was underway from bullying. Worse yet, there was no way for me to contain it, and Dad's understanding about that one incident was of little use to me given the far larger problem I was facing.

It should be noted that there was never another attempt at school to trip me with my lunch tray in hand. That was mostly due to the fact that soon thereafter I stopped eating lunch at school, along with the tragedy of the school burning down that fall. I had no connection to the latter event, just for clarity's sake.

The fall of my freshman year, I had found a way to dodge those upperclassmen during lunch. The easiest way was just to avoid the lunchroom. Of course, this did not help my being a small guy.

Early in my freshman year I found a nook in the corner of the old school near the elementary entrance, and just simply waited for the noon hour to be over. A few times my cousin who was a schoolteacher passed with her brood of students and nodded. Those were hard days to get through, but when I found an exit strategy I employed it.

For all the horrible side effects from which the school district suffered after the fire that destroyed the classic-looking schoolhouse, I must say it did have at least one positive aspect.

My friend, Todd, always brought a packed lunch, and I would try to pocket an apple or something from home. We ate in a variety of locations given the upheaval in the months after the fire. We witnessed mobile classrooms brought in, and at times a general state of chaos lingering about the place.

Since I could not tell my parents about the bullying, and what was happening to me at school, I started to save my lunch money, and added it to my small but steadily growing savings for family Christmas presents. That would be the way it was for the rest of my years in high school as I never again ate lunch at school.

For the rest of her life I never told Mom the whole story, but I do know there were always crackers and peanut butter or bread and cheese or such as a snack when I got home from school on the counter. The snacks carried me over until supper. Preparing snacks may have been 'the Mom thing' to do, but I also wonder at some level if she didn't have an inkling of larger issues at play. She wondered about things, I am sure, even if she was not sure as to what they might all mean.

With classes spread out all over after the fire, Todd and I found places to be safe and also to have fun. One of the grand places was in the science lab with the teacher who would almost hold court if he were in a good mood. I still recall some principle of science playing out in dramatic fashion with a Bunsen burner, and wonderful hues from the flame as a bit of this or that element was added to the mix. The science lab was always a gentle, and relaxing place to be.

But the best of the lot when it came to a most wonderful personality who always smiled, and seemed sincere was the literature teacher. I found it easy being in his class, not only for the topic he taught, but also due to how he conducted himself. I recall often looking at him, and thinking that at some point that is how I probably would look when I got older. The teacher was slim, average height and looks, and wore sport jackets that had a patch on the outer sleeve at the elbow. He loved to read, and seemed so confident as he stood in front the classroom. I had a crush on him, but knew what attracted me most to him was his sense of self, something I was trying to figure out in my own life.

I know that I let him down when I failed to follow through on a forensics meet that I had signed up for in my freshman year. He was working on a solid team that he could take to competition, and I had worked hard to not only memorize my piece, but also strongly deliver it. In my bedroom, or behind the garage, or in front of him I was able to march through the whole piece. But as the time neared to when I was to stand in front of others, I was plagued in my own mind about how I looked, my weight, but more importantly how I was feeling about myself. I had already internalized a lot of the bullying. At the time my feelings were just one large mass of stormy confusion.

Today I would phrase those feelings as not being able to project to others who I truly was. Instead I was left feeling inside like everything which was slurred against me from the bullies was perhaps who I really was. In that sense the bullies were victors.

I was 'sick' the day of the competition held at another school, and I know it upset my instructor. I liked him, and my letting him down only added to the utter dismay I was feeling about everything.

Even so, it was clear that Todd and I were still allowed extra latitude around him, and that he liked the quirky ways we worked to make him laugh. One of the most memorable moments with him was one that perhaps in retrospect we took a wee bit more liberty than we should have. But I will never apologize for the smile it created then, or the one that still crosses my face. It remains as one of the most silly, and rather hilarious stunts Todd and I both were able to pull off.

Todd and I were in the same study hall, and were able to get out at the same time. We met up at Todd's locker where we retrieved an old telephone, a white glove, and a white towel. We headed to the literature teacher's room, where a class was in session. With a stuffy looking appearance, akin to that of a waiter in a fancy restaurant, Todd had the towel over his lower left arm with the white-gloved hand holding the phone. The long cord ended in my hands in the hallway. As Todd opened the door and headed toward the teacher, I connected the wires to a battery pack and the phone rang. With a deep British sounding accent Todd said, "Sir, it is for you."

From the hallway I could see the instructor smile and laugh, and then moved Todd to the door while saying, "Get out of here." He came to the door, looked out at us and said we could not really be doing this type of thing. The fact he had a smile the whole time told us he indeed found the act funny and clever.

That was the amazing thing about Todd. He was picked on for being whatever some people wanted to make him out to be, and yet he had a sense of humor, and timing with his lines while telling a joke that was as if he had no worry in the world. What I was not to really clue into until years later was that he was hiding all the slings and slurs of the world behind comedy. If anyone really needed someone wiser and older to talk to, it was Todd.

That protective mechanism of comedy lasted as long as Todd could make it work. He dealt with the mean verbal taunts by spending weekends writing truly hilarious satirical pieces about the issues of the day, and those who hurt his feelings while in school. Each Monday I was eagerly waiting to find out what his latest folder of papers would contain. There was much potential in his ability to skewer with humorous words, and drawings that stung just as hard as those that were flung at him. I have often wondered if he would have been a writer for *Saturday Night Live*, or a show such as *South Park*. He had that much potential.

In our last year of high school Todd told me he had dreams about one guy in our class, perhaps the best looking if the girls were to be the judges on the matter. Todd really liked him, and in fact the two were friends. It was then that Todd told me he was gay. It was no big deal. I already knew that. But I was the first one he was ever speaking the words to verbally. In reality, it was a huge deal.

That afternoon I told him I was gay too, and that was that.

The fact was that being gay, in and of itself, was never a big deal for me. It was just a part of my makeup like brown hair, and a love for reading. Looking back I recall when I was very young one of the guys working at Shippy Shoes in Stevens Point was a favorite of mine when the family stopped in for footwear. Though it would be years before I understood why that was, I do know that I never personally felt any desire to be anyone other than who I was.

I sometimes read about people who use drugs and alcohol as a means to deal with who they are, instead of just embracing themselves. I never turned to chemicals to deal with life. In that respect I was a very well adjusted and healthy person, as I never loathed the person I was born to be.

I have heard often of the angst, guilt, inner tension, and countless other feelings that some people grapple with when 'coming out'. I never had any of that inner turmoil, or questioning. I was the person I was born to be, and was comfortable with it.

What I had no ability to cope with, however, was the mean and vile nature of others about things for which they had no first-hand knowledge concerning my life. In small towns, especially, that small-mindedness can then take on a life of its own, and be most cruel.

What made being gay troublesome for me was the lack of understanding from others who came to conclusions based on perceptions that were faulty. When that bigotry turned into terrifying words and physical assaults, it was devastating. I recall that Todd and I both told each other that since we had been friends since fourth grade, and had been through so much together, we would always be buddies long after high school was over.

One of the themes that continues to trouble me even after the many years since this bullying took place for Todd and me was the lack of anyone to really talk with concerning the problem. Todd had no more of a resource to fall back on than I did. While we each had good and caring parents, the same group of wholesome well-meaning friends who made up our small circle at school, the fact remains that we were all teenagers, and everyone was facing their own set of complicated issues that demanded attention. None of us had the life experiences with which to assist anyone else.

It is for that reason that I have long advocated for mentoring programs aimed at helping certain segments of society. Helping someone through one-on-one dialogue that bridges the gulf between a young person's fears and the way that life changes as we get older and move forward is a vital antidote to bullying. Part of the problem of being bullied is the fear that it creates, the negative self-connotation that starts to manifest itself, and the belief that somehow nothing will ever change. Mentors who are older and have been shaped and molded by life experiences have a strong foundation to help others understand the process of coming to terms with one's self. That is the essence of The Trevor Project: You Are Not Alone. (I have included a list of resources for kids like Todd and I were in the appendix of this book.)

In 2000, though I was very opposed to the candidacy of George Bush for president, I penned him a very personal and strongly worded letter in support of one idea that he championed. His support for mentoring programs was indeed the correct policy stand to take, and one towards which I wish more candidates would lend their efforts. Gay teenagers need to know that they are not alone, and that people care and are willing to be engaged to make their lives as productive and note-worthy for all the right reasons in the high school years as for any other student population.

My grade school years led to my loss of self-confidence which really took a hit as the teenage years neared. Those years are so layered with complexity under the best of conditions, and if anyone is slightly not marching in the same line or acting in the same fashion as 'everyone else' there is a terrible price to pay. Kids can be the meanest creatures on earth, which is why there needs to be teachers, and school personnel who can oversee and guide youngsters to a more healthy way of viewing themselves, and as a consequence interacting with others.

We must have parents who raise children with the social standards that allow for the respecting of others when it comes to diversity. If a parent finds it wrong to steal, drink to excess, and cheat on their spouse it is likely that those moral codes will be handed down to the next generation. The same is true for the traits of not allowing for bigotry, racial epitaphs, or stereotyping. Placing the Golden Rule which we use to recite as, "Do unto others as you would have them do unto you" (Matthew 7:12) back into the homes of Americans would do much to end some of the most outlandish acts that take place in our society.

At my high school there was no counselor who was prepared to deal with the issue of sexual orientation, and frankly there was no teacher who really wanted to make a complete smack down of the offenders, as well intentioned as a couple teachers were at the time.

Part of the reason this happened was based on the time period in which I was a teenager. While there were places in the nation far more open-minded than where I lived, it should be remembered that it was also when the first gay character on TV was even written into a script. Being forward leaning on matters at that time still must be placed in context.

Billy Crystal played Johnny Dallas in the ABC program *Soap*. While Phil Donahue was using his talk show, as were others to address many social issues. For the rural areas, such as my hometown, it appeared to me that few people in my hometown were listening. That is not a harsh statement about Hancock; almost any rural area could be labeled in the same way.

From my adult perspective it is just utterly bizarre to think of those bullies as having such a force over my life. That is the craziness that comes with bullying. It is mean, grotesque, without logic, and in the midst of the madness seemingly without a real escape. The victims of bullying feel trapped as they have no real life experiences to fall back on to show how the problem can be addressed, and often have not developed the social network to have others help deal with the matter.

For me the undermining of my self-confidence started with two factors that played out hand-in-hand. Being thin and lacking sport skills painted a sign on my forehead that read, "Kick me, and when I am down put sand in my hair". No joke. How kids are not raised to value diversity, and appreciate differences is based on a whole set of criteria. Part of the problem was based on the time period I was raised, the fact that some parents just raised bullies, and I grew up in a small town in rural Wisconsin where out-dated thinking often clung to people like manure to the cleats of a boot.

Today with the societal changes that are taking place, along with more news sources, and social media there is headway taking place by shining a light on bullying, and working with young people to find a way forward. It was hard, however, to always be the fish swimming upstream, but that is how I often felt.

It is hard to describe the feeling I had at age thirteen when getting up to home plate with a baseball bat while looking out at the other team spread across the field. I would hear someone encouraging the other kids to all move in closer. The perception was of course that the skinny kid will merely muff the ball.

"Easy out for sure," one of them would mutter. That is not what a teenage guy wants to hear. Talk about crushing confidence at an awkward age in life. Had I been the psychical education instructor who in this case was a rather out of shape man who often read the newspaper when class was indoors, I would not have allowed such behavior to occur. There are ways to handle boys, but he repeatedly missed the mark.

To begin with, had I been the teacher I would have not allowed only the good players to select the teams. With all the boys in a cluster at the start, the faces that soon remained were the guys who had no sports skills such as me. Ultimately kids like me had to head to one of the teams as there were no others to select, and there were the usual groans about losing a mere gym class contest because they had to be saddled with someone they deemed unworthy.

As an adult I can see how the teacher could have handled such situations. But was not that teacher an adult himself at the time that such things took place under his supervision? Was he not an adult at the time, like all the other teachers and administrative staff at the school? Is it not the same for every teacher and staff member across the nation now?

That is my point.

An opportunity that might have turned into a learning moment for those young impressionable minds was missed when the same old reasoning about boys and sports was allowed to continue. The type of thinking about how the teacher ran his gym class is just as foreign to me as the color of blankets that hospitals once used when sending babies home. There is no place for any of that in modern society.

So there I was at bat, and so much of the team in the field had moved forward in unison. It was an awkward moment for me. The first pitch was about to commence. And then the teenage anger that was stored deeply within me found a way to be released. With absolute resolve the bat met the ball. The arc of white reached up. The ball flew beyond the expectations of the ones who were so cock-sure in the field.

That afternoon in eighth grade at the baseball diamond located at the Hancock School just a short distance from the rows of pine trees near the playground equipment proved far more important to my future than I could ever have known at the time.

It would be a journey getting to the place where I could look back at that event and place it in perspective. At the time it was just one more dreadful reminder that I was somehow different, at least in how people perceived me. I had no real muscle mass that caused that ball to soar. It was just pure anger that connected with the ball. I am sure that if they had let me bat over and over I could have replicated that first hit multiple times. I had lots of anger to cash in; in anger, I was rich.

I was already tired of being defined by other students as a weakling, sissy, and worse. When those guys moved in towards the infield thinking I was going to play the part they had constructed for me, I got mad. I had been mad many times before when the taunts and meanness piled on--the difference was that I was armed with a bat and I had a way to unleash that anger. No one knew why the ball flew as it did, and when it was over everyone thought it was that I had lucked out. I knew better.

Though slender I could run fast, and loved to have the opportunity to play games, but admittedly was not gifted for sports. Somehow I wound up with a left-handed glove as a kid, which makes sense I guess, as I am left-handed. Unluckily though, I can only throw with any degree of success with my left hand, which as anyone reading this might conclude certainly slows down the process of a fast-action baseball game. My awkwardness really made for some loud comments, as well, from fellow players who only saw their self-worth wrapped up in sports. (This situation could have been another teaching moment for the gym teacher of my youth.)

Essentially, I was doomed. At home there was never any way to foster my development with sports. I never recall any of the baseball throwing or football passes that seem common among siblings. The one time I ever recall playing some buckets with my brother, and then for just a couple of minutes, took place at home before the old barn was torn down. The hoop was located on the south side of the structure, and for whatever reason he picked up the basketball and we shot a few. The fact that I can recall only one instance of bonding in this way speaks volumes, I think, about why we never formed a relationship.

I am not sure to what degree Dad played baseball with my brother in his early years, but by the time I was old enough for sports there was no interest from Dad if I learned to catch a ball, or hike a football. That is just a fact. At one level as I got older and reflected on that it felt bad, but I must say in the same breath I never much thought about sports to encourage the process along either. In time, Dad and I would bond on other things, but it never would be over sports.

By the time I was born my Dad was age forty-two, and was probably tired of raising kids, and even more of tossing a ball. I do not fault him for that, and rather accept it as a part of being the youngest in the family.

I never thought about the Milwaukee Braves, now the Brewers, in the way my brother did when he was a youngster. When I was born in 1962 he wrote letters to my Mom while she was in the Wild Rose Hospital. In some detail he described games he had heard broadcast on the radio, and his hopes for the team. As I read the letters again while writing this chapter it is so clear how different our interests were as kids, and I wonder, but will never know to what degree that interest was encouraged by my parents.

Living in a rural area with no other kids my age to play

with or interact with in any way meant there was never a chance to become more proficient with my gross motor skills. While I was blessed with grandparents, and relatives as neighbors there were none my age to be playing any sport, or naturally with the inclination to do so.

Sports were also not something much talked about in our home, as there was no television in those years where the games could be watched. As I grew older I cared less for sports as they only meant embarrassment in one way or another, and with no one to show me why they might be fun I moved on to areas of life that did enthuse me.

All of this talk of sports boils down to one simple truth. I was being judged for skills I did not profess to have, nor had I sought out. I was not being evaluated by my peers for the qualities I did possess. I was singled out and made to feel so different, so useless at times that I am somewhat astonished that I made it through that period at all.

My friend Todd did not. Todd committed suicide in September 1980, at the age of eighteen. We had only just graduated high school. My Mom knew instantly that there was no good news coming to our doorstep the evening a squad car pulled into the driveway. As I sat at the dinner table, in the place Mom always sat, a representative of the Sheriff's office, maybe even the Sheriff himself, sat in the chair I used for mealtime. He told me that my best friend was dead—"the result of suicide".

I still recall Mom yelling out the south kitchen screened window to my Dad working in the garden to get to the house. My Dad stood alongside the refrigerator as my Mom sat next to me at the table. For the longest time, the officer just reached across the table and held one of my hands. We talked. I never saw him again, and years later thought if I had the chance he deserved munificent thanks for the humanity he showed me that night.

There was no note of explanation from Todd about why the event happened as it did. There were no words of hurt or outrage. It seemed as if the suicidal act itself was to be all that needed conveying. I knew in my heart what had happened, and it ripped deep.

Later that night when it was almost dark, I got on my sneakers and ran to the woods way up south of the house. I got far enough into the towering pines where I knew I could yell, scream, and curse at everyone and everything. I could not fathom why God had allowed this to happen, and why there was no one to stop it, including me. When I had emptied my first volley of anger, I walked back to the house.

I had spoken to Todd the day before he died, and we had made tentative plans to head to Stevens Point to hang out and have some fun. We had not done that very often, even though he had access to a car. Only a handful of such excursions to the Point were ever made since Todd had attained a license.

I noted nothing in that final conversation with Todd that seemed out of the ordinary. He made comments to the effect that everyone was back to high school, but the fact we did not have to be there was a good thing. I agreed.

As I look back on the totality of this whole story the thing that is the most sad and gut-wrenching is that Todd's life was just starting to pull away from the madness. It didn't matter. There seemed no way to see beyond the past. Todd should have had every reason to think that something good could happen. High school for us had ended. He could have had every reason to see that good was on the horizon, and yet could not.

The strength of bullies, and the harm they cause is not just with the instant pain they inflict with verbal taunts or punches, but the emotional pain and distress they lodge within a person's very inner core. The damage to the other's sense of self is the most heinous part of what they inflict on others.

I wish that Todd could have seen or sensed that brighter lights and better people were over the hill following high school. Sometimes hope in small town America is not enough to break through the dark nights in search of a new dawn. That is the tragic truth too often with young isolated gay people. Too often we read of youngsters who search out a permanent solution to a temporary problem. We need to be better prepared to notice when bullying occurs, and act to intervene to stop it when it happens. This is especially true for those in professions where they interact with young people regularly.

Over the decades, and especially in the last several years, I wonder what Todd would say about the progress this nation has made with the issues that seemed so daunting when we were teenagers. Today many schools allow gay dates for proms, college students are open and excepting of gay friends, major companies have domestic partner benefits, political candidates seek out gay voters, and gay marriage is going to be allowed everywhere, I predict, in the next few years.

One of the most important changes in many of our schools is the advent of GSAs, Gay Straight Alliances. The goal of most of these alliances is to make a school community safe while creating a welcoming environment for all students. As this alliance approach proves, many of the answers to the problems start with common sense attitudes about how we treat others. These alliances show us that we should echo how we ourselves wish to be treated. We are back to the 'Golden Rule' again.

I wish Todd could have found some way to hang on, and had a better support network, which I acknowledge with much reflection over the years should have included myself. I was floundering too, and yet wish I could have been better equipped to offer insight to his state of mind, or provided sounder advice, and a more hopeful message to impart. I have carried guilt about this for years. There is never an answer to these questions, and yet over time I have asked them.

Random acts of kindness leave a real mark on people. One of our high school teachers witnessed a verbal incident in the hallway aimed directly at me. He motioned me into his classroom, and closed the door. He knew what was happening, and wanted me to know that all of it would be over when high school was finished. "Everything changes," he said. "You just have to believe it, and just make it through the rest of high school." He told me that once I had left school, and was doing something interesting with my life all that was currently happening would fade away with time.

It Gets Better are the essential words at the heart of Dan Savage's campaign by the same name. His message of hope is aimed at teenagers today. "It gets better," my teacher told me. He was absolutely correct, yet it begs two questions.

First, why should I have had to somehow 'make it through', and have any less opportunity to have memorable years in high school than the ones tormenting me? Why should the bulk of the heavy shouldering of the matter have been placed upon me?

The second question that stood out like a red light bulb pulsating in the dark was that since he knew full well what was happening, why did he not take the next steps up the administrative ladder and make sure it ended? Why were the punks who threw the verbal slings not the ones taken into the classroom, and then admonished?

I understand on a real human level the teacher was trying to reach me, and help me. But as an adult I see it was too little, and aimed not totally in the correct direction. Let's try not to further injure the victim.

When I cursed and cried in the woods the night that my friend Todd died, my anger and disgust ran across the faces of my past and left no one untouched. I was angry with everyone. Including myself.

Following Todd's death I was in deep distress. I still liked who I was on the inside. I had my interests in broadcasting, history, and books. But there remained nothing that I could see on the horizon that was offering any hope. I was eighteen, not yet enrolled in higher education, unemployed, and did not even have a driver's license. I had no close friends with whom I could talk; in fact, I had no one I could honestly confide in or anyone I could ask to help me process everything that was happening. I had never been in a darker place in my life.

Years later my Mom would finally tell me that some were worried that I too might commit suicide during those months. While I was floundering and depressed, I never viewed suicide as an option. I wanted to live. In spite of everything that had happened over the years I felt there was something for which to live. I needed to process everything. I had to find somehow a way to believe that something good could happen for me.

The lessons from the books I had read during those years came to mind. During that time I recalled over and over the story of Theodore Roosevelt losing his wife and mother on the same day in 1884. While his Mom passed away from typhoid fever, his wife would die just a few hours later from Bright's disease. It was following this double tragedy that the future President retreated to the Dakota territories to find himself and start anew. I knew there was a lesson to be found in his life. Rough times can be fierce, but there is always a new chapter to be written.

The moral of Roosevelt's story seemed logical in a rational way of thinking. It also all seemed so far removed from my life in Hancock. Emotionally I pulled back and only let those things that interested me make contact. I immersed myself in the presidential election coverage that was intensely under way that fall as Ronald Reagan worked to defeat President Carter. I read weekly news magazines, books, and listened to 'Chicago Ed' on the radio.

I recall during those weeks and months at shutting the door to my bedroom, which was an addition at the end of the house. It had been built as the family had grown, but had no heat, so it required the door to be open to allow warm air to flow. That winter there were times the temperature fell so far that I could see my breath, and while my Mom wanted the door to be opened at night I demanded that it be shut. I just wanted to be alone. I wrapped up in the blankets on the bed, and listened to the radio late at night.

I had lots of feelings and thoughts that I could not honestly express to anyone, and so being alone was just easier instead of pretending things were fine with 'happy talk'. There are times when solitude is easier, though wonderful friends like the ones I would come to have in my life in years to come would have been ideal. There are times when we are wrong about solitude being easier. It is sometimes preferable to have those close friends with which to talk and share ideas.

In 1987, once I started working with a state legislator in Madison, which allowed me health care coverage, I sought help from a therapist to allow me to more efficiently process all of the turmoil from those high school years. I had so much that still needed to be resolved. Going to seek professional help was one of the best decisions I ever made. Nothing is better than talking things over and coming to understand why feelings exist, and how to react to them in a more constructive way. (Rosalynn Carter, our former First Lady, has fought for years to destigmatize good mental health care. I applaud her.)

My therapist at the time suggested that my wanting to have the room so very cold following Todd's death was a part of my mind needing something else for me to feel instead of the constant pain of loss, and the confusion about where my life was to go. We also talked about the bullies, and what made them act so recklessly. While I still harbored deep feelings about what they had done the therapist put their lives into a larger context in which to be viewed. Being teenagers, they also were seeking to understand themselves and the world around them. They too may have had questions about their sexuality as often those who strike out in the fashion they did have latent feelings that are trying to be understood. While many of their contemporaries might leave the area for college perhaps they only saw a very limited future for themselves in the area where they were raised. My therapist humanized the bullies more than I wanted to hear, but we still sat there and talked, as that is what I wanted, and needed.

It proved to be exceedingly beneficial to talk, and share my feelings in that protected space week after week. It has always baffled me why there is such a mystery, and at times a reluctance to seek out therapy. Getting in touch with feelings is never easy, but it serves a purpose.

When my Mom passed away I again sought the aide of a therapist. Mary, a trainer of communications and inner healing was an exceedingly compassionate person, and insightful. She asked me what I wanted to accomplish in our sessions. She sat and just listened as I listed off what I needed. When I had finished my recitation, she told me that many people come to her and spend weeks trying to get to what I had enunciated clearly at the outset. My goals for our sessions were not lofty. I needed to find ways to move through my grief, and get to another place.

My sessions with Mary were not complicated. I talked and she listened. The therapist never overly interjected herself in to what we were talking about from one week to the next. As if by some magical spell, though, the talking melted away the pain. I gained understanding in to my own process of grieving. I developed coping skills which helped me to make it through the next several years as slowly I said goodbye to my Dad as well.

I am stronger as a person from being in touch and honest with all facets of my life. Others at times say men just need to "Buck it up". Keeping things inside is not 'manly'; it is in fact the weak way to live life. Never having to confront and deal honestly with feelings and emotions is not only counter-productive in how to live but it also lessens the quality of life. I personally am not willing to sacrifice quality of living for the sake of my perceived manhood.

I wish there was a way to know precisely how I turned the page that winter after Todd's death. Really, all I have to offer as an answer was that time allowed me to let it happen. At some point I started to dream again about what I wanted from life. More importantly still, I began to take concrete steps to move forward.

Following Todd's passing, I again thought about the day in eighth grade when I popped a baseball over the heads of those who thought I could never do it. The more I thought things through, the more I would be damned if those who had plagued me in high school were also going to decide my future. There was just no way in hell that I was going to allow others to set the parameters for my life, or confine me any longer. My new mission became a deeply personal one. I would live my life authentically. All others with opinions on my future could respectfully remain silent.

Perhaps I needed enough of a period of time to get the feisty side of my personality to break through and dominate. Some deep down gritty determination that had started with anger sprouted into a resolve to make my life what I wanted it to be. I commenced plotting my next exit strategy. This one was going to be different though. This new stratagem would be healthier for me in the long run.

As I thought about my prospects the one thing that seemed to be my best route out of Hancock was to follow my interests in radio. With that I decided to go to broadcasting school. My latest exit strategy was not an elaborate plan. By taking those first small steps, I felt a sense of empowerment. Life was going to go my way for once.

Cost was the main factor in my decision to apply at Trans American School of Broadcasting in Wausau where I was enrolled starting in September 1981. Looking back it was the right thing to do. In ways I could never have imagined, my time at Trans American not only allowed me some education in which to proceed with my life, but more importantly allowed me to heal. For the first time in my life I liked who I saw in the mirror, and knew the guy smiling back was just fine the way he was. If one ever needs my definition of being rich, that would be it.

I had no way of knowing it would be the people I met and the friends made while at school who would be so helpful. And, they helped me without knowing they were a part of the process. Over and over my classmates renewed my faith in the future by showing me that diversity is a good thing. Thriving on small ideas or limiting the experiences life afforded was not a part of the mindset that made up my broadcasting class. In later years when thinking about the group of students who comprised my class I would laugh to myself how political conservatives would say this just shows that the media, of which we all wanted to be a part, were only big liberals!

The first impression I had of my class seated for the opening lecture was how they all seemed more like me than of those who I had left behind from high school. That really struck me. It wasn't that we dressed alike, or looked alike. It wasn't even that we were all interested in broadcasting. Instead we all had certain areas of interest that were different from the rank and file. I very much appreciated that quality in my then-classmates.

Some were very in tune with the contemporary music scene and bands, others wanted to know more about how the legal system worked so as to cover the court system. One was so sure he was about to be the next major play-by-play announcer that he kept his own set of stats while watching sporting events just so he was ready when his chance came. Everyone had a dream, and everyone seemed to have faith that whatever he or she held close inside was possible.

This in not to say the atmosphere was somehow geeky, in fact it was quite the opposite. It was a lively, dynamic place where lots of ideas and energy flowed. It was clearly a more focused and mature atmosphere than I had ever known previously. I felt comfortable from the beginning.

Seated on the left of me in class was Bruce who remains one of my longest-running friends. To my left was Bob, a blond-haired guy with a fantastic laugh.

Bruce was a bit reserved, and more mature than most in the class, but what struck me, other than his NPR-type voice was that from the first day he always carried a really nice, professional looking briefcase. Inside his case was everything neatly placed, from his books, pens, a tie that was rolled perfectly, and an umbrella. It was not the common way to bring what was needed to class for guys our age, and so in some way it might be easy to think he stood out. In reality, Bruce blended in with everyone else who seemed to all have their individual ways of being, and he was equally comfortable with that fact. It was not lost on me that Bruce was very confident in his way of 'being'. As simple an act of carrying a briefcase may be, the daily ritual struck me. He liked what he did, and was going to do it his way.

Meanwhile Bob and I struck up a friendship that was easy and natural after knowing each other only for a short time. Somewhere along the way a running joke had developed about Bob needing to teach me how to drink, as I had no background on that front at all. So after many laughs about this we made plans for an evening at the Scott Street Pub, a popular little spot not far from the school. It was there that I drank the first full beer of my life. I related to him that nugget of information, and he laughed, and then asked if I was serious. Indeed I was.

Though I did not explain it to Bob that night, my upbringing was vastly different than how many now view the years of childhood and teen experiences. My family grew up, as my Mom would describe it when angry when not having the house the way she wanted it as "living back in the sticks". We had one family car, and Dad used it for work, and after his long day there was no running the kids around for this or that club or outing. I grew up without other young people around, and I did not hang out with a bunch of friends who held parties or drank endlessly. In short, I did not know much about Wisconsin's omnipresent drinking culture. It would be very hard for any contemporary teenager to fathom spending an entire weekend at home doing domestic things, and then know that was the way the following weekend was also to be spent.

More importantly still, my Mom did not allow alcohol in the house. We did not sit in church every Sunday but there were certain codes that were observed, and so when an association that worked with the town board, where my father served as supervisor would bring a basket of nuts and fruit it was graciously accepted, and much appreciated. The year Mogen David wine was offered as a present, it too was greeted with a smile. I knew the wine would never stay in the house. The question was only how it would disappear. The next morning as I left the house to get on the school bus I found the answer. The snow bank on the right side of the steps from the back door was a crimson color.

Years after I had moved to Madison I kept a few bottles of really good beer in the basement, and my Mom informed me that the plucky act met with stern disapproval from someone in the family. I was never sure if that was just another thing that was viewed as my 'getting away' with something since I was the youngest, or not. Mom and I would also laugh over the years about how someone wanted me banned from the house when I pierced my left ear while working at WDOR. At times it felt like I was close to the *Twilight Zone*.

The beer stayed in the basement, and the earring remained for years. And somewhere over time my Mom softened her ban on alcohol, and even made an ice-cream container of what is known as 'slush' that never froze when placed in the freezer given its high alcoholic content. When added to Seven-Up for a holiday, Mom's slush was quite tasty. I can add though that one day, I went to the freezer to get some of the slush, and it was gone. Remarking that there was no way my parents could have used all the slush themselves, I was informed that it had been there for so many years that she felt it was no longer "good". Fearing it had spoiled, Mom had disposed of it! That should tell you everything you need to know about how alcohol was viewed in my family.

There should be no mistaking the fact I was, and remain a serious lightweight when it comes to alcohol. That was soon discovered as I sat with Bob; it was determined that perhaps playing darts, talking, and laughing would be more enjoyable, and that became the order of the night. I felt free while hanging out with a friend who over the school year would continually serve me as a reminder that life indeed was good.

There was also Ivan who while I would never know very well as a student at school stood out for me as someone who was living authentically, and proud of it. Ivan came from Upper Michigan, was my age, and gay. No one had to ask or wonder. He was, and that was it. No one sat in judgment of him, or excluded him. In fact, he was loved for his campy and spirited way, along with his sharp wit. I would often wonder where he obtained all his self-assurance and how he came to be so self-aware. I never had more than fleeting conversations with him, but always sensed someone who was a bit wiser than his years.

After moving to Madison I again ran into Ivan, and discovered that he was operating a business, Madison's Tea Room, a restaurant situated directly across the Capitol Square from my ground floor office window. It was therefore shocking to look out the window upon getting to work in February 1989, the morning following the mayoral primary election, and finding his store front taped off with yellow crime tape.

Ivan had been murdered in his business during the night; he had been stabbed more than 30 times according to the police report. His killer would be sentenced to life in prison for first-degree intentional homicide. It was a horrible and chilling event for Madison. On a personal level, Ivan's passing made me very sad since I knew him to be rather remarkable.

It also while in broadcasting school I met another longtime friend who made a lasting impression on me. While rounding the corner of Mister Bob's, the former downtown motel made into apartment efficiencies where many of the broadcasting students lived, I ran into someone I had not yet met, but seen from a distance during the fall. It was a snowy Saturday afternoon, when I heard the first words from George of Fargo, North Dakota.

"Know where I can find a snow shovel? My car is stuck."

I told him that perhaps at the front desk someone might know, and so together we went in search of a shovel. After helping dig out his car which truly was lodged in the middle of the driveway on the backside of the building, he suggested we head to a video arcade. At first it seemed a strange segue from what we had been doing, but over time I was to come to see his spontaneity play out over and over.

George was talkative, funny, very personable, and I was

soon to discover that he was very good at video games. I had never played such games but I was ready to learn. Video games could be instantly addictive. That afternoon, I first played Centipede, and loved it.

While driving around Wausau George would tune his radio dial to a local rock station. One song would get more volume than any other during those months. To this day there is no way not to hear *My Sharona* and not think back to those carefree days when windows would be down with breezes blowing as we laughed and shared time.

Another of our impromptu moments had us in his car trying to find a Mexican eatery. The trip took us out of the city. The car developed a motor problem and we were forced to walk for a bit. At the outset, we thought the restaurant was only a short distance way. George's sandal came undone as we trekked, the sun was getting warmer, and clouds were gathering and lowering. We came upon a business where we planned to use the phone to call someone for a ride, when a kind stranger in a pickup truck gave us a ride back to the inner city. As we rode along it started to rain. That should have been a bad day by most reckonings. But it was not. We never stopped talking, laughing, and proceeding forward with our plans. George does not live as close today as I would like, but over the decades it only takes one phone call to again connect, and again know that a real friend is on the other end of the line.

George surely found me to be "small-town" as much as I found him to be a "city-boy". Those months his friendship allowed me to grow as a person, laugh heartily, and never once feel like I needed to be anyone other than who I was. That remains the best definition of friendship that I know.

So much of what I was feeling and experiencing during those months at broadcasting school were things that most everyone else had experienced in high school. I knew that, and yet I was thrilled with where I was, and what I was learning not only every day in the classroom but also with the social interactions from those around me. I was being accepted readily by new friends, and the burst of energy I felt within was thrilling.

Bullying had caused me to delay living and kept me from experiencing things during high school. I was making up for lost time and pushing my way forward. My self-confidence started to expand. I felt great. I fell in love for the first time during those months, and while it was never to be recognized I knew I wanted it to happen again. I was fine with learning and stumbling, and even being bruised at times as long as the path led me forward. I no longer doubted my every move, but instead continued to assert myself. I no longer asked if something could happen, but instead how it might happen faster.

Months after school started, during a long conversation with others late into the night I was asked how it was that after starting the semester as a rather shy guy I had opened up and become a different person. I never really answered that question, as it was too complicated. There was a release to my personality, and everything that had been pent up over the years was coming out. I was at heart an outgoing person, loving to tell a joke, and sharing time with others. If I had answered fully, my response would have been that all of those classmates were the reason as to why I had changed. For the first time in my life I felt like I belonged, and was welcomed for just being myself. I was so ready to live and heal, and I had no desire to be anywhere other than with that group. That was the answer to their question.

After being in Madison for a couple of years I decided it was time to try and make a difference for someone else, by taking some of my experiences, and trying to assist someone else. I signed up for *Big Brothers of Dane County*. I had created healthy exit strategies for myself that had worked, and I knew I was not alone in needing ways to find a path forward. The reasons for having problems and issues were many, but at the end of the day everyone can use a friend to talk with, and know there is support. There was a continuing segment on one of the local news channels about the need for people such as myself to be matched with an ever-growing number of young people. Since I had the time, and energy I spoke with the agency.

Within a few weeks I was being introduced to Chris at a local McDonald's. He was talkative, inquisitive, and also very fond of French fries. We were going to hit it off just fine. There are so many kids in need of our time and commitment as a society. I knew of his family situation, and hoped just to be a weekly reminder that one person, other than his Mom who was a very smart and caring woman, might be able to hear what he had to say.

Week after week we did a whole assortment of things. Off to the zoo, the putting green, one of my family reunions, but perhaps the greatest fun we had was climbing to the interior painting at the top of dome in the statehouse. It was a Saturday morning, and following the required sampling of donuts at the Dane County Farmers' Market Chris and I headed into the Capitol. As we roamed about and looked at everything that fascinated him I noticed a door that was never open--but now unlocked and gaping wide with a beckoning appeal.

We entered and climbed up a long staircase, being careful on some steps that were way unsafe, and ventured onwards until we were directly under the painting that seemed so small when looking up from the ground floor. Chris looked down, and his smile is one I still find remarkably clear in my mind. We touched the painting (briefly, just to say we had done it), looked around and started the climb back down. I had hoped that no one had somehow closed and locked the door while we were inside the dome! He was taken with the whole building, and truth be told that adventure leaves me still pondering who the bigger kid was that day.

Even though we had fun outings I also tried to make sure we also talked about the things that mattered to him. He was easy to get chatting away, and so with a gentle question on my part we were able to talk about what he thought and hoped. He was able to just talk about anything or nothing at all, depending on the day. Regardless, I was there to listen, and hopefully provide nuggets of thoughtful conversation or advice.

We never know how every story ends when it comes to our involvement in someone else's life. Over time I lost contact with Chris but I hope that something I did or said lingered and made a difference with how his life turned out. That is not some egotistical need for myself but rather a sincere wish for someone who made an impression on me.

I really feel that we are our brother's keeper in this path of life we walk. My issues may be different from the person who passes me when walking down the street. We all need to reach out and try to make a difference for others when we can. Chris showed me that putting time and energy into shaping tomorrow is worth the effort. Everyone needs to be lifted up at times, and whereas the students at broadcasting school had done that for me, I wanted in some way to pay back what had been given to me.

Years later after leaving the statehouse I worked as a program director for a non-profit that arranged for mentors to be placed with teenagers who were already in group homes. If these young teens did not set their paths in a more positive direction, things were surely to get worse. Part of my job was to speak with the teenagers, and do an assessment for placement with a mentor.

One of the first to sit in the office with me looked every part the average male teenager. He was in a group home which demonstrated to me that there was a lot going on behind those eyes, even if the eyes seemingly only reflected the lights of the office.

I never anticipated, however, the words he spoke in such a plain and powerful way when responding to a question as to why he wanted a mentor. It was not so he could get away from the group home, or catch a burger or pizza, or even toss a football at a park. No, the reason this young man wanted a mentor was distinct. With all seriousness, he declared: "I want someone to talk with; I want someone to hear what I have to say."

For me hearing those words rang like a stark bell. It was what I had felt at his age. The very thing that I needed at one time in my life so very much, and was unable to articulate the need for, or attain was what this troubled teenager was so simply able to state. This time there was an adult who was listening to what was being said. I was not about to let the ball drop.

If there is a lesson to be learned anywhere within this chapter let it be to make sure that bullying is never allowed to happen, and to make sure the young people in our life have at least one person who is always there to listen, and be non-judgmental. It must be recognized that bullying happens in large part because first there is a bully who taunts, demeans, and harms another be it in psychical or emotional ways. But there also needs to be a clear recognition that those who bully are often allowed to do so because there are others who witness such acts and never take the initiative to make sure that it does not continue.

The second to last time I was at my family home in Hancock was in September 2011. That day I spent some time looking out the windows of the old home. James left me alone to be with my thoughts for a few minutes. I quietly said good bye to the past. I was sad, but I felt it was the perfect ending to this chapter of my life.

As I stood looking out the south windows of my bedroom lots of images flashed through my mind. So many memories bounced around. Some of them were happy ones about when I 'played radio' or watched the snow pile high on the trees or picnic table in the back yard. Others were far less cheerful, and yet they too were part of the life that I had led while a resident of that room.

Life had changed for me since I was the roughly ten year old boy who went from the small bedroom to the larger one vacated when my brother moved out on his own. At one time I had not weighed a hundred pounds while looking out those panes of glass. As I stood there that afternoon I was nearly one hundred sixty pounds, and instead of the insecure and bullied kid who at times never wanted to leave those four walls to head to another day at school, I was now a sure-footed, experienced, confident, determined man.

I had sought the help that I needed to be able to stand up against anyone who thought they could treat me unfairly. I felt good about myself. I knew that there were those over time who had doubted my resolve, but now there were clear lines drawn on a whole host of issues over which I would never relent as I moved on in life. No one again would make faulty assumptions about the grit I now claim as my own, carry with me, and bring forth and muster for the path I now walk.

Bullies be damned!

A southerly facing pane of glass captured the afternoon sun that day. As I nostalgically looked out the window, my childhood bedroom window, on that afternoon the light scintillated. The flash of a smile reflected back at me. A beautiful and broad smile. And, I really loved the guy who was wearing it.

Illustrations

Illustrations

1. Geneva and Royce Humphrey on their wedding day 1947
2. Geneva graduates as Salutatorian from Hancock High School 1946
3. Gregory about six months old
4. Royce with 'Bessie' at the family homestead in Coloma
5. Gregory, lean and lanky, at Yellowstone National Park 1975
6. Gregory, age seventeen, in front of 'the barn' at family home
7. Gov. Tony Earl and Gregory aboard Utopia in Sturgeon Bay 1986
8. State Representative Lary Swoboda and Gregory at a Tourism Committee hearing in Madison
9. Hancock home in the midst of a real old-fashioned snowstorm
10. Family home—the lawn trimmed and the rocks leading up the driveway 2000
11. Gregory reaches for the hand of presidential candidate Bill Clinton. He also shook hands with Al Gore, standing to the left of Clinton, at the Wisconsin statehouse 1992.
12. Coveted yellow ticket allowing Gregory's family to stand in front for the Truman-style campaign train stop in Plover as President Bush sought reelection 1992.
13. "Fly me to the moon, let me play among those stars."
14. Former U.S. Senator George McGovern, a political hero of Gregory's in Madison for a book signing.
15. Geneva's kitchen was always the place to sit and relax, with the coffee pot plugged in and waiting to be poured.
16. Royce and Geneva celebrate fifty years of marriage; with Grandma Schwarz, Royce, Geneva, and Gregory 1997
17. Work bench that Royce made for Gregory when he was a boy on the day Gregory took it to Madison 2010.
18. James and Gregory celebrate their first holiday as a couple at Gregory's parent's dining room, November 2000.
19. James' Maine home also had a kitchen where family and smiles abounded; James, his Mom Marion, and Dad Robert 2001.
20. James and Mom shared stories, smiles and laughter over the years. Taken for Gregory's birthday, July 14, 2007.
21. Geneva loved flowers, and enjoyed this rose garden in Canada.
22. Looking out the living room windows onto the front lawn on the second to last time Gregory was in the family home.
23. James and Gregory continue to walk their shared road together.

124 *Illustrations*

1

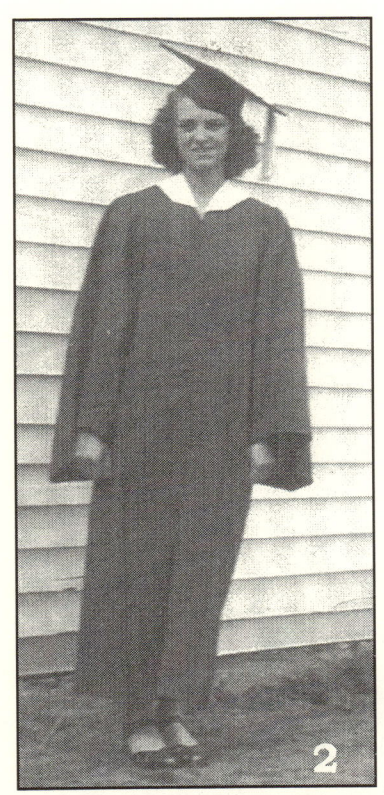

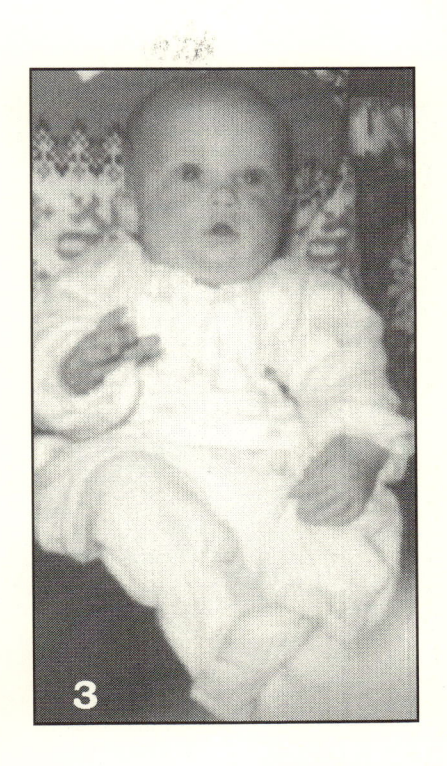

Illustrations **125**

Illustrations

Illustrations 127

7

8

128 *Illustrations*

10

130   *Illustrations*

Illustrations **131**

15

Illustrations

16

17

18

Illustrations **135**

19

20

21

22

Illustrations **137**

23

> *"The final test of a gentleman is his respect for those who can be of no possible service to him."*
>
> —William Lyon Phelps

Lary
(With one 'R')

Lary: *If you could choose to be one or the other would it be Bob Haldeman or John Ehrlichman?*

Gregory: *Neither. I would be John Dean.*

There were many constants in my working relationship with State Representative Lary Swoboda. (I'll just simply call him Lary here.) The most genuine and truly fascinating was that we both shared a great curiosity and interest in the life of the former President Richard Nixon. The political intrigue that surrounded Nixon made for dynamic and thought-provoking discussions in our office which served the First Assembly District consisting of Door, Kewaunee, and a sliver of Brown Counties; the same could be said for those times when Lary and I traveled the state for committee hearings and political events.

How did Rosemary Woods contort herself so as to make her claims about the eighteen-minute gap on the tape seem credible? What might have happened had Nixon just destroyed the tapes? Was not the *Checker's Address* one of the best political moments for speech-making on television? Should Nixon have had less hard-headed 'gate keepers' at the door of the Oval Office? How would China have been brought into the world community had Nixon not been elected in 1968?

There has never been a more perfect fit for a discussion about Nixon than that which Lary was able to provide. I have never met anyone who could counter with ideas as Lary could about the life and times of one of the most interesting and complicated men to ever occupy the White House. Decades later I can still make that statement. In that respect I miss the time spent with the former legislator.

It is still amazing to think of Nixon running and winning for Congress in 1946, being elected to the U.S. Senate in 1950, securing two terms as vice-president starting in 1952, being defeated for president in 1960 and governor in 1962, only to turn around and win two terms as president starting in 1968, resigning in one of the major political scandals in our history in 1974, and then resurrecting himself as an elder statesman and author in his final years. There was no end to the conversations that Lary and I had about this giant on the political and international stage, even though we very often disagreed with Nixon's policies and tactics.

While Lary had been a witness over the decades as Nixon made news and stood on the world stage, I had started to follow Nixon in the dark days of Watergate as he stood before the nation alerting all to his plea "I am not a crook". Lary was enthralled with the constitutional crisis that had shaken the nation, whereas it was the international drama Nixon had created by deal-making with nations such as China and the USSR that made me aware of how important his role in public life had been. While I too was much intrigued with the 'Saturday Night Massacre', I was also fascinated with 'ping-pong diplomacy'.

The home of Lary Swoboda in Luxemburg contained countless books, and I suspect they neared a thousand. The first time I laid eyes on all of them there was surely a look of amazement that crossed my face. Books were everywhere, and while not organized in any way, the collection included what I suspect was every book about Nixon that had ever been published.

Over my years of reading and buying books about Nixon—which number over fifty on my shelves—the books that I own about the former President have long been the most numerous about any one person in my collection. Abraham Lincoln comes in second place, with Jimmy Carter in third place for the number of books.

Among those books my favorite concerning Nixon is *The Making of the President 1968* by Teddy White, a writer and political pundit who earned my respect and admiration. *Lincoln* by David Herbert Donald remains the essential read on my shelves about our most important president. When President Clinton was leaving office in 2000, he was asked if there was one book that the new leader of this nation should read, and he suggested this powerful and insightful text. The book that jumps off my shelves when it comes to Carter would be *An Hour before Daylight* by the former President himself.

There were so many books in Lary's home that near the end of his life when the local community was unable to raise the needed funds to start a small library, he donated enough of his own collection to start a small library in a room at the local town hall. I must say that was one of the best stories about Lary that could ever be told. What a grand and lasting statement about someone who understood the power of a book, and the joy to be found within its cover! This, I feel, is the ultimate tribute to the man I knew.

There were many afternoons while working with Lary at the Capitol that he would come out to my desk and say, "Should we take a little walk?" I was never aware of any other legislator and staff having a regular routine like ours, and so it felt often like slipping out of class to play hookey when the sun was out, and the warm breezes were blowing.

"Should we take a little walk?" was the cue that we were heading down State Street to the many used bookstores that lined the way. These were some of my favorite haunts the first years I lived in Madison. Searching through the large array of topics and delights that lined the shelves made me very aware I needed an eighth day of the week to be invented just to read. The stores had that warm musty scent of old books that I have always found appealing. The stacks would rise over my head, and often require the use of a small step ladder, or a climb on a nearby chair.

Lary and I would browse, and then compare what we had found and walk back to the office where we would complete the tasks left for the day. Those excursions were some of the fondest memories I have of the time we spent together. Even after the differences that would separate us in the years to come I still have a genuine smile about the walks that always increased the physical height of my bedside book reading pile.

The very first time I was ever in the car with Lary behind the wheel, was also the last time. I had arrived at Lary's home for some campaign work in the district prior to my being hired in his legislative office in Madison. We had the agenda for the afternoon planned, and I got into the passenger seat. It was, after all, his car we were taking for the trip.

Lary put the car in reverse and it became a wild amusement ride akin to something I had only experienced at the Waushara County Fair. With my stomach lurching upwards and legs reflexively clenching together we sped in to reverse at a very fast clip barreling towards the end of the drive. As he looked for traffic I asked the only question that needed to be posed?

> Gregory: *"Would you like me to drive?"*
> Lary: *"Would you? I hardly ever drive myself."*

I first met Lary Swoboda when I was reporting on the State Assembly Agriculture Committee meeting that he brought to Door County. As Chairperson he wanted to show his constituents that he had a committee that mattered, and was able to convert their desires into legislative bills aimed at resolving whatever problems they had. Nothing says your local state representative cares more than to have a full committee of legislators listening intently to local woes and concerns. When it comes to farmers, they always bring along a basket-full of issues that can try the patience of any well-meaning elected official. So when I write that legislators at the front table listened intently, it says a great deal.

The afternoon of the public hearing alerted me to two things about our local representative as he came forward for an interview in the hallway. The first was that this man was short in stature. In the years to come, I would learn at the statehouse there was a saying among Republicans that the only claim to fame Lary Swoboda had was as the shortest legislator serving in the body.

Few ever knew how much this impacted Lary, as he never much talked about it. Once, however, when we traveled down East Washington Avenue for dinner he was peeved about some matter that was not going his way under the dome. It was then he spoke about the tall and urbane Speaker of the Assembly, Tom Loftus, and said there was no way he could ever be like him. It struck me odd that after all the years Lary had served, and represented the same number of constituents as any other member, that he harbored such feelings. I reminded Lary that it was because of rural elected Democrats, such as himself, which allowed for Loftus, who I liked very much, to be the Speaker. It was the same argument I always reminded others about when the clash of rural and urban interests took place.

The second thing that struck me that first time I spoke with Lary was that he was unable to look me in the eye during our radio interview. There seemed a point in the distance down the hall upon which he focused, and while giving full and complete responses to my questioning about the local cherry producer's concerns, he never looked at the one with whom he was talking. I thought that odd from a politician, and remarked about it once I was back at the radio station.

The station I worked for was solid Republican, and therefore no one was a strong supporter of Lary, a Democrat. The biggest thorn Lary posed for the GOP was the fact he kept winning every time he ran for his seat. In fact, Lary was the first Democrat to win that Assembly seat in over one hundred years, and would hold it for nearly twenty-five years before taking an appointment, and thereby leaving the legislature. When watching him work the local parades, it was not possible to miss the warm and affectionate greetings of "Uncle Lary" from the folks assembled on the sidewalks. He was truly one of the locals.

When I started working in radio I knew reporting news was where the tire met the road. I wanted to conduct interviews, and cover politics. There had been a love of politics brewing within in me from the time I had started to read history books, and mixing that passion with broadcasting was where I was heading. I would later recognize how fortunate I was to see politics and news from both sides of the divide.

The first national conventions that we were able to watch on television from our home were in 1976. I was addicted to the coverage, and followed intently both the Democratic and Republican events. I thought it must have been the height of excitement to be a reporter and have a large headset to walk around the convention floor. I imagined myself following the rumors, and interviewing the players who made the drama unfold.

I also wondered what it must be like behind the stage where the real power players were gathering and plotting how best to win a national campaign. There was no way for me to get enough of the intrigue, and over the days of the two conventions the fourteen year-old me was pasted to the floor in front of the television.

The only time I recall being somewhere other than watching the coverage was when my Mom told me Grandma and Aunt Evie needed help with shucking some corn. We sat on the door step of my Uncle and Aunt's home with what I thought was a mountain of corn. I recall talking about the convention while we stripped the ears down for canning. As soon as we had finished, it was back to Walter Cronkite.

As I worked in radio my interests in a variety of topics deepened. I loved broadcasting, covering the local meetings, and some political events. I was also growing to care more about policy, and was forming ever more clearly shaped views about the role of government, and the way to solve the issues that confronted our state and nation.

I had objectivity, front and center, while on the air, and could for instance interview, write, and report a news story about Kevin Hermening who came to the station one afternoon on a GOP swing to media outlets. He had been the youngest hostage held in Iran during the embassy crisis, and I got to interview him in a side studio.

My Hermening interview was more a dialogue as I found him engaging, and was really interested in what he had to say. He was trying to find a political opening to launch a campaign, and was making use of the microphone to buttress his case for cutting spending in Washington. In time, he would unsuccessfully challenge Congressman Dave Obey in northwest Wisconsin.

I knew he was being put out on the political stump for partisan reasons, in hopes of advancing his name brand. Had he already been an elected official I would have handled the news report differently. He showed up at the station hoping to increase his name recognition, and political identity with the aspiration of becoming someone with a title, and wanted to use the station for his benefit. I needed to fashion my report in such a way that omitted my views towards his conservative points while at the same time not allowing him to have free PR during the news. That type of rounded objectivity was something I tried to maintain throughout my time on the air, and I think I did it successfully. I felt that if it was not proper for an announcer to interject political sentiment, then it was equally true that traveling politicos from both parties should also be kept in check.

With my growing interest in politics, and needing to find new avenues to explore I decided to attend one of the meetings of the Door County Democrats. The thing that struck me instantly was that I was the youngest person in the room—and that I was not the only liberal in the county—even though we were then a minority on the thumb of Wisconsin. I started to attend the meetings every month, and volunteered to assist with projects such as the Annual Fish Boil in Jacksonport, aimed at promoting the party and making money for political purposes.

I also loved staffing the party's fair booth. We had a place near one of the large doors in one of the exhibition buildings. It was easy to step from behind the table at the booth and more directly interact with fairgoers. I reached out to people, and found in so doing that I was moving miles away from the lack of confidence that surrounded me as a teenager. I was coming into my own with greater clarity, and finding my foundation was more solid. Politics for me was not only something I enjoyed and found intellectually appealing, it was also a real way to grow as a person and become more assured of the man I was becoming.

I was no longer tentative when engaging a stranger in conversation. I was able to wing a conversation with someone I had just met as I did on the radio with the faceless listeners. I could pose some question about either an upcoming election or issue that was making the headlines while shaking hands. I felt solid and weighted those days of the fair, and most comfortable in my skin.

It was also at this time in my life that I started working on campaigns by going door to door asking for the support of voters for candidates running for public office. I must say the first lesson I learned was that football Sundays were taboo for such activity! Interrupting the sacred time of those who prayed to the gatherings at Lambeau Field garnered me more four-letter words than I could have predicted.

Aside from that I was to gain much from the experiences of walking to a stranger's door, knocking and not only handing off a piece of literature, but engaging in conversation. Over time, I could feel the past limitations that seemed to be in control of me become akin to how we drop winter clothes when spring bursts forth. Whatever I needed for self- confidence to move forward for the rest of my life was provided with those early volunteer jobs in local politics.

This all would prove useful when I started my job at the Capitol and started to rub shoulders with others who at times had more skills, experiences, and formal education than I had. I never took a step back, or let myself be made to feel that somehow my point should not be made or registered. I knew how to play the political game too, and was not shy in demonstrating it.

As I worked at the local level I became aware that some people in the party liked my energy, and welcomed the fact that I was not shy to state what needed to be known. While I was broadcasting as Trevor James on WDOR, I was writing Letters to the Editor in the *Door County Advocate* and the *Algoma Record Herald* as Gregory Humphrey. I was demonstrating that I was not timid when it came to saying what needed to be heard.

Door County Democrats told me that the county was so Republican and conservative that even in church or in bowling leagues many kept their political affiliations under cover. That struck me as odd, and something I never understood. I saw such numerical disadvantages as more evidence as to why Democrats needed to be clearer and increasingly vocal about the positions that we held. It was that vim and vigor that some party members found attractive.

I readily admit that being in my early twenties, and full of ambition and dreams meant I was not concerned about what strangers thought, and I certainly was not timid about making points concerning the issues of the day. It was in part due to my forth-rightness that attracted attention when the opening for chairperson of the party occurred. Transplants from Chicago who lived in Jacksonport were among those who told me I needed to seek the chairmanship, and securing that position would be the first step to running for political office.

When I decided to run for party chair, I began by calling some of the people I had met along the way as a volunteer. I called a few of the union men who worked in the shipbuilding industry, and got the commitment of support from well-established members of the party.

Dorothy Mosgaller was among them and she helped me win against an opponent who had a longer resume, and who could really call Door County home. Dorothy was involved with local housing for senior citizens, and from time to time had me over for dinner. We formed a friendship that lasted for years, and when her husband Bill died I was honored to be a pallbearer.

Dorothy was one of the dyed-in-the-wool Democrats who talked of the Kennedy Administration as if it were just yesterday that JFK was playing with his children on the lawn of the White House. Every day her edition of the *Capital Times*, the state's most progressive newspaper, would arrive at her home. When Reagan's name was mentioned on the news the shaking of her head would start, and the pondering of what the nation liked about him would start anew.

What most impressed me about Dorothy was the continuing faith in the political process she demonstrated when it came to making changes in our country. I still recall her telling me I needed to find a girl to marry so that when it was my time to run for political office I would have a family. Though I never mentioned it to her, my faith in the political process was aimed at making it so such marriages of convenience were not required.

I was learning to talk the language of politics; I wanted to build support for a job that would allow me to be more involved and see the process of politics play out more closely. I wanted to share in the excitement of state party conventions, along with dealing with candidates. I also wanted to help shape our message as a local party.

The night I was elected chairperson produced a wonderful feeling inside. Following the meeting I went back to the station where Trevor James wrote a news story about Gregory Humphrey. There were clearly lines that blurred, and ethics of all sorts that got tangled, but the story was news, and it was written in a purely fact-based fashion. There were ways to have opinions, I was learning, and also write with clarity and objectivity.

I am not sure that such an arrangement would be tolerated in any radio market anymore, or should be, given the hyper-sensitivity that everything political has now reached. I think it worked in my case as I was sensitive to the dual roles I played, was effective at my job on the air, and mature about how I handled my political work. I also think my friendly persona helped to disarm any who might have had problems with the matter.

What I did not know at the time of becoming chairperson was that the general manager of WDOR had been the GOP chair for eight years in the 1960s. What might have been an awkward and difficult situation in the workplace actually became one of the events that made for better relations between us. There was more for us to talk about, and it was clear, even though we disagreed on issues, that we cared enough to be involved and put some skin in the game. It was the first time, but not the last, that my appreciation for my political opposites would rise above partisanship.

Late that night I went to Country Kitchen near the edge of Sturgeon Bay and ordered one of their breakfast skillets that was all the rage at the time. It was served on a dark brown platter with a matching mug for tea. I sat there alone and recall looking out the window and thinking how most people would not see this event as very impressive, but for me the election was huge, and showed how far I had traveled from the events of my teenage years.

Lary: *"Let's go across the street and hear what the political buzz is tonight."*
Gregory: *"Sure. That sounds great."*

As county chair I worked on expanding the membership, increasing our revenues, and strove to get Democrats elected. I was able to work at making things happen that were just plain exciting, and which allowed me to see politics up close where it could be better understood and appreciated.

In 1986 I asked Fred Peterson of the famed Peterson Shipbuilding family, and owner of the "Utopia", a large sailing vessel that had voyaged around the globe, to give Governor Tony Earl, and a group of contributing Democrats a bit of a trip around Sturgeon Bay. I admit it was a bit gutsy to ask, and again this might be chalked up to being young, but Fred was just a classy older man; we got along just fine. There was perfect harmony on board. Fred was proud of his boat, and honored to have the Governor out for a trip; my fellow Democrats were pleased to be there, and I was gleeful about having it all work out.

I truly loved the adrenaline flow that came from that political work, and was struck, as in the case of the boat ride, how people from different ends of the political divide could unite. People who might be grousing about property taxes, environmental policy, or the need for more transportation funds were able to find common bonds while relaxing and viewing the beauty of Door County.

In 2006, I chatted again with Tony Earl at a reception for singer Denyce Graves following a remarkable concert appearance at Overture Hall in Madison. We talked about the years that had gone by, and reflected back to the time when the tone and style of politics was gentler, and seemingly less rhetorically driven.

The former Governor knew a boatload about state politics, the upsides of winning, as well as the sting of defeat. Through it all, as I reminded him, he was always a gentleman and gracious. His eyes still flashed, and his words still had precision and honesty; laced often with humorous phrasing which allows him to be a great storyteller.

The thing that struck me about Earl in 1986 was his genuineness, which was not a trait I noticed in every politician I would come to know. He was solid enough with his own set of principles that he would not campaign on Sundays when running for re-election, even though many tried to convince him otherwise. That type of person with strong inner convictions has always moved me in his or her direction.

When I asked Earl if he missed the excitement of the campaign trail he flatly stated he did not since politics has become just plain mean and nasty. He told stories of how he would have heated disagreements with his opponents, but at the end of the day the common bonds of friendship took control, and the arguments were retired. He added the personal assaults aimed at each other makes politics harsher, and less fun.

One of the things I recall about his 1986 trip to Door County was talking with a man a few years older than me who was working on the staff of the Governor. He was involved with the Council on Lesbian and Gay Issues that was set up by Earl. I remarked with pleasure that the Governor had created the council, and how much progress I thought this would provide on a host of issues. While thanking me for my comments he was quite clear in telling me that this should not be discussed in the area during the election.

I liked this man, respected him, and knew him to be intelligent, as I had talked with him on the phone a few times prior to the Governor's trip. I disagreed with him, however, about the constituency he felt he was helping. While it was true that the GOP alternative that election year would not be a champion for gay rights, it was also true that there resided all over the state people who were interested in the work of the council. Voters in liberal areas were aware of the council, and those gay citizens in small towns needed to know they had a Governor who was alert to their needs too. Were those issues concerning the council so volatile at the time that it was better to run them under the radar for the larger goal of winning an election?

Those types of questions about issues are posed and considered all the time concerning elections. I have never held to the timid view when it comes to politics or the reasons support is given to a candidate. While I fully understand politics and the urge to win come Election Day I also think that when given the opportunity to lead it should not be squandered. Leadership is not, in my view, walking the top of a fence, but rather taking firm stands and using logic and skill to win an election.

Campaigning and policy issues often compete, but I have always found myself on the side of social progress. I think that good policy makes for good politics, and as such did not heed the wish of Earl's staffer that day in Door County.

Tony Earl would lose the election to Tommy Thompson, but it was not over the issue of a council, a council that at the end of day most citizens were never even fully aware. A Thompson campaign ad over the location of a new prison along with the never-ending woes over property taxes would be the basis for the final results.

I do think, however, if more people had been more outspoken and engaged on the issues that the council promoted, there would be more progress on those matters to impact positively today's generation. It also needs to be stated that being reticent when given the power to act is one of the failings of too many who work in the political process. I have little time for those who urge caution when it comes to mobilizing mass determination to effect needed social change. I prefer those who lead.

Gregory, driving: *"Here is the walking list for the doors we need to knock on today."*
Lary, riding along: *"I never follow those things. That is not how I campaign."* With that, Lary takes list and discards it in to the back seat with a dismissive backwards toss.

There were some truly impressive moments when Lary would rise above all the characterizations others would make of him, and show that he was a solid politician. I was traveling with him during one of the first campaign treks we would make while I served as chairperson. Traveling up the thumb of Door County I was aware from the Democratic Party what small communities we needed to stop at, and which doors we needed to have Lary give some face-time to with voters who we knew were his supporters.

While Lary fully understood the need to chat, shake hands, and be seen he would have nothing to do with a list that only had certain names on it. "People talk" was his short answer as to why he would not use a list. "People will ask, 'Why did he not stop at my house?' I know he stopped for the guy on the other side of the street." Lary was the ultimate politician who shook everybody's hand, listened with humor and patience to often truly crazy comments, and then promised to look into whatever was being said.

That last part was something I was never able to connect logically to the larger role of being a state representative. With limited time in the day, only so much energy to be given, and a larger raft of real issues and problems to be resolved, why did Lary think every hair-brained idea and out-of-the-ballpark complaint deserved a response? "They all have the same weight of being a citizen, and I owe everyone equal consideration", was something I heard over and over from him. While that is a most noble and upstanding way to view the role of a legislator, I still think making every day count in office makes more sense, and thereby positively effects a larger number of people more deeply, rather than spending time on a constituent who had problems securing a mail-order bride, or trying to stop a member of the coast guard from dating a married woman, as one irate husband requested of the legislator's office.

There were those times that Lary knew his staff was just not going to take on certain cases, and so there Lary would sit at his desk in his office and make calls to people who must have thought him half-baked, trying to find some avenue of recourse for a constituent everyone else would have forgotten. That is why when it came time to comment on the Lary's death in the fall of 2012, I wrote that Lary was the 'Constituent's Best Friend'.

1991. The Wisconsin State Assembly chambers are packed with people wishing to comment on allowing eighteen year-olds the right to drink in Wisconsin. The proposed Act authored by Lary. With the first Gulf War underway Lary felt that if you were brave enough to fight and die for your country you should be able to order a beer in a bar. Lary, his talking points in hand and waiting at the back of chambers to be first speaker at the committee hearing whispers in my ear:

Lary: *"Are we fighting Iran or Iraq?"*
Gregory, thinking silently 'Dear God'...: *"Iraq".*

A few months after I started in Lary's office a new friend in the building commented to me that people had noticed a change in Lary since I started working with him. He was on time for meetings, was more organized, and that his office appointments were reported to be more structured, and as a consequence shorter. I had no idea at the time I accepted Lary's job offer that part of my duties would be to make him more organized. I must say at once I never reached the level that I wanted, but there at least were square corners to the often needless piles of paper that he felt should be kept in his office.

I received my job offer while attending the Kewaunee County Democratic Christmas Party in 1986. I had traveled down to the event in order to meet people, and also to show that we were united as a party in our larger goals. I also went because, well, it was a fiesta! It was snowing and cold, and when the party was about over Lary told me of his desire to hire me for an opening in his office.

Lary had made it possible for me to meet and chat face-to-face with Democratic Caucus staff several months prior. What I really wanted, however, was to work in a legislative office, and kept gently pressing the case following the 1986 election. He was aware that I wanted to work at the Capitol.

Lary had called me one night at the radio station in mid-November, following the election, and told me that there was no staff opening in his office, and though I was diplomatic on the phone, I felt crushed after hanging up the receiver. I had constantly worked hard at both the radio job, and also my tasks as chairperson, and when the election was over I was left with only a radio job.

But the next day I was up and kept pushing forward, while not relenting at contacting people I knew, and making it known I surely wanted to work in Madison. I had heard rumors for months that there might be an opening in Lary's office, and if a good word could be said for me I would be appreciative.

So it was very pleasing to be pulled aside at the Christmas Party and told the job in his office was mine if I wanted it. I told Lary I would be thrilled for the opportunity, and that I would never let him down.

The drive back to Sturgeon Bay that night was electrifying. I put the music from WSM in Nashville on loud, skidded home over the snow, went to bed but was unable to sleep. I was up early the next morning and off to the radio station.

Some wondered why I was in so early given my air shift was hours away. I made contact with the general manager, and sat down in the plush brown chair in front of his desk. When I informed him of my new job, and that I would be departing before Christmas he at once considered the staff shortage.

"Can't you stay past the holidays," he asked?

I had not had one Christmas off in the four years since starting work at WDOR, and there was no way I was about to miss another family holiday. Plus, I had a few details to attend to, such as locating an apartment in Madison, organizing a few personal matters in my life, along with some needed down-time to relax. Someone else would need to spin the Christmas records that year at the station.

Later that day I called Lary and let him know I could start the first day of the new session, which was also the day Tommy Thompson would be sworn into office for the first time.

I rented my first apartment of my own in Madison on Hancock Street, a few blocks from the Capitol. I had lived in a small space in a house while in Sturgeon Bay, and was very pleased to have my own place once I moved to the capital. I spruced things up, brought books from my home in Hancock, bought a little tea pot and a special mug, and called it home.

That first morning I walked to the Capitol in a blue suit from JC Penney for ninety-nine dollars, a suit for which I still have the sales slip as it remains a wonderful memento from that time in my life. (As a side note, ninety-nine dollars in 1987 had the same buying power as two hundred three current dollars.) The suit was part of a Christmas present from my folks, and whereas I never had up to that time much reason to dress up for work, I was most eager to start a new trend. I had a nice red tie that said "I'm here", which I had practiced tying numerous times that morning so it looked just as I wanted. I almost succeeded in tying a perfect Windsor. Almost.

I cannot give voice to the emotion that caught in my throat as I neared the Capitol Square, walking in the winter chill up the isthmus to the Wisconsin Capitol building that I had worked very hard to make my place of employment. The building is massive and imposing but what it represents truly moves me, and I knew as I walked up those steps that first morning that all sorts of drama would be unfolding within the stoned walls. My mind surely rushed over headlines that I had read in years past, and now I was about to be a small part of the process I found so captivating.

I had changed my hair-style considerably since leaving Sturgeon Bay, combing it all back so as to look a bit older and more seasoned, and was feeling most confident, even with all the new surroundings closing around me. As I walked that morning to work I was really in my element. That is something I have often thought about over the many years since, and know it was meant to be that I was employed at the statehouse. I was really sure of myself, but not in a cocky fashion, but just a most serene and sure-footed way. From the beginning, I just sensed I belonged there. Where in other jobs on the first day there were nerves, all I could feel that morning was pure excitement.

That first day was filled with ceremony and pomp as the inauguration for a new Governor, the entire Assembly and half the Senate took place. There was a real sense of democracy unfolding that day, and it seemed the elected officials understood the higher purpose about why they had run for office as they raised their hands and swore an oath. That feeling would be evident to me each time inauguration day would take place. That is one time in our frenzied political climate that our ideals seem to trump partisanship, and that is a good thing. It is almost as if a sense of renewal bathes the process, if only for a short time.

That evening, Lary, those close to his campaign, and I went out for dinner. Days later, politics would emerge again as the driving force in the building, but for a few hours the first day of my new job consisted of a most humbling mood not only for the elected officials, but also for me. It was a long way—far more than miles that had brought me from Hancock to a ground floor office that looked out onto State Street.

Over the months I would learn a great deal, but perhaps the first lesson was how politically challenging even the job I had as a Research Assistant, otherwise known as an administrative aide and committee clerk, could be when there were those back in the district opposed to the fact I was hired.

Shortly after starting my job Lary wanted a press release to the local papers and media concerning the new addition to his office. Being the person in the office charged with handling the media, and writing the releases I again found myself writing about myself as I had when working in radio. The release was brief, and factual.

There was no way to have predicted that some women in Kewaunee County who found it their mission to overturn Roe v. Wade would turn on me, and force Lary to feel the heat. They were quite concerned about the Letters to the Editor that I had penned relating to abortion while living in Door County, and serving as chairperson of the county party. I had staked out a clear pro-choice position. These women were adamant that Lary replace me in the office with someone who championed placing their head in the sand.

Lary confided that we needed to stem the issue, and since I presented myself very well he thought a meeting in the district with those who were all in a lather would be a wise move. I advised Lary that he might want to alert the women to the fact he runs his office, and will make the decision as to who is employed. Nothing is more unseemly than having the tail wag the dog, but clearly a small group of constituents were attempting to do just that very thing. Lary always liked it when he could look to be in charge, and giving him the construct of how to handle this matter while making him the leader was the perfect political starting point—both for me, but also for him.

On a Saturday morning at a local gathering spot in Kewaunee County we entered to find a gaggle of women upon whom I had never set my eyes looking sternly in my direction. I felt they were waiting for my head to spin and for some scene reminiscent of *The Exorcist* to play out. Instead I walked over to each of them, introduced myself and shook their hand. I offered pleasantries to each of them. Disarming political opponents in ways they cannot refuse is always the best choice.

In the conversation that followed they brought up my letters and views. I reminded them that it was very accurate to say I agreed with the 1973 Supreme Court decision, but that it was also true Lary cast the votes on the Assembly floor, should any issue regarding abortion require legislative action.

Lary made his pronouncement after listening to the women that he selected the best people to make sure the legislative office worked most effectively for the people he represented, and that I would indeed be staying in my job. The women truly thought they were going to make an elected official change his mind about his hiring decision, and though they put their best face on as we all exited, it was clear they were not pleased. Such is politics.

I truly loved my days working in the statehouse. It was more than just the chance to see legislation crafted and move through what at times seemed like a painfully slow and purposely stodgy process, but it was also the little things that made me smile.

Lobbying groups always have legislative days at the Capitol where the attempt to sway elected officials to vote on important bills for their cause is attempted with office visits and constituent out-reach. It was tradition that these groups would also host an after-work event where *hors d'oeuvres* and beer and wine would be provided for legislators and staff who wanted to attend. I enjoyed meeting people, and talking about the news of the day, and finding out where others thought the fate of pending legislation rested.

    The bankers always had one of the most lavish affairs, and so it was not surprising to see an ice sculpture set up near the place where the light refreshments were being served. Lary was in front of me holding some overly sweet non-alcoholic concoction that was made beet-red with grenadine which he never failed to order. I can still see him reach out for one of the thin and elegant strands of ice on the sculpture, snap it off, and add it to his drink. I asked God to make me invisible from anyone who had also witnessed the act. My prayers were small.

    I found stashed in a hallway on one of the upper floors of the Capitol an old wooden chair on wheels with a cushioned seat that leaned way back. The chair had been used for many decades on the floor of the State Assembly, but with renovations underway and new chairs arriving there was a removal effort underway for the older ones. The chair did not slide along as smoothly as it probably once did, and so it took time to get it down to the office on the ground floor. Pushing it down the hallway I started to sense the history that came with it, and knew that it would stand apart from the rest of the furniture in the office. This only made the chair more special for me.

    For the rest of my time working in the Assembly my scavenged chair sat behind my desk. There was one attempt from the person in charge of renovations to the building to have my chair removed, as it did not look the part of everything else in the office, but I would hear nothing of it. There was a sense of the past that was etched into that chair, and I was sure there had been over time more than one starchy legislator that had to be stern while sitting in it. Though I was often found with a smile on my face when at work, I too could be tough when required. The chair stayed.

    I had in front of my desk a shoulder high partition of sorts (the kind that line the modern cubicle office structures) that had a soft backing. The partition allowed me to display my growing collection of political buttons ranging from the era of FDR to the 1992 elections. Over and over it was a wonderful way for all sorts of people who came to the office, perhaps in some contentious state of mind, to be persuaded to talk about something else that then perhaps might make for a friendlier meeting. I recall one of the lobbyists who frequented our office often bringing someone new to show off the collection. There were also those on the legislative page staff who appreciated history and would stop by, talk. Over time, we would become friends.

    Perhaps no other more humorous moment occurred than

when Jim, a colleague and friend, came back from a conference in Ohio. He worked on the fourth floor. I was busy working on some constituent matter when the phone rang. My friend asked that I come to his office.

Jim knew that I was an Elvis fan and had spotted a lamp made from cast plaster that had the face and shoulders of 'The King' in concert mode. The bust of Elvis was topped with a large blue and white satin lampshade with a hint of gold piping for trim which added that extra over-the-top quality to the piece. I shan't mention how a thirty-six inch high original 1977 Elvis lamp, created shortly after the King's disappearance, makes any walk to the ground floor of the Capitol just a bit more memorable.

I will never forget the looks the lamp generated as I entered the elevator, or the heads that turned as I walked down the hall to my office. The lamp stayed in my office for several days and made whatever conversation people may have had about the political pins on my partition pale in comparison.

"Elvis has left the building!"

After a short stay in the Wisconsin State Capitol, Elvis took up residence in Hancock. He sat on a low rise night stand in my old bedroom for years. My Mother, God bless her, kept him neatly dusted and cared for him like everything else in her home. He rather "grew on her" over time and she found his presence less objectionable, though not entirely acceptable. When James and I found out that we would be moving to downtown Madison in the spring of 2007, she took me aside one Sunday afternoon and said, "Gregory, dear. Now that you are going to have a place all of your own, don't you think Elvis would like to go and live with you?" I acquiesced and James and I loaded Elvis up in to the back seat of my car, strapped him in with the seat belt and drove home.

Elvis is in the bedroom now. His pale blue jumpsuit and lampshade look quite smart against the 'lava blue' wall we painted for him. A few weeks after he moved in, Mom was talking with James and said while snickering, "Ha...ha! Now Elvis lives at your place!" James replied with a smile, "Don't laugh at me, old woman, or I will bring him back!" With a look of abject terror in her eyes and a grin of hilarity on her lips, Mom retorted, "You wouldn't dare!" He wouldn't actually. James has come to accept Elvis in his life as Mom had to do years earlier.

Only a few months after starting my job in the Capitol, a most unbelievable opportunity presented itself. I grabbed the chance with both hands. There was a conference of state legislatures meeting in Washington, D.C., and Lary wanted me to attend. He asked me to accompany him and his wife, Jan. Taking my first trip on an airplane, and getting to see the nation's capital was just about the ultimate experience I could envision at the time. (The only thing that would be as memorable was heading to Graceland with my best friend only a few years later.)

The morning of our flight, I was quite uncertain, given my knack for throwing up on the fair rides, how I would fare on a plane. I prepared a peanut butter sandwich and ate it to calm my stomach prior to arriving at the airport, and then took not one—but two—Dramamine just to make sure that I would not be ill. They say at times that less is more. In this case, I thought to myself, "If less was more, then think how much more MORE would be!" Gulp. And down went the pills.

As our plane sat on the tarmac getting ready to take off, I was still quite nervous. I had a bit of concern about how the plane would actually stay in the air. Suddenly there arose some hustle and bustle at the front of the cabin. A passenger had fallen ill due to a heart situation, and needed to be removed from the aircraft. Strangely, witnessing the medical situation on the flight did not make me more nervous. The pills I had recently taken made me rather sedate.

I had a window seat, and really was impressed as the land just slipped away from underneath the plane. The engines roared, pushing us up and over the city, taking us to a destination I had only read about over the years in the history books that had been almost like friends to me.

While at the conference, one item that we took note of, and talked about with others led us to produce a major amendment during an upcoming budget process. It had to do with the way that the State would protect shipwreck sites on the Great Lakes. Making sure that shipwrecks are safeguarded from vandals, and that those historic sites are used for tourism was something that came from our time in Washington. There are many such sites off the shores of the Door Peninsula, and along the coasts of Wisconsin. Too often some of the artifacts were stolen by others. With state funding and oversight we started a process to reverse that trend, and ensure access for all who wanted to enjoy seeing these historic sites. This program continues to this day; I know that my work on the issue lives on.

Building on resources with which we came in contact during those working meetings of the conference led to support from important supporters of the shipwreck protection cause from places around the region, including Chicago. With a groundswell of support from those who understood the need to preserve historic sites, we were able to pass our amendment once back in Madison. We were able to convince Lary's colleagues in the Legislature that by studying shipwrecks, one develops an appreciation for the critical role these vessels played in the development of the region and a respect for the men and women that worked the lakes. Today the Wisconsin State Historical Society manages a large underwater archaeology program for the benefit of everyone.

Jan, Lary and I also had time to do some sightseeing. The places I had read about in the books all of a sudden were tangible. There is an enormity to democracy that plays out in Washington as the historical sites demand to be viewed and honored. There is no way not to stand at the base of the Lincoln Memorial and not swim with emotions concerning the great hopes and causes that moved the sixteenth President to action.

We were at General Lee's home that looks out over the Potomac and Washington, watched the changing of the guard at Arlington National Cemetery, and stood where President Kennedy and Robert Kennedy are buried. We toured the White House, and visited some members of the congressional delegation on Capitol Hill. I saw the old Senate Chambers, and Statuary Hall. There is no way not to feel history, or be moved in countless ways while visiting these sites.

More historically significant than my sightseeing was what was taking place over at the White House then. While we were in Washington, the Tower Report was handed down. The 1987 report regarded the Iran-Contra scandal during the presidency of Ronald Reagan. Lary headed to one of the places where the report was for sale, and since it had just been released there were piles as high as my shoulders in row after row with all sorts of people grabbing a couple as they headed toward the cashier. The report represented an unusual exercise in government: a President coming under fire from a panel that he himself appointed and that was headed by a senior member of his own party. The panel, which included Edmund S. Muskie, a former Senator from Maine and later Secretary of State, and Brent Scowcroft, a former general and national security adviser, only lent added weight to the report's criticisms, and increased pressure on the President to respond effectively. We felt lucky to be on the ground floor, so to speak, by having one of the early copies of the report.

The most memorable time during that trip was the night when I was left to my own devices. My hotel was located only a couple blocks from the White House. It was rainy and so I changed into jeans, grabbed my umbrella, and walked out the large front doors of the hotel, past the doorman. I headed in the direction of the White House. With the gentle rain, the lights which illuminated the most powerful residence in the nation, and the imposing fence that surrounds the edifice--I just slowly walked and soaked it all in with every step. At one point I tried chatting with a guard at a small entry post. I didn't get very far with my chatter. I noted on the guard's face that he had seen the 'out-of-town' look in which I was awash. I thanked him for his time and continued on my way. I walked for a long time around the outside gate of the White House, and every now and then in one of the lit windows I could see movement from inside.

I knew that night, regardless of whether I ever had another opportunity to again visit the nation's capital, it would never look so intense or feel as special as it did as I stood in the rain and felt a sense of the power that makes this nation so grand.

Working in the statehouse allowed me the opportunity to meet and talk with a variety of people that I never thought would be possible only a few years earlier. As a teenager I had watched Lucille Ball in one of her creations as the secretary for the banker, Mr. Mooney (who she affectionately called 'Mr. Money'). She was star-struck with the Hollywood names that were often clients at the bank.

Over my teenage years, and as I became an adult, I had watched and followed national politics but never in my wildest imagination did I ever think a time would come when there would be a chance to see these people up close, or watch them work a crowd.

Since 1988 was a presidential election year, and Madison was a perfect place for political activists to engage with a candidate for the primary election, there was more than ample opportunity to meet the candidates as they visited the capitol to 'press the flesh'. It was very easy to see and hear them as they attempted to gain supporters and funders for their races.

If one ever talks about the benefits statehouse employees get from their jobs, let me be the first to say they are not all related to money or accrued sick-leave. For me, the chance to see the nation's politicians up close, watch them work a crowd, or hear as they framed their message in an important primary state was priceless. My interest in how those presidential candidates operated, handled themselves, staged events, and constructed their arguments was genuine. The process was utterly fascinating. Better yet, a handshake and quick conversation was better than a pay raise!

I not only had the opportunity to see democratic candidates, but also wanted to witness the movers and shakers in the Republican Party, if and when they came to Madison. Since the State Capital is a very liberal area, and Dane County progressive in its political identity, it was less common to see a Republican make a visit. I was delighted then to be able to get really close to Vice-President George Herbert Walker Bush when he paid a visit to Madison on a campaign swing the spring of 1988.

It was a Saturday morning, and I was standing alongside staunch Republicans who seemed to be having the time of their lives--to be honest, so was I. There was no way not to have almost as many friends on the Republican side of the aisle as the Democratic one when it came to the workplace, and it was easy to get the needed ticket for the Bush event. I not only had access, but was able to stand right up close to witness what I had previously only read about in newspapers concerning one of the major movers and shakers from the political world.

Bush would be the first ever elected figure of his stature with whom I would come to have the opportunity to shake hands. His visit was a captivating experience, almost as good as having been in the press box for Reagan's visit to Oshkosh. Prior to this I had been to state political conventions and had the chance to talk for a few minutes with Jesse Jackson, Governor Bill Clinton and Governor Michael Dukakis but being only a matter of yards from the Vice-President as he made a campaign speech was heady stuff for a former boy from Hancock. You can just sense the power that accompanies such an individual, be it the image that is cultivated from press reports over the years, or the knowledge of the role he played in government. Whatever the genesis, my being right up front in the thick of the action made for a truly memorable occasion.

The Vice-President and his wife Barbara were on small riser of a stage at a hotel complex in Madison. He gave a spirited campaign speech and then reached out in that way every politician does to show he is one with the voter, and shook hands with those assembled. I was in the first couple rows of standing people, and reached out for the handshake that I still vividly recall. There is no partisanship in this additional thought, but he had the softest hands on a man I had ever felt. I have shaken many a politician's hand but nothing came close for softness than that of the Vice-President.

I know Bush 41 had a far more complex mind and introspective ability when it came to policy than his son Bush 43 was ever to possess. Over the years when the name Bush is tarred due to the actions of 43, I am always mindful there was a vast intellectual difference between father and son.

Of all the elected politicians I would see over the years it would be Bush 41 that I was to see the most often. The only sitting president's hand I have shaken was that of Bush 41. What made it even better was the ability to share the day with a nephew who also was able to shake his hand, and participate in one of those great American political campaign rallies during a spirited contest for the White House in the fall of 1992.

As we both arrived at the Waukesha campaign rally I noted at once that we were a bit late. As a result we stood for the speech in the back of a large outdoor space at the Expo Center. The weather was cool, and I think it had rained a bit earlier in the day. But after years of practice at getting the handshake from a candidate I was not about to let the fact we were not near the front deter us. So I told my nephew as the speech ended, and the music struck the volume that makes shivers go up and down your spine that he needed to follow me, and stay close. I had been to a number of rallies, and knew how to make every footstep count. I started a direct move to my left and along the perimeter of the fence. Up and around we went. I knew the vast majority of rally-goers were going to leave, and we needed to be out of their way, while at the same time angling towards the candidate. We were soon located at stage left and all of a sudden working the rope line was President Bush followed by the gracious, sweetly smiling, and perfectly necklaced First Lady Barbara Bush.

Up to that moment, the President of the United States and his wife were always just a television image, or black and white news photo in the morning newspaper, or as we had just seen figures viewed from the back of a campaign rally. Now all that was dwarfed as mere feet were separating the leader of the free world from the handshake my nephew and I would never forget. To say my heart was racing at that moment would be a severe understatement.

Time stands still for an instant. There comes recognition of the enormity of the moment. The President of the United States has your hand in his. Politics passes and history is in control. It is simply the most intense feeling, and one that still catches me and makes me stop and replay the event in my head.

I knew then I was a pretty cool uncle, and hope over the years that those who trekked with me to the Bush rallies in 1992 will think the same, and recall with a smile how lucky we were to witness history.

The most politically romantic event of that 1992 season was yet to come. Accompanied by seven of my family members, I was about to see something that was straight out of the history books. There will never again be a moment for my family like the one which played out in Plover on October 31, 1992. That brisk Saturday, George Bush and his family were making an old-fashioned train ride in the image of Truman and conducting whistle stops along the way.

In Plover, the Presidential stop would be made at the same station where my Mom first stepped onto the soil of Wisconsin. After leaving Ozone, Arkansas for the hope of a better farm and a better life in Waushara County, Plover was the place where my Mom and her family had stepped off the train. Tired but anxious, the family was content to have arrived safely. The night that the train arrived in the sleepy Wisconsin town, my Grandfather Herman was carrying all the money the family had from the sale of the Ozone farm. It was carefully tucked away in a pocket near his chest. Now, Mom was there, not as a child, but as a Mother and Grandmother to see a President of the United States. The ground upon which we were standing seemed almost hallowed.

    I had secured the prized yellow tickets (yes, the color of one's tickets for these rallies is all important) from a Republican friend at the statehouse that not only allowed us access to the event, but to the all-important staging area up front. My parents, and the other family members parked cars some distance from the old train depot, and walked into the cold blustery wind to the place we needed to converge in order to get into the main rally area. Once those gates were opened we made a 'diplomatic dash' that combined our intent to get up close to the event without seeming to be pushy. The folks were slower but that was fine since all that was required was for someone to stake out the place we wanted to stand. Obviously, we needed to be directly in front of the stage where the President and his family would congregate and speak. And that is where all eight of us stood.

    It was as if Bush 41 were ripping a page from the Harry Truman campaign of 1948. The presidential campaign that year was winding down to the final days and hours. President Bush was campaigning around the nation and commenting along the way about how he was reading David McCullough's latest book *Truman*. That in turn created a sensation for history buffs around the country. By connecting himself to Truman it was hoped that he too could win the election as Harry did in 1948. Bush aspired to a come-from-behind victory.

    We waited a long time. I had instructed everyone to be ready to roll out of Hancock on time, and be prepared to wait. It was good advice and well worth it. Light snow flurries swirled through the air, even some ice pellets stung our face at times, but there was energy and enthusiasm as many thousands descended on the train depot. The crowd's noise picked up. The stamping of feet to keep people warm resonated off the paved depot platforms.

    In later news accounts, we would all would discover that it was that frigid day in Wisconsin when President Bush was told of his fate by his internal pollsters. Things were not looking good. In spite of everything, there were still campaign stops to be made, and Bush was traveling Wisconsin by train, working over-time at making his Truman moment come true.

My family did not grow up in the city. These types of events were not in our normal routine. This event was something I could make happen for my folks, and while I admit to having a little pride about pulling us all together with the needed tickets, there was an even more over-powering sense of history that was soon to be rolling down the tracks.

The large spotlights that were required to make the event visible to the crowd and allow for the media to do their job were switched on; looking up into the lights' bright glow, the flakes of snow were visible. The stage was set in a rustic Midwestern tone with corn shocks, and pumpkins to add not only to the festive nature of fall, but also to be reminiscent of a traditional Halloween. A band had been playing and that kept the audience tapping their feet. An announcer conveyed one of those conversational-toned messages to the crowd at about 5:00 P.M. The message was loud, clear, and surely heard all over the region: "Ladies and Gentleman. I have just been informed that the President's train is only a mile away". With that, there was a roar of the crowd that was simply deafening. A few seconds passed. Off in the distance, and to the left of where we stood, the stark lonesome sound of the train whistle from the powerful locomotive carved its way through the brisk air and landed on the ears of the assembled crowd. The President's train was rounding a bend and coming into the train depot at Plover. We were no more than twenty feet from the podium, and so close that we could feel the rumble of the tracks carrying the Presidential car.

The crowd exploded with cheers as the sleek locomotive brought the long line of train cars to a halt in front of the crowd. The President and his family were waving and ready to embrace the people. The crowd was highly partisan, as it should be, for such an occasion. It was one old-fashioned down-home type political gathering that evoked every page from the musky-scented books of my youth, and pulled everyone who was there to witness it back to a grander time of how politics once was conducted in America.

As the event ended and the Bushes entered the train the lights of the dining cars came on, and the linen covered tables were visible as dark suited waiters moved around arranging for a meal before the next whistle stop. The wait staff appeared poised and sure footed in the way they walked and leaned over the tables. As I watched from the outside there seemed to me to be a sense from those inside that this moment was not likely to ever happen in this a way again. The political whistle stops of history were coming to an end.

My family would have loved to have been able to join the President and his family and staff for the meal on the train. Instead, we had a pleasant meal at a small restaurant in the Plover area. We were chilled to the bone. I know Mom and I warmed up to the largest and hottest bowl of soup that the chef offered. Like everyone else at the table that evening there was a smile. Mom and Dad talked about that day for the rest of their lives.

"We never would have thought of doing anything like that," was the way Mom often would reflect back on the day. Dad often reminded me that some of the people he knew in Hancock could not believe he was able to get so close to the President. Dad was still a Republican when Bush 41 came to town; he wasn't by the time Bush 43 left office.

The other Republican who I met when he came to Madison, a city that is not fertile ground for conservatives, was Senator Bob Dole. He visited the Capitol on behalf of the state party.

I was working in the office, and a buddy on the other side of the aisle knew when the Senator's SUV was going to wind its way up one of the circled drives of the Capitol, and drop him off. I made my way to the designated area, and stood outside with a mere handful of people as two vehicles came up the drive. With a dark suit and a rather serious exterior he exited his vehicle and with his left hand, met those who wished to say hello.

As always the pen he held in his crippled hand was meant to deflect the fact that he was an injured veteran. Dole seemed thinner in real life, but there was firmness to his footsteps and sureness to the gait of his walk as he entered the building that conveyed to me there was no doubt he was a political leader. He projected the aura of someone who needed to be reckoned with, and that is a most important first impression any politician wants to impart.

In 1988 one of the nicest and most sincere of candidates ran for the presidency. Illinois Senator Paul Simon was perhaps the most approachable politician I have ever met. If there was someone who seemed 'one of the people' it was this smaller man with a bow tie and big glasses. When he stopped by the Capitol for a noon-time rally and greeted folks, it seemed to me as though he worked on the Square and had just wandered over for an afternoon stroll with state workers. He chatted and bantered as if he had known the folks who came to see him for many years. Simon had a most affable way of interacting with voters, and came across as genuine, and voters pick up on that trait. As a former editor-publisher of a newspaper, and then a senator with liberal ideas it is clear why I found him most remarkable.

In 1988 I was enthralled with the words, style, and foundations of the Jesse Jackson campaign. I gravitated towards his mission of inclusion of all groups into a national mosaic. His words spoke to me personally. His discourse centered on a metaphor: the United States represented to him various pieces of cloth that did not mean much by themselves. Assemble all those various little pieces of cloth together and they become a grand quilt. The patchwork idea connected with how I viewed our national needs at the time. I also was mindful that he was on the correct path about how our nation spent far too much on military spending, and that we too often felt compelled to use the weapons that we had amassed.

I had first met Jackson in Stevens Point at a State Democratic Convention, and had been able to get a pair of tickets for my family to participate at a Sunday morning rally with the Chicago-based minister. The three of us sat in the front row, right-hand side, and as Jackson took the stage he noticed my young niece wearing a cute dress and waved at her while making a comment about how nice she looked.

The ability of Jackson to carry a crowd and move them to action through passion was something I was able to witness numerous times over the years as he came to Madison either as a candidate or while working to elect others to office. It was the night before the April Presidential primary election in 1988 that his campaign made a stop in the office where I worked. My office desk was on the ground floor; next to the State Street entrance. Directly out my window and on the steps leading down and away from the building, Jackson was to hold his last major rally before the polls opened. In advance of this rally our office was informed for security reasons that my window needed to stay shut and the blind closed. The hallway that led from the rotunda down to the revolving doors that exited to the rally site was filled with serious-minded security men.

Prior to the event a couple of Jackson's assistants stopped by and asked if they could leave their heavier jackets inside on a chair. The place would be unlocked as there was no way anyone was taking anything given the number of security men all about. I asked if there was a way to meet again the candidate, and was instructed to wait in the hallway.

I still have no way of knowing if the Jackson team jogged down the hallway for security reasons or because they felt they were late. Perhaps, this was a technique Jackson used to release pent up energy. All the same, a phalanx of large muscled African-American men in suits along with the presidential candidate were jogging in a spirited pace down the hall. (If I were the type of person to enjoy running, I might have joined them.) As the team approached my office, one of the advance team I had met pulled Jackson over. Jackson stopped, smiled, and shook my hand. I told him that his campaign meant a great deal to so many who felt they often had no voice to represent them. He replied, "Let's go win this election", and made his way towards the doors, again at a half jog.

Outside as the late afternoon sun set, Jackson delivered one of his famous barn-burners of an address, leaving people holding hands with the person alongside whom they were standing. I had found a spot next to the building and looked out at the faces, but I will never forget the one next to me. A man I did not know, about my age, had tears running down his face as Jackson vocalized the hopes of the nation and painted the picture of what America could look like if we all worked together.

Throughout the 1988 presidential election season, I wore Jackson's campaign button on my jacket. I had been a supporter of Jackson in 1984, but was not able to campaign and work in his behalf to the degree I had wished. In 1988 I was more pro-active. The most amusing part of this story was that Lary was far more conservative than I was. While with him in the district one day he asked me what his constituents might think about me wearing my Jackson button. I told him that I hoped the voters might ask about Jackson so I could tell them of the message he offered for America. This seemed to make Lary mighty nervous; he sensed that I was serious. He never talked about the button again, though I knew he thought it might harm him among some conservatives.

In 1992 I attended a rally at the statehouse for Bill Clinton and Al Gore. Tens of thousands were in attendance. My best friend Brad and I marveled at the moment. The weather was perfect, with sunshine and warm temperatures. The King Street entrance to the Capitol made for the perfect back drop to a major campaign appearance. A growing sense of confidence that this was the team who could win the White House for the Democrats was palpable. Months after the election the photographer for the Assembly Democratic Caucus came to our office and told me he had finally developed all the pictures he had taken the evening of the Clinton rally. He thought I might be interested one of the snapshots in particular. The photographer then handed an envelope to me with a single photo inside. I treasure that picture very much and have included it as an illustration in this book. It shows me with my hand reaching up for Clinton's hand. I had the handshake that evening of both Clinton and Gore.

For political junkies these types of encounters create joy and enthusiasm. For someone who harbored secret dreams and saw no way to ever think they could come true, the picture of Bill Clinton and me remains more than just a remarkable memory from a campaign rally. It speaks to how hard I had pushed to get to Madison and work in the Capitol. The side view of my broad smile underscores the pleasure I felt at reaching my goal.

At the top of the list of all the national figures I so very much wanted to meet was Senator Ted Kennedy. It was never to be. When he became sick, I knew it would never happen. At the time of his death I was melancholy. I reflected on his life while the news accounts filled the airwaves. All the memories of the Kennedy clan flooded back to me. I was missing more than just one of my political heroes. I was also missing a part of America that had somehow slipped away into yesteryear.

Many years ago at the statehouse I knew a woman who had grown up during the Depression. She married a soldier who went to fight in World War II, and loved and revered both Presidents Roosevelt and Truman. She read constantly about this period of time and thought often about the larger-than-life political and military leaders who led the nation to victory. I recall telling her once that the History Channel concentrated too much on the 'the big war', which only made her wonder if I had any sense of history at all! I could never understand why she felt so nostalgic about such a comparatively limited period in our nation's history.

At the time of Kennedy's passing, I found myself oddly in something of the same 'condition' as this woman was in the years I knew her. While I have broader interests for history than she did, I feel most at ease with that cast of characters from my childhood and early adult years. While I am certainly contemporary, I also am clearly nostalgic.

The Kennedy family had always represented a world of political excitement and drama. As a teenager Ted Kennedy would become the person I most respected as the philosophical model for what I felt a political leader should sound like on the important issues. Like many my age, there had always been a Senator Kennedy to lead the charge.

Then he was gone.

As I watched the old newsreels the week of Kennedy's passing, it became very clear that not only was he gone, but also a whole era had ended. The finality of it all seemed more real, as if more official because of the death of Ted Kennedy.

Throughout the Kennedy retrospective coverage I noted that off camera reporters would be talking in the newsreels, and just by the voice I could identity Roger Mudd, John Chancellor, and David

Brinkley. There too among the grainy images was Frank Reynolds who I had so admired as a teenager. While we currently have a myriad of reporters and anchors on the all-news cable channels, I seriously doubt if thirty years from now we will, as a nation, be able to connect as easily to the sound of their voices. That isn't to say that today's reporters are not hard working, but with so many competing voices it will be harder for anyone of them to be exalted above the crowd. I also believe, with no arrow aimed anywhere, that many are not, nor ever will be heavyweights of the kind that are forever etched on the old newsreels that ran constantly during the Kennedy memorials.

The same is likely true of the many elected officials in office today. How many Senators today upon their deaths will produce the outpouring of emotion that we saw with the passing of Ted Kennedy? As much as I admire former House Speaker Pelosi, she is a mere shadow to the legendary Tip O'Neill. Now there was a politician! On the world stage there once was Mao, Brezhnev, and Thatcher. More modern leaders such as Xi, Putin, and Cameron just lack any of the sizzle of an earlier age. Granted the times and events also make a leader, but still there is a lack of larger-than-life gravitas in so many of today's world leaders.

The chapter of a larger universal book turned a page when Ted Kennedy died. I am deeply saddened by it. I am not ready to let the past slip away. I certainly follow along with the latest twists and turns of the world (as a news junkie I need to) but like the lady I knew back at the statehouse, I will also be turning back the pages and rereading the times that were somehow more comforting to me. The chapters from our universal past which I will reread will include that cast of characters from the world stage of my childhood. I like a good story, especially about those who were genuinely larger than life.

One of the most pleasant interactions with someone I had not previously met occurred when Supreme Court Justice Shirley Abrahamson received a request from a school in Lary Swoboda's assembly district. Justice Abrahamson had been invited to give an address marking a special occasion. She would need a ride to the district, and then also need to be at a conference the following evening in Stevens Point. If we could somehow work out the travel plans for such a combination of needs she would be pleased to make the address. Our office made every effort to make it possible. It took me roughly twenty seconds to see the conclusion so everyone could have what they needed to make this event possible. We arranged many of the details and sent word over to the Justice's office. The Justice replied favorably and accepted the kind offers we had made. She agreed to be a part of the community of celebrants that day, which afforded me one of the most memorable road trips I would have in the job.

On the day of the event, I pulled my car to the location along the entrance to the statehouse as the Justice brought out a large stash of books in a cloth bag, along with a suitcase. She got into the car, fastened her seatbelt, and we started talking. I cannot express the pleasure it was to have such a lively conversation for three hours as we headed to the district. She was inquisitive, humorous, and delighted in odd stories I shared about my days in both broadcasting and politics. She offered insights into law and her life. The following afternoon I took her to Stevens Point for her conference and recall that it was cold and rainy, but through the entire trip she was upbeat and the conversation never-ending.

The following week when I returned from lunch I noticed a small envelope under the door to my Capitol office. Inside was a handwritten note from Justice Abrahamson thanking me for the courtesy of a ride and such a nice time talking and laughing. It was I who was the one who needed to say thanks for such a wonderful time. What a truly wonderful woman! Wisconsin can be proud of the work she has done on the court since her appointment to the bench in 1976 by Governor Patrick Lucey; she has served as Chief Justice since August 1996.

It was almost noon and my best friend, Brad Kelly, who also worked at the statehouse, came down to see if I wanted to catch some lunch. I told him I needed to first make sure that Lary had everything he needed as session was underway. I started to grab my suit jacket and came to find it missing from where I had placed it. I was stunned, and yet needed to head to the chamber. There I met Lary, who sat nearest one of the swinging doors which had a window, allowing me to get his attention. Brad was standing behind me poking his finger in my back to make me laugh as we both saw where my suit jacket was. Lary had grabbed my jacket, which in no way matched his slacks, and as I had a height of five feet ten inches—and he did not—Lary looked like he was dressing up in his father's jacket.

One of the most interesting, and frustrating parts of working in an assembly legislative office was the political campaigns that took place every two years. While I loved the various components of what made an election compelling drama, a certain intensity to the whole affair cropped up when the politics of my job and campaigning joined together. It was rather stressful. The reason for the drama was that what should have been one of the traditional races for Lary in 1988 turned out to be one for the history books at that time.

For the most part the work in the office consisted of committee assignments, and making sure the bills that Lary had authored were making it through the process. Keeping some constituents happy, and making sure the press was aware of the work we were doing comprised the other portion of the job.

I loved the policy angle of the job; I was in charge of press relations. I also very much enjoyed planning for the election, the framing language for the brochures, door knocking, and planning for the debates in the district. I can honestly say I had a visceral reaction to our Republican opponent. I felt he was often disdainful of Lary. It stemmed from more than political differences; it was as if the GOP did not think Lary were qualified to be the representative, and that irritated me greatly. I had met what the GOP sent to Madison. I could assure anyone based on that criteria Lary was more than qualified. More than that, Lary was working towards his Ph.D. in education administration, and whether one liked his politics or not he was heads above the rank and file legislator when it came to having a plan for his life and sticking to it.

When it came to 1988, the election memory that most comes to mind is my throwing up. My faulty digestive system found no blame in the election returns, but rather in the stress of being involved in a campaign for State Assembly that was at the time the most costly Wisconsin had ever witnessed. It is one thing to report on campaigns, and quite another to be in the heart of a heated political race. For as much as I felt very fortunate to have had experiences at both ends of the story when it comes to these events, I admit to having been a bit nauseated at the time.

As the race grew more intense, and the GOP made it historic by throwing over $50,000 into an assembly campaign, I started to stress. By the morning before the election, I was ill to my stomach and I spent the day at my home in Madison. While drinking herbal tea and eating soft foods I watched Bernie Shaw on CNN. I felt miserable physically, and knew the results would be dreadful for the Dukakis campaign, which affected me morally too. A cloud of defeat is oppressive, but I tried to see beyond it. On Election Night, I was back in the first assembly district where our team secured a comfortable victory. What a relief!

What struck me at the time was the placement of 'THE phone call' between the two candidates once the race was over. It did not take place the night of the election but instead was made by our political opponent the next morning. I will never forget the short sentences and rather stern facial expression from Lary as he took the call in his kitchen. After the money and fight that the GOP had thrown at him, all Lary could offer was a short display of being courteous, and no more. I could not fault him for that.

After the election our campaign had some political buttons produced. You read that right. We produced a political campaign button *after* the election. The campaign had been so grueling that we needed some way to alert others to the insanity we had endured. Essentially, we printed buttons which made us feel good about what had happened. The buttons read, "I Survived Tommy Thompson's $50,000 Club". Today, people consider $50,000 to be start-up money for an assembly race, but at that time it was a huge expenditure. More importantly, I need to add that $50,000 is only what was *reported* as having been spent. The actual amount from our opponents was far higher.

There was a silver lining to this whole period. The morning after winning the election, a number of us gathered at a little diner in Luxemburg. I treated myself for the first time to a Belgian waffle with lots of fruit, and heavy on the whipping cream. We had won the election. My appetite was back. Life again was good.

I recall at the time I had thought about our stress level in the hectic weeks of the campaign, and tried in some way to compare it to the absolute intensity of a presidential election. I could not make it compute, and still have no way of knowing how people survive the ordeal of a national race. While I had always been a most enthusiastic spectator of election night returns, I had now been in the middle of a race as it played out for state assembly. My job and livelihood was attached to the outcome. Changes in policy for the whole state would have been in the offing had the GOP been successful in unseating Lary and securing a working majority in the Assembly. Though I have never lost my zeal and excitement over campaigns or elections, that first taste of campaign life deepened my appreciation for the sweat and toil of making sure every vote is obtained during a race.

Election nights for me were in large part the stories from history books which weaved pictures and impressions upon my mind of Abraham Lincoln staying in the Springfield, Illinois telegraph office until nearly 2:00 A.M. to find out that he had won the 1860 presidential election. Or, knowing that Richard Nixon having won in 1968, closed himself off in his library and turned the record player up high to be moved by the musical score from *Victory At Sea*. This time, history moved in closer. It was sitting next to me on the couch. As Lary secured another two-year term in the assembly, George H. W. Bush was being elected in a very comfortable fashion across the nation as president.

⁂

Every four years in October, I am seized with an excitement which clings tightly straight on through Election Night. Autumn winds add a nip to the air. Colored leaves lose their grip from the place they called home for months. The scent of wood smoke wafts about. Canvassers with clipboards come 'a-knockin'. Lawn signs sprout. Candidates bounce up onto quickly erected stages decorated in patriotic bunting while crowds roar. All the while predictions are offered with either hopeful anticipation or dreaded pessimism.

I knocked on doors in Sturgeon Bay and Algoma in the fall of 1988. I felt the same as when I was just a freshman in high school, watching and reading about the 1976 match-up between President Ford and Jimmy Carter. That was the first time I followed a presidential race. My political maturity was not yet formed and so I was 'supporting' President Ford who had the backing of my rural conservative-leaning family.

The family gathered in the living room for the returns, but we went to bed that night not knowing the outcome of the race. When I woke up the race was still in limbo, and Ford had not yet conceded. I jumped on the bus as it arrived, always too early it seemed for the nearly one hour ride to school. I chatted with the bus driver, who told me there was certainty Carter would prevail. I could tell she wanted him to win, and I let her know Dad wanted Ford to be the victor.

That night on television I recall the images of Jimmy Carter and his family at their family home in Plains, Georgia. In the years since, I have come to compare those videos in the same light as that of President Ford following cancer surgery for his wife, Betty, shortly after his assuming the presidency. In each case the humanizing of these men made an impression on me that lingers. Regardless of the political combat, it is important that we recognize the human connection that bridges us as Americans. In time I was to form my own views that were independent of my family's, and become confident of Carter's abilities even when much of the nation seemed to reject such sentiments.

By the time 1980 rolled around there was no doubt where my political perspectives were headed, and they were not with my Dad's party. For the first time I voted, and while many sons might recall a fishing trip or ball game while bonding with their father I can think of no other event that clicked better for us than his picking me up as we headed for the small village polling place in Hancock. Dad always felt his fighting in WWII was for the bigger reasons concerning the freedoms we enjoyed, and perhaps none more important than that of voting. It was not lost on him that I was so interested in the election, and so eager to vote for the first time.

It did not matter to either of us that we cancelled each other's votes out that election. Upon leaving the building we encountered Leslie Wetmore, who worked with Dad, and he gave me thumbs up as praise for taking the time to vote. From there it was home for the dinner which Mom had prepared, and on to watching the reported returns.

At the end of the evening, after the election was called, Mom popped into my bedroom and remarked that perhaps Reagan's victory would not be so bad, and everything would work out. I never thought that to be her most sage observation, though she was usually an optimist in general. She always enjoyed watching new families move into the White House, regardless of their partisan natures. I would have been happy to have extended the Carter's lease for another four year term.

The following presidential election would prove to be one of the more gratifying ones as I was able to broadcast from WDOR as the results were coming in from the nation and around Door County. With our national feed from ABC News, along with a reporter at the local courthouse, I was able to weave the narrative of the night, throw in tidbits and trivia, and anchor the proceedings from the studio. I had prepared a binder of all sorts of information on state races and historical oddities that made their way over the airwaves that night. If one can ever be 'in their element' that was certainly one of the moments for me.

The 1984 presidential election will forever be recalled as a night when the national Democratic ticket imploded, but one where I was pleased with the product WDOR put out over the airwaves. After it was all over, and the station had signed off shortly after midnight a friend and I met at Country Kitchen in Sturgeon Bay. I still recall the dark ceramic platter that housed the eggs and hash browns and the tea-pot brought to our booth. We talked far into the early morning hours, recapping events, and talking politics. Though I was not making much money, and had not really decided how to make it to my next career goal there remains a glow in my memory about that time of my life.

In 1992 I recall the beaming face of my best friend Brad. On the morning after the election, we headed to get coffee in the basement of the Capitol. "So this is what it feels like to win!" he gleefully said on the staircase. This was the first time that a presidential candidate we had voted for won the election! Brad and I knew there is nothing like java served up with a side of political victory. Even if it were only from John's Coffee Shop, located in the basement of the State Capitol, there was reason to grab a cup and smile.

I knew that as enthralled as I was with politics there was really no way I wanted to actually run for office. While I loved policy and knew shaping it would have been tremendously rewarding I could not fathom giving up so much of my time for the constant attention that constituents demand, and in some cases deserve. For all the differences I have with the other side of the political aisle I have never been one to lump all elected officials in one group and disparage them. Those who decide to run and serve the nation are to be respected for the work they undertake, even when we disagree with their policy directions or political philosophy.

I am often on the opposite side of the political debate from many when it comes to the topic of increasing a legislator's salary, which is different from *per diem*, a practice that I know first-hand needs to be adjusted and better regulated. Making sure that a legislator is actually in Madison, and working on legislative business so as to meet the criteria of earning *per diem*, a daily allotment for housing and food, will make for less reluctance at adjusting the salary for these jobs.

I have always stressed that being a member of the state legislature is not a regular job, as the duties extend far beyond time spent in the office, or what most would consider a normal workday. To be sure, each legislator chose the path of being a public servant, and so should not be felt sorry for when having very full days. There is a need to have truly committed elected officials serve the public, and pay should be in line with their duties and time worked. I strongly feel that a healthy salary should be looked at as a way to encourage talented people to serve.

The idea of public service being a noble calling is something that we have long forgotten. The fact is, party affiliation aside, each member of the legislature had the desire to put themselves up to the rigors of a campaign and public inspection in order to serve the greater good. In the midst of all the jokes, we often forget that public service can be a grueling occupation, and really deserves our appreciation.

I saw the demands of the job up close while working with Lary. There was never a time when he was out in public that someone did not stop to talk with him about an issue, pose a question, or have a constituent need that he felt required a response. I have witnessed people walking alongside him during parades to ask something, catch his arm after church services, or talk with him while he filled his car's gas tank. Anytime we went out for dinner, he never left a restaurant without constituent needs noted on napkins. I watched as he used a piece of the butcher's wrapping paper to make notes one day as a constituent grabbed him in the grocery store. And believe it or not, I even witnessed someone 'needing' his time at the funeral home during his mother's wake. The calm that he showed in all these instances, multiplied day after day, is not unlike many representatives. Granted, some work harder than others, but the vast majority on both sides of the aisle do a great deal of serious and weighty work. To pretend that these jobs are easy, and should not be compensated at a reasonable rate is just absurd. During harsh economic times many workers will see no pay increase, and even suffer job layoffs, but to use that as an argument against a pay increase for legislators is simply mixing apples and oranges.

One of the fondest nights I recall from working in the capitol was on a Friday during a long arduous budget battle. Behind the chambers where the members sit is a simply magnificent parlor where wonderful old pictures are hung, massive tables and chairs are arrayed, and a true sense of history can be felt. I started working in the building before air conditioning or computers. The stone structure of the Capitol seemed steamy at times, and even stifling if not near an open window. As the hours nudged past midnight and the wrangling continued on the floor the page staff opened up the massive windows in the parlor, lifting up the large panes and letting in the most cooling and receptive breezes I am sure to have ever felt. I pulled one of the large chairs closer to the frame that was as low as my feet. I sat there with other staff as lobbyists ran around in the panicked mode they seem to always display. I have often thought the rapid and frantic movements of a chipmunk as it scatters every which way is the most appropriate way to describe a lobbyist when trying to juggle what needs doing during budget deliberations.

Sitting there after a sixteen hour work day might have been a reason to wonder what I was doing wrong in my life. I was serene and really at peace as I heard the debate behind me from the legislators, while the breezes filled the parlor, and friends gossiped. We all looked out across the Capitol Square and knew we had truly unique jobs.

Lary would decide to seek election as Wisconsin School Superintendent in 1993, placing himself in a crowded primary contest. While it was really a most remarkable few months to see a campaign of this type, getting to travel along with Lary at times as he sought name recognition, and press coverage, it also was clear that the final phase of his political career was in progress.

I am not sure how Lary really felt about his chances at becoming one of the top two contenders following the primary, but I never had any illusions. Lary had the intellect needed to run the office, and had some ideas about education policy that really were grounded in thoughtful consideration. But, Lary was never going to win the race because he did not have the political gravitas and smoothness required to get the nod of the voters statewide.

Over the years Lary had not worked at making sure he owned the political heft needed when it came to this type of an election. He was still walking on egg shells with tepid remarks for his constituents over this and that issue when confronted in his district. How could he project his own political identity in a statewide race, and thereby make people feel he was sure-footed enough to be elected and serve as School Superintendent? It is far different to shake hands of the voters in Sister Bay and Kewaunee than try and secure serious press coverage and respect in Eau Claire and Milwaukee.

In the end, Lary came in fourth place, and I knew the writing was on the wall following that race in so far as it concerned his time in the legislature. He no longer had the desire to be in Madison doing the same job he had done for nearly a quarter of a century.

No one could blame Lary for wanting to move on. It was interesting, however, that Governor Thompson's administration also wanted to help Lary move along, so that a Republican could take the seat, and assist the GOP in gaining a majority in the chamber. If Lary could not be removed from his seat in an election, why not give him a job with a salary that he could not resist?

After what appeared to the press and others at the time as a comical undertaking, it was finally announced in an edition of the morning paper that Lary would be the State Director of *Americorps*, a program started under the leadership of President Clinton.

While I was understanding of Lary's desire to find something new to do with his life, I was not impressed at all with his lack of candor to me about the job he was offered. I was fully aware of the backdoor negotiations which were underway with the Governor's office, but when the final deal was struck I had to read about it in the paper rather than be told to my face from the man I made sure looked good since 1987 and was prepared for the work of the day.

I do not countenance such cowardly behavior from anyone.

I always bought the morning papers. That day, I held the edition in my hand. On the front page was the news that shook the Capitol. With paper in hand I walked directly to Lary's desk, and shoved it under his nose, dislodging his pen from whatever he was writing at the time.

"We need to talk about that story" were his words to me.

"We have nothing to discuss," I said, and left him alone. That morning the staff of his office refused to answer the phones, and let all the calls directly land on his shoulders. I was not in any way going to handle any interference for his actions going forward. Within a couple days he was gone from the legislative office for the last time.

I felt that I had earned a more forthcoming and honest approach to learning about his job than to pick up the newspaper *en route* to the office, and learn that while he had a new position, I was out of a job. The ethical aspect to the way the last pages of this story played out left me thinking as much about human nature as it did about the next chapter of my own life.

There need not be a lack of honor and respect in political offices from those who benefit year after year from the labors of staff who work to make sure legislation is passed, voters' needs are met, favorable press is created, and future election success is secured. Why it is not obvious to have a two-way street where fairness abounds when it comes to the type of issue I confronted remains a mystery.

I stayed for a few couple more months in the office keeping the citizens in the district connected to their state government in the absence of a state representative. At the time of my departure, a number of my friends threw me a going away party. I was shocked to see them standing in the office after returning from a coffee break that Brad had easily lured me to without a hint that something was planned.

When we returned it was really most kind and wonderful to find the grouping of friends I enjoyed working with in the building waiting in the office. As I scanned the faces I knew how very much I would miss them on a daily basis.

That day there was a wonderful chocolate cake to enjoy and my friends presented me with a gift of a shortwave radio which I still love and use to hear the news from around the globe. It has been on my desk for nineteen years, and is a reminder that there are good people in my life. Those faces, and party time in the office was very touching, and remains a moment I will never forget. I was so grateful for the loyalty of my friends, especially in the absence of the same from the representative I had faithfully served.

It was over a year before Lary and I talked again, and then it was quite formal and a matter-of-fact conversation. Over the following years Lary and I saw each other a handful of times, but it was never the same between us, and never did he offer an explanation for how things had ended in 1994. I also never asked. There was no way I wanted some contrived answer to a matter that I had moved past.

The very last time Lary and I met was at a meeting in 2006 when he wanted to again seek election to the Assembly. He had been replaced at *AmeriCorps* after a couple of years, and had done some other work in educational pursuits, but wanted to be back in the statehouse.

I told Lary it was a mistake to run again, and that unless he had a strong desire to make a special issue his cause, which I knew he did not care to do, then he needed to leave the idea of a race behind. There was nothing to be gained from again placing his name on a ballot. Too many politicians do not know when to walk off the stage I reminded him, and usually it only resulted in embarrassment when they tried for one more winning hand. He heard what I said, but did not listen. We left on diplomatic terms, but we never were to see each other again. Lary did run for the Assembly in 2006, and lost the election to his Republican opponent fifty-seven to forty-two percent.

I had told Lary at the time I was hired in 1986 that I would always do my best for him. Though things ended between us not as I had wished, I still made an effort to make sure at his death that he was remembered with dignity and honor.

In a column which first appeared on my blog, *Caffeinated Politics*, and then was reprinted in the *Door County Advocate*, a major paper in his district, I made known Lary's deep regard for his constituents along with his constant work to assist them.

> "I am not sure what will be placed on the grave marker for former State Representative Lary Swoboda, the Luxemburg Democrat who passed away on Sunday at the age of 73. But I think the most appropriate wording would be something akin to 'Constituent's Best Friend'.
>
> While Swoboda had a special interest in education policy, and made efforts to find an equitable way to lower property taxes, his greatest emphasis on any given day was making sure his constituents were taken care of, their needs met, and their problems resolved. While anyone can make that statement about a member of the legislature, I can attest

to the fact in Swoboda's case it was true.

When Swoboda first arrived in his Madison office each week he would pull from his pockets and brief case bits of paper with scribbled notes. Someone from the barber shop wanted a Blue Book; a guy from the market had a homestead credit problem; a business person needed to have his plans moved faster through the then DIHLR; a woman at a fish fry had drinking water concerns and needed DNR assistance.

I asked him on many occasions why he felt so connected to his constituents, and devoted as much time to clearing up their concerns.

He would always respond that he felt they needed to have a local connection to their state government, and to know the programs that were paid for with their tax dollars was money well spent.

One of the things that all had to respect about Swoboda was his desire to truly keep his marriage working while serving all the years in the legislature. He often told me there was no way he could have been in political office for the number of years he had, and left his wife in the district while he worked in Madison. So while there were some jokes about always seeing his wife, Jan, around the Capitol there was also a larger commitment to being a married couple that was taking place.

Over the decades many faces of the elected ones come and go under the Capitol dome. Some are remembered for political moves, and policy changes. Others will just fade away into history.

At the end of Lary Swoboda's story one thing remains clear and stands out.

There was never a better friend to the average constituent than that of Lary Swoboda.

It may not be on his grave stone.

But it is the truth."

I would not have replaced those years working in the statehouse for anything. They gave me a deeper appreciation for the importance of government, a first-hand understanding as to why we need strong contemplative reasoning when it comes to crafting policy, and a continuing and abiding faith in our political institutions—even when they move slowly or in the opposite direction of where I wish they would head. With time, deeper understanding, and personal reflections the world of politics has more depth and meaning to me, but one thing has never been altered. I can say my foundation of excitement about our government, and the world of politics has not been dulled, but instead enhanced. I remain very much an optimist about our future as a state and nation.

Before concluding, I will make here a bit of a post script. As I wrote this chapter a new book was published and released that caught my attention. Several great previews about the work landed in the book sections of newspapers, and each one made the book look quite remarkable. *Ike and Dick* by Jeffrey Frank examines the strange, powerful, and complicated political arrangement between Dwight D. Eisenhower and Richard Nixon. As soon as I had read the review in the *Wall Street Journal* I bought a copy from Amazon. It arrived as the construction of this chapter was in progress, and I had to smile as Lary would have loved this edition. On the front cover, in small letters, is printed: "Advance Uncorrected Proofs—Not For Sale".

Years after leaving my job I wrote a note to a friend who was hoping to get a job in the state capitol. Knowing how difficult and frustrating it can be, I wanted him to know his hard work was worth the time, and emotional investment. I closed my note to him with the following about how he should conduct himself once employed under the dome--it was the way I met each day when I went to work in that wonderful building, and I hope is the way others seek to do their job when fortunate enough to work there in the years to come.

> "...in your job make each day count, and affect change in every way possible; honor the public's trust in every action you take."
> —Gregory

Lary (With one 'R')

Lary (With one 'R')

The first fall of snow is not only an event, it is a magical event. You go to bed in one kind of a world and wake up in another quite different, and if this is not enchantment then where is it to be found?

—J.B. Priestly

Feel that Breeze!

"Heavy snow and strong winds continue to bear down over the region, and now at least one county is pulling its plows off the roads until the main portion of the storm has moved past the area. While the Portage County Sheriff's Department advises that no one venture out on the roads this evening as driving conditions have continued to deteriorate, Wood County authorities report they are pulling their plows off the roads until 4:00 A.M. tomorrow morning as the blowing and drifting is making it impossible for the plow operators to see where they are driving. Keep it tuned to WSPT Stevens Point for the latest weather reports, and do not forget that tomorrow morning we will have a full run-down of the school closings and other cancellations. Meanwhile back music to warm your mood..."

On many a snowy morning as a boy I would turn the radio on earlier than usual to see if there were any reason even to think of school, let alone get up and prepare for the bus to arrive. As is still the custom, the schools not holding classes due to inclement weather were read aloud in alphabetical order. That list was repeated periodically over the radio for those "just tuning in". With deep breaths of hopefulness I waited as patiently as a kid could for the name *Tri-County School in Plainfield* to be read from that list.

I recall there were more snow days in my youth than what kids get to experience now. We had real winter weather with which to contend while I was growing up. This is not to say that my recollections are akin to the stories of my parents who seemed to walk uphill both going and coming from school. The winters were indeed more robust and character forming in the years I attended classes. Anyone who wishes not to believe that climate change is occurring only need to talk with someone who has lived for a few decades in the northern half of Wisconsin to better understand that weather conditions have been altered due to mankind's handiwork on the planet.

On those days when the snow piled high and school was cancelled there were many times Mom would look out the living room window, and remark that the passing car was the first one out on the road. Then Mom would continue looking out a southern-facing window to watch and see if the car had made it up the way to the intersection at the corner. She wanted to know if the vehicle turned, or continued onwards. When the snow was light and fluffy, there would be a cloud of white trailing the vehicle. Snow that lifts and is carried off on the winds is stunning and always accompanied a good storm.

Our stretch of country road was prone to drifting with an open field on one side. Winter weather would often close County KK down with dense drifts of snow. There were times when the car my Mom was watching from her southerly vantage point had to turn around, unable to continue. The high drifts created an impasse. Mom understood these U-turns in the road as confirmation of the severity of the storm. Should it be a cancelled school day she might add 'they made the right decision'. Mom would then be confronted with a different reality. I might be 'underfoot' all day. I knew she was happy to have me home instead of 'out in it', as she would phrase it. She always seemed to enjoy our snow days spent together.

Though it may be hard for some to believe, there were other times when no traffic would be on our road for days due to the heavy snow, and blowing winds. A car in the driveway might have its front end nearly covered over, and the back door to the house might be drifted shut. Dad would need to shovel his way in to the house once he arrived home from work.

Mom had her own snow day traditions. The soup pot would come out, a ham bone from the freezer would follow, and bean soup would then simmer for most of the afternoon. It would be ready to be served when Dad was able to come home for a meal. The windows in the kitchen would steam up, and the comforting aroma of home cooking would greet Dad as he entered the house. While Mom carried the soup to the table, Dad regaled us with stories from his day's work.

Dad would only come home for supper when he thought he could take a break from the plowing. While eating, he would talk of how bad the roads were from the storm. I loved to hear him tell us how the ramps on the highway were icy and slick, or 'they can't get through up on '73', but my Mom never seemed to find the adventure in a snowstorm that I did.

Many times I recall my Dad saying they would need to 'bring in the Oshkosh'. Those were magic words to me as a young boy. I knew then that the storm was a real nasty one since the Oshkosh was a double-bladed snow truck that would not only push the snow off the roads, but also mound it far off on the shoulders. I suspected that to ride in one was a bit like taking a mini spaceship ride, extra loud and bumpy.

Indeed, a ride in the Oshkosh would have been tremendous fun. Just the same, there was nothing better for really pushing the snow into high banks then when Mom's brother would pass on our roads driving the motor grader with a huge wing plow attached to it. After he made his trip down the roads, the piles of snow could be over half way up a telephone pole.

I rode a few times in my Dad's snowplow while he raised heck with the drifts and ice on the highway. Sitting up so high and seeing the snow plume off the wide blade was perfect fun. I still get goosebumps thinking about those rides all these years later. After one school event, Dad was to pick me up and drive home. The weather forced him to change plans rather dramatically. Instead of pulling up in the Buick, Dad pulled along the school in the large, beefy county truck outfitted with a snowplow. I climbed up in to the truck, gave a bit of a wave to my friends still waiting, and Dad put the vehicle in to gear. No kid could ever have felt more proud to have a parent pick him from school.

Dad loved driving that snow plow truck for the county. He was kind and generous, and was 'made for' the job. I tried in various ways to engage a county truck and driver to lead the funeral procession for my Father. I wanted very much that one of those trucks accompany Dad on his final journey as the hearse wound its way from the church past the family home, and then to the cemetery. The County could not find a way to make it happen. I was so disappointed. My Dad never failed to find a way to make sure the passage was clear for countless travelers during all the storms; I wish the County which he had so faithfully served could have found a way to honor him in this way. No one will know how much that truck leading the procession would have meant to him, or me, as that was so much a part of Dad's life.

Feel that Breeze!

After a good ole winter storm and the roads again were passable, Dad would come home and get caught up on his sleep. He worked long hours when snow fell. When he was awake again, he would tell Mom and me that we had to see how some of the roads looked with their snow banks. I think he enjoyed the snowdrifts too, once they were no longer extending themselves out into the traffic lanes. Off in the family car we headed down the back roads and I was amazed at the huge piles of snow mile after mile in the ditches, and banking off into the fields. I would remark that they would be perfect for sledding, and my mother would instantly reply, "You would be hit by a car." She may have been right, but so was I. She tended to see more potential accidents about to occur; I only saw reasons for excitement.

The huge blasts of artic air or heavy snow would remind us that winter had really settled in and we would start reflecting on what the national weather service had predicted for the season. We would recall together the earlier reports and ascertain if they indeed had been accurate. When it came to such talks there was no better source for some fun than to think back to the late weeks of summer and refresh our memories about the Woolly Bear caterpillars. All my life I can recall first my Grandmother, and then my Mom making winter predictions for either a cold or snowy winter or a mild one based on the stripe of little fall caterpillar.

Legend has it that a wider middle brown section on the insect means a milder winter season is approaching. Conversely, a narrow brown band is said to predict a harsh winter. Without a better sampling of data, that is to say without having made a more exhaustive search for wooly caterpillars, it was hard to determine if enough of the insects had the same type of stripe. Without better records, it is possible that we just kept finding the same wooly caterpillar in the yard over and over. Our science was not conclusive, but rather awesomely speculative, which suited us just fine too.

There were other folk legends as well that got attention around our dinner table. Others spoke of the timing of the first crash of thunder in the early spring, or the arrival of the first hard frost in fall. We were asked: "Did the acorns set on heavy this year, or did the leaves fall from the trees early? Did you hear the formation of geese flying over, and heading south already?" We didn't really need to know about the oak trees or the Canadian geese; we already had wooly caterpillars.

Another source of weather lore intrigued me as a kid. In

fact, the *Old Farmer's Almanac* still does. I am not making any claim that the *Almanac* has any more or less understanding of the ultimate outcome of the seasons than the caterpillar, but I will say it is a most novel publication. Who cannot warm to the nuggets such as "a fire hard to kindle means bad weather" or "black bears head to winter dens now"? The *Almanac* was correct more often than not, and my nose told me so. I would look at the charts and predictions in the fall and when it was reported "ragweed in bloom now", I sneezed in agreement.

We always had a copy of the small-sized yellow-jacketed publication back home, and it was fun to read both the articles, and their ads which could best be described as quaint. Best of all were the weather predictions that dominated a section of each edition. Accurate by luck or not, the predictions were highlighted with small icons and graphics along with old folklore, and are always fun to read.

Over the years James' Mom would send a copy our way late in the fall, and come January, I would be comparing the scene out my window to the printed predictions within its pages. I could always dial Marion up and talk about what was going on; she had already 'pre-read' the copy she had sent me, so she knew of what I was speaking first hand. There is still something about the old-fashioned look and tone of the publication that makes me aware everything need not be slick, or 'new and improved' to be important to our lives, or bring a smile.

Like my own Mother, James' Mom read avidly and clipped articles from the paper. Several times a month an envelope from Maine would arrive in our mail box with newspaper clippings that his Mom had selected for us. Her weekly grouping would include a wide assortment of news that might deal with everything from strange sightings of moose, interesting columns regarding political events, notations about strange weather phenomena or even cartoons from the funny pages. She had been sending James newspaper clippings from the time he left home for Middlebury College, and then during his studies in Europe. Her mailings were such a regular occurrence that we eventually supplied the address labels to make it easier for her to send the clippings our way.

In almost every mailing there was a notation on one or two clippings which said something akin to "Gregory needs to read this" or "blog about this". I will never forget when she sent me the 12,000 calorie per day diet menu that Olympic swimmer Michael Phelps followed. She told me to mimic his diet so as to put on more weight. She knew just what I needed.

The last mailing from James's Mom came in early November 2011. Days earlier, she had been diagnosed with a very aggressive form of cancer. Marion passed away, Tuesday, December 20,

2011, at her home with family caring for her. It was a devastating time for all of us.

One of my first memories of Marion is of her looking up at the Maine sky in the evening and reciting her own favorite weather predicting adage. "Red sky in the morning, sailors take warning," she'd state. Her face seemed to reflect a real sense of dread, as though she had been out to sea herself or had been home waiting for a loved one to return on his boat. "But red skies at night, sailor's delight!" Her face lit up. Marion lived for those red skies of the evening over the coast of Maine; if she could have lived in a lighthouse, she would have, just to be able to see the sky painted pink more often.

One of my favorite memories of Marion is from 2002 when I first visited the Maine coast. Marion and I were seated out in the sunshine with her husband Robert, and James. We had travelled to visit at the Vaughn family home, long-time friends of the family. Dinnertime was fast approaching; fresh lobsters were brought to the table. It had already been quite a day for me. I was fascinated at seeing an ocean for the first time, tasting the salty water, and also taking a small lobster trawler, named the *Judith L Sullivan*, out to where the lobsters were contained in a crate underwater. The crustaceans that the host and I had gone out on the water to fetch were soon to be lunch!

Marion sat across from me as a lobster was placed on my plate, and I suspect my face must have shown how far from the ocean my hometown actually was. "Where do I begin?" I thought to myself. I will never forget how Marion went through the steps for me of getting the shell separated and the meat out. Those instructions were the start of a love affair with lobster that only continues to grow.

Many a time Marion would call or write and tell us in Madison what the lobster prices in Maine were. Living near the ocean, Marion would chant, "Lobster is cheaper than steak today!" Lobsters were always far cheaper than what they were in the Midwest. In 2006, Marion sent me an email that summed up her desire for everyone to understand how to eat lobster: *"Had a nice ride to Greenville on the 15th. Stopped at a new eats place there. 2 out-of-state guys there had lobster dinner with the clams. Didn't know how to eat a clam nor how to pick a lobster. I resisted giving lessons but when they threw away the bodies without picking them, I nearly lost it. --Mom"* In Marion's kitchen, almost no part of the lobster went to waste, and especially not all the yummy stuff inside the body. From that she would make soups and dips for chips.

Marion also liked to make fun with us at times. During the final weeks of her life, she called me one day and said I needed to be at her home in fifteen minutes as the lobsters would be ready.

Feel that Breeze! **189**

The sixteen hundred miles separating us at the time didn't matter. If I did not make it in time, a small portion of what I was supposed to have had would make her kitty very pleased. She didn't say who would get the remainder of my crustacean.

My first experience on the Maine coast nearly a decade ago was magnified many times over when during that trip a pot full of boiled lobsters was placed on Marion's kitchen table. I had never seen anything like it before, and recall telling my Mom about the meal. Instead of being impressed with the seafood Mom instead was more interested in pictures of the Wilson kitchen cabinets! I still recall my Mom having Dad look at the picture of Marion's custom-designed, deep-well cabinets and wondering when she might have some just like them.

Now that Marion is gone, I miss not getting my copy of the *Farmer's Almanac* in the mail with her handwritten annotations. She was always pointing out the parts she thought I needed to read first. She readily agreed with Mom's wooly caterpillar method of predicting weather, and always added that if you counted how many stars were inside the ring of the moon as it began to snow, you could tell how many inches of snow would fall in the night. That was harder for me to verify here in the city than it would have been in the country, but I saw no reason why it wouldn't be true. Even today, though more rare here in the Midwest than in Maine, I never fail to stop and admire a good deep red sunset and think of James' Mom, who shared a love of weather predicting with me. "Red skies at night, sailor's delight!" Good night, Marion.

Some of my friends were thrilled when the World Series was to hit the airwaves; I was in a state of excitement when weather reports that demanded the kind of attention which made radio announcers take on the serious persona that stood apart from their regular easy-going style. When weather bulletins were read, it could almost make for manic actions around our home. My folks seemed to think every storm might be 'the last storm.'

Just to be clear, weather always played a larger role in our home than for that of my friends. My Dad worked for the County, and throughout the year his job often was directly impacted by the weather. Weather too was a part of the daily conversation that flowed in our home. James has pointed out that he had never spoken as often of the weather as since moving to Wisconsin, and more intriguingly still, attending a family function at the Humphrey home.

Today I am far more conscious of the weather reports than almost anyone living in our neighborhood. The most severe weather might be predicted from the National Storm Center, and yet a large percentage of local residents seem unaware as they pass our corner. I know this to be true because so many stop to chat. Folks look at clouds that have no chance of dumping any precipitation, and muse about how much rain we are going to get overnight. Others can see the storm coming on the horizon as it crosses the lake and have no idea if it will impact us. It continues to amuse me how close we are to the weather every day, and yet how many are seemingly clueless about the basics of what they are experiencing.

As a boy in summer it might be the hottest day of the year when the corn could be *heard* growing in the fields. If you were quiet enough, you could perceive the gentle cracking and popping sound of the ears growing in length and breadth. If I had had skills in music composition, I would have written a symphony for this musical event all on its own. On good corn-growing days, my Dad would muse about the state of the concrete on the highway, and if it might buckle and cause a 'blow-up'. An actual crack up happening on the highway would stop the planning for a picnic, delay a birthday gathering, or alter plans to head to the market. Work came first because people's safety was at risk.

Or, it could be a winter day when the very last thing most people think about is heading into the blanket of white that was falling down and swirling about due to high winds. In winter as soon as the threat of a major storm was reported there was planning so Dad could get some needed rest before he would head in to Mother Nature's fury for the long hours of plowing and salting the thoroughfares.

There was no way to predict what would happen, but there was no doubt when the phone rang on a blistering day, or when the snow started to pile up, odds were that Dad was about to be taken away from his family. That was the only part about weather events that I never liked.

When I was a teenager, there was an Easter snowstorm that dumped heavy wet snow on the region. Though I rode with Uncle Bob and Aunt Evie along with Grandma to church that morning, it was doubtful, I thought, that the large meal Mom had planned would be served in the fashion, or at the time she was hoping. On days like that we waited until hearing from Dad before knowing when to call my siblings and tell them to come over. There was always the chance that the best-laid plans would be upended due to the circumstances.

Coming home once from a Saturday shopping trip to Stevens Point, I saw first-hand the buckling of pavement in the heat.

Feel that Breeze! **191**

I was just a boy then. For miles things had slowed on the highway. Thinking it was a traffic accident we were relieved to see that instead part of the road had just buckled, and not something more tragic. As soon as we noticed the trouble though, my Dad was talking about what he needed to do once he dropped us off at home. He would need to call his workmate, Walt, and get the truck loaded with some patching tar. He needed extra traffic cones, he reasoned, given it was a weekend and the volume of vehicles were heavier. There was a list forming in Dad's mind about all that needed to be done, and in the hours to come that list would be expertly executed. The patch in the road would be so smooth that no one could tell there had been anything amiss only hours earlier.

When really young, I wondered why Dad just did not get another job that would not take him out into the storms, and away from home. With time I came to see Dad's role in the midst of such storms as one that impacted not just the family economy but also the comings and goings of countless people who relied on what he did. People had doctor's appointments and parent-teacher conferences at school; workers could not take another day off of work. The main roads had to be kept cleared. Making everyone else's life just a little easier was Dad's job.

Dad was mindful that he served a larger role than just holding a job. He made every effort to have the stretches of pavement that he maintained to be some of the best in the state. Part of that mindset came from his upbringing, and some just was a part of his genetic makeup. He felt he was to do his job as best as one could--be it at home, or at work. People relied on him to do things just that well.

Over the decades that my Mom delayed meals, or postponed plans she came to have a different view of the need to have every inch of the roads in pristine condition. With humor she would often say in the final years of Dad's employment that no one else would ever make sure the roads were in such perfect condition, and added, "Do you think they will just shut the highway down without your plowing and salting when you retire?" She had made many a meal that had gotten cold, waited long nights for his return home, and gotten up at strange hours to heat food and make sure he was not over-extended with his duties. If Dad drove the county plow, it was Mom who worried about making sure all the other parts of the family unit were running smoothly during storms.

Dad's involvement with weather-based concerns did not have to be the result of his work; it could also be from his duties as an elected official. There were many times that unexpectedly a call would come in after a harsh and wild thunderstorm which landed trees on the town roads. Dad served for forty years as Town Supervisor for Hancock. His duties as a Supervisor gave him the responsibility of locating someone to clear away the debris. In the spring after the heavy winter snows of my childhood there were times he needed to go and assess the flooding of roads along with the frozen culverts that were not functioning as hoped.

I sometimes tagged along on the culvert inspection missions, and loved to see the fields that had once grown corn and potatoes completely under water from the spring melts. Even more thrilling was when Dad would go slowly through the water that covered the roads, as the very culverts we were inspecting were impotent to deal with the volume of winter run-off. The sloshing of the water on the underside of the car was a sound I had not often heard, and it made the kid in me giggle. Dad undoubtedly understood something very different and was worried for the undercarriage of his car being hit with all that extra salt solution.

Over the years of my childhood there was always the reminder that weather, even when cloudy, wet, and blustery could also be perfect. My Mom turned rainy days when one might think otherwise as being gloomy into an afternoon that was warm and cozy inside. She came to make me understand that such days were a great time to read or get caught up on something that was always meant to get done.

Mom would undertake little projects straight off her 'to do' list. Sometimes she would sort through the closet in the dining room. It was filled with cloth and sewing projects. She had a large cardboard box layered with countless folded pieces of cloth of assorted colors. I still recall the distinctive scent of the cloth. It was neither musty nor old, but rather fresh and crisp smelling. The cloth always seemed ready to be laid out and used for some purpose.

Mom would set up her sewing machine, and from time to time ask me to help her thread the bobbin since there was less daylight when the clouds lowered outside. Bending over and slipping the thread into the eye of the needle was easy, and she might remark how quickly I had completed my task. Then, there was a flurry of sewing and stitching on the project. Sewing seemed like an activity perfectly suited for a dreary day outside.

While Mom worked, I would stretch out on the floor nearby with books and paper and find ways to be content. When it was colder outside it was best to lay out in front of the stove and feel the warmth flow from it.

To this day, I love the gray wet days when there is no work

to be done outside. James and I curl up, read or complete 'office stuff'. There is a certain charm to the last autumn duties as the cold winds blow knowing that for a few months things slow down and other indoor projects can be become the focus of our daily lives. Mom nourished this idea of how to view gray skies, and I will forever love her for it.

Over the years I have much enjoyed a sense of glee when television meteorologists get to use the latest computer systems and gadgets to follow storms and predict where they are heading. While I am no fan of 'reality television', I am always impressed and addicted to the weather systems that demand full coverage. I can watch severe weather programming and be totally engrossed with the developments as they unfold.

"This is WTMB, Tomah, We interrupt this broadcast for a special weather statement at 7:38. All evening we have been following the series of intense thunderstorms that has been moving in a northeasterly direction throughout southwestern Wisconsin. The National Weather Service has issued a severe thunderstorm warning for Adams and Marquette Counties until 8:15 and Waushara County until 8:40. Large hail and destructive winds have been associated with this band of storms that stretches from a line south of Mauston to just north of Baraboo. Campers in the Castle Rock area are to take to places of safety immediately. Large trees have been reported downed from this line of storms along with property damage reported in Richland County. We will keep you posted throughout the evening on this developing weather story."

I often told my Mom she worried too much about storms, and she always had a stock response. "Someone has to worry." I never was able to place that into any useful context, and just accepted it as part of her personae. Nothing ever truly bad happened from the storms, but she was going to be prepared just the same.

Mom would have been a great military leader; she was prepared for all eventualities, and I loved her for it. She had a mental list of things that needed to be done when storms moved through, and had determination that everything would be ready when the first blasts from a wind bank cut loose. Mom sprang into action when the threat of severe weather was reported on the radio. We would monitor the reports over the scratchy AM signals as the static competed with the announcer.

     Mom filled large yellow containers with water and placed them in the bathtub. All the major appliances were unplugged so they would not be burnt out from a lighting strike. All windows were shut and fastened except when tornadoes were probable and only then one was left slightly ajar for the expressed purpose of equalizing air pressure inside the home. She also had us kids make sure everything was picked up outside. Bikes got put away, clothes were taken off the line, the hoe and rake were stored safely back in the barn, and all the doors on all of the outbuildings closed securely.

     Mom had a file box which she took to the basement. The box contained all the important information any homeowner needs to access in case of an emergency. The only thing we lacked was an air raid siren. Mom would have had one located in the backyard for the full effect of a looming disaster had she had her druthers.

     When green roiling clouds, or dark blue ones with the ominous white portion indicative of strong winds got close, the entire family went to the basement. Depending on where the storm was heading would determine which side of the basement we would shelter.

     Only two times did the drama of potential tornado danger make me queasy. The first time was when Dad did not respond quickly enough to Mom's marshaling us to safety. Her plea rose above the crash of the thunder. "Get down here!" she yelled so loudly that it still lingers in my mind's ear. Let me underscore it was not a suggestion for him to move. It was an order. As a small boy, the world seemed to me to be very unsafe anywhere except in the concrete bunker of the basement when a storm brewed.

     The second time a storm really unnerved me was as we all huddled in the basement as the winds lashed and raked the homestead. With a tremendous crash we all looked about and Dad craned his neck to look out a casement window. Dad wondered out loud if a part of the roof had been taken away. I recall inching up the wooden steps after it was safe and peering upwards with great dread at what might be seen, or not seen. To great relief all was fine that evening, with only a very large branch of a tree having broken loose and thrown close to the house.

     Given the role that weather played in the life of my family, I think it interesting to note that not twenty-four hours prior to my Dad's passing, a powerful tornado would pummel the landscape near my family's home.

     A tornado formed near County Road G and Buttercup Avenue in far eastern Adams County. Damage was noted to some homes and areas of trees, especially along Buttercup Avenue as the storm tracked into Waushara County. Several center-post irrigation systems were destroyed, torn apart and placed like one might twist a plastic straw and then toss it on the tabletop. Some roof damage to homes and power poles, less than half-a-mile from our home, was observed as James and I viewed it the following morning. The tornado weakened to EF0 over most of its path as it continued to areas southeast of Hancock before dissipating. Visual inspection revealed that straight line winds destroyed telephone poles, and trees were uprooted or broken off at their midsection. Road ways were blocked and in need of clearing. The whole area looked to have been under attack. The winds, though, they just missed our property.

That final huge storm of my Dad's life took place on Sunday April 10, 2011, about 6:30 P.M. It was an EF1 Tornado located 5 miles southwest of Hancock.

The power of the storm seemed to fit into the narrative of what was happening to Dad at home. Strong forces were at work, unpredictable in the exact course they would take, but all knew that both outside and inside the house there was nothing to do but hold on tight and let the storm pass. Some storms rip up trees and toss the picnic tables about while other storms take a soul.

I am likely alone in my gratitude for that storm. The tempest allowed Dad to have something else to think about the final night of his life. James and I had something exciting to talk about with him as he listened to the reports of the damage just up the road. He was certainly going back in his mind to the days when he would have picked up the phone and started the process of making sure the roads were cleared of limbs, and large trunks cut up to be hauled away. Dad's memories were only eclipsed by his infirmities. Hats off to that one last meteorological hoorah!

Be they preparations for the cleaning up after a storm, or in advance of one bearing down on the western portion of the county where we lived, my parents always exercised an abundance of caution. I too as a boy felt the need to organize the essentials, the things I could not live without should the house blow away. For the sake of clarity, I mention that these 'essentials' were not the same kinds of 'essentials' that I stored on my workbench out in the barn.

As a young boy, I commandeered a very small green suitcase with a nice tight latch that was probably no larger than fifteen inches by ten inches. I figured that the small green valise was large enough to hold what I needed to make it through whatever Mother

Nature had in store for us.

    Following one storm that knocked out our electricity, Dad placed a call to the local long-time Hancock electrician, Johnnie, asking for assistance. He liked my Dad a great deal, and so not long after the call his knock was heard on the back door. Dad greeted him and let him inside the house, exchanging pleasantries and tales of the conditions outside. In the kitchen, Johnnie inquired why I was lugging around the little suitcase. While the contents of the case weren't top secret, I was reluctant to open the case for fear that the storm might surge and I would lose its contents foolishly. That would have just been bum luck for sure. Johnnie finally coaxed me to open up my treasure trove. Stashed inside among other small items were several of my Big Little Books, which were my favorite reads at the time, and a small flat Hersey candy bar, in case I got the munchies. Johnnie took a few coins from his pocket and added them to my contents. Perhaps he thought I needed bus fare! Nonetheless, I admired his generosity.

    Obviously my parents felt they had more pragmatic attitudes about wild weather, as they would have recalled the horrific storms that had pounded the area in the early years of their marriage. On September 26, 1951 a category F4 (max. wind speeds 207-260 mph) tornado blasted its way 17.4 miles outside of Hancock. That storm killed 6 people and injured 3 more. Another F4 tornado on April 19, 1957, 28 miles from Hancock killed one person. Otherwise stated, from the perspective of data collected over time, and released in 2011, the Hancock-area shows historical tornado activity is above the Wisconsin state average, and is 117% greater than the overall U.S. average. Just hearing those numbers would have made my Mom start gathering supplies and begin preparing for the big one!

    As I got older I started to see weather in a whole different perspective than my parents. I saw the grandeur, energy, and beauty that Mother Nature provided over and over with fascinating downpours, blizzards, windstorms, and even hail. As I read and started to understand the science behind the weather systems that blew through I lost any desire to hunker down in the basement when the thunderstorms started to unfold.

    We find that often elusive sense of security in a loved-one's embrace. Mother felt safest when she had all of us tucked in under her wings in the basement. Her mother, my Grandma Schwarz, was a bit different. Weather phenomena were something she also enjoyed, but I need to state right up front that I never saw her willingly walk out into a rain storm or a gale. I do recall standing with her, her arm around my shoulder, at the screen door of her home. She left the door ajar during what my childish understanding thought to be a massive storm. The crashing thunder and bolts of lightning were grand, but there was nothing to fear if Grandma herself was willing to be there in the midst of it all.

I had never experienced a storm in that way before, watching it descend all around, viewing it up close and personal. I absolutely loved the way Grandma watched it, and knew this type of fun could be had at our home too. The question became, of course, how do I convince Mom that letting me ride out the storm from above ground would be a good idea? I knew instinctively that the "But Grandma said..." path of argumentation would likely not produce the results I hoped. My plan would take more thought than that. Moments spent watching storms with Grandma demonstrated two things. The first was that weather was clearly something to be enjoyed, and secondly and perhaps most importantly weather can be viewed up close even when it is wild and unpredictable. That understanding is something I have carried with me every day of my life, even though my parents seemed at odds with how I viewed the dramas playing out above our heads.

Every kid has that time when they are no longer Mom's little boy. For some it might be a week away at camp, or no longer confiding secrets as had once been done. In my case it was when I no longer was willing to head to the basement for storms. There came a time when I stood at the windows upstairs, and watched the storm unfold outside. I do not recall that it felt liberating as I never felt over controlled or stifled as a kid, but instead was just pleased to see the storm up close. I did not think much about that at the time, and in fact my growing up moment never registered until my Mom and I chatted many years later over coffee at the dinner table. She remarked that she knew I was getting older when I no longer wanted to come to the basement when it stormed.

As a teenager reading about how hail formed, lightning was generated, or anvil-shaped thunderheads were created was perhaps the time I also wondered how many occupations I wanted to pursue as an adult. I loved the never-ending story weather created, the excitement it churned up as the dangerous storms approached, and once again how the meteorologists were tuned in and listened to by the public. There was a time I wanted to seriously work in the field of meteorology.

At the age of fifty I am not sure if one is blessed or cursed with wanting to pursue a wide variety of interests. While I clearly count my curiosity about almost everything to be a blessing it goes without saying that even if I were overly talented—which I am not—there would still be only so many weeks in a month, and years in a lifetime. At the end of my time there will still be so much left undone that I want to try and about which I want to learn more.

When asked about what I wanted to be when I grew up, I had thoughts about how it might be useful to be a teacher, adventuresome to be an astronaut, and civic-minded to be a politician. In the past decade, I also have added bakery owner to the list. There are none of the old-fashioned sweet delights to be found in our Madison neighborhood, the kind that made Grandma's house such a special place to be when cinnamon buns were being rolled out on one of her classic well-used baking pans. If I had enough money, I would open a good neighborhood bakery nearby.

Meteorology would have also been a lot of fun. I never had the math skills required to pursue weather forecasting, though; I have long been convinced that mixing letters and numbers in math problems is the devil's work, and to be avoided entirely. Luckily, weather phenomena have never lost my attention. My heart races when a report of kick and snort weather moves into my area.

No one should assume that I am one of those who loves to see the events unfold from inside while pressing my nose to the windowpane. While it is true that Windex is used more often in our home following major weather systems it is also true that I can always be found out in the bluster and chaos that Mother Nature sends in my direction.

On August 18, 2005, when James and I lived on the West Side of Madison, I had a real encounter with a tornado, and it was most remarkable. At about 7:15 P.M. we had started on what was our nightly walk around the neighborhood. Clouds built up from the northwest; conditions did not warrant us not taking our walk. About three fourths of a mile from home the emergency sirens sounded, and while the sky looked more threatening, it still did not appear from our vantage point that we should walk faster. We did though decide to turn and start back for home.

The clouds and darkness did move in quickly as we neared our apartment. At one point, I made James stop and just look at the lightning. It was so different from anything I had seen before. No bolts of lightning, but instead elaborate laser light formations bejeweled the sky.

By the time we got home the sun was shining on the opposite side of the street and people were on their balconies looking into the sky with hands shading their eyes. James went indoors while I stayed in the driveway and observed the sky. It appeared, though falsely, as though the storm has skirted the west side of the city. Our neighbor came home in his car and said "What are you doing out here?" He told me that the sky was violent looking, and the trees in our area were blocking what was happening. I told him he just had to watch the clouds, as it was truly amazing. He agreed, got out of the car and put his garage door up, just in case he had to run in side for cover.

What happened next was a sight I had never seen before. From here to the end of this account it took only minutes. Looking northwest the horizon area of the sky was orange and not threatening. The clouds midway in the sky started boiling from the bottom. It looked like a pot on the stove in a full rolling boil. It appeared as though the contents of the pot were being violently shifted as the heat sent water down and then thrust it up again, over and over. This movement continued, intensified, and moved in our direction.

Then a rotation started. While not tight, the spin was clockwise, circular and quite large. My neighbor asked me, "Do you smell that?" I was not paying attention to my nose, but when asked did smell a distinct odor, not a bad stench, not really a chemical smell, but something that was part of a downdraft of wind. Later a local meteorologist told me that was likely ozone-3. I gather it was from the lightning overhead and the turbulent winds which brought the smell to the ground.

At that time my neighbor ran inside.

I stayed where I was in the driveway, and watched as this cloud formation became more defined and moved off in a somewhat southeasterly direction. I ran into the street, (there was not one single car anywhere) and observed it as I ran for about a block until the trees blocked my view. In the street the gray clouds that I had seen overhead had turned into a white comma shape in the sky. I knew I had seen a tornado form and watched it as it moved away.

I ran back home and bounded upstairs. James had the news on and within a minute Channel 27 reported that a tornado had struck their station, just about 2 miles away from where we lived. After about three or four minutes of that report, hard rains descended on our area, lashing the windows and beating on the roof. Never before had I witnessed Mother Nature in so foul a mood close up. It was a little frightening, and yet it was something I just could not stop looking at. James told me that I didn't even have the good sense to come in from the rain. This may be true, but I have never heard anyone say that I would go out into a deluge.

But that is exactly what I like to do.

LaRoccas was the first restaurant we visited after moving to the isthmus. It offered good downhome-style Italian cooking and the traditional charm of an authentic Italian family. It was a continuing pleasure to order their food. One evening, after having ordered a slice of meat lasagna and some fettuccini a la Vito (in a light white wine sauce with seafood and named for the restaurant's owner), we walked to pick the order up. A few light sprinkles fell as we made our way back home. We decided to sit inside our home to eat rather than out on the lawn as we hoped. The rains began to fall a bit more steadily.

While the forecasters had predicted wild weather it really did not appear all that bad. As we sat at the dinner table the light shower turned into quite a rain. It then ramped up and turned into a harsh downpour. I got up from the table, and looked out windows from all sides of our home, and then opened the door to look out the front stoop.

"James," I shouted, "you have to see this!" Running through the rooms he reached the door and looked out. It was a real Madison monsoon, and the noise it made was loud and intense; a storm like this demanded to be experienced. "Come on, get out here!" I shouted.

"I think I will watch it from the windows," James replied. With that attitude James never would have been selected to travel with Lewis and Clark!

I, on the other hand, might have been asked to lead the expedition. Since I had no reason not to, I grabbed the largest umbrella we owned and slipped on my sandals. On the stoop and down the steps I went into the almost deafening downfall of rain. The wind whipped the falling gusher. As I peered up from under the umbrella I could see the top of the trees in our neighborhood swaying heavily. With almost a demented madness, the rain poured down on the pavement, cars, and of course my back and legs. Even with the umbrella the back of my shirt was soaked instantly, and my shorts stuck to my legs. It felt great!

I did a half-skip-run along the sidewalk and to the street corner where the roiling waters from two different directions crashed and churned, struggling to enter the curb drain. No use. The water's force surged. The flooding took the water wherever it wanted to travel, crossed over the street, and into the next block. The waves kept coming with conviction down the sidewalk. They banked up and over my feet and ankles. (The lesson here might be to always have sandals at the ready to wear, as you never know when a walk in the rain is just around the corner.)

When I made it back into the entryway of our home after a bit more walking and feeling the intensity of the downburst I was met with "Your mother said you did not know enough to come in out of the rain. This is worse, you willingly walked out into it!"

Yes, and what a wonderful experience.

I slipped into a very hot shower and as I did it was clear the sirens in the city were going off. In seconds James rushed in to alert me of the tornado warning. All I could say, with a heart full of regret, was: "I came inside too early!"

I have always enjoyed the wind.

At our Madison home most days there is a wind blowing. Regardless of the month or season there is always a breeze, and often a brisk one that reminds me that the air currents are always struggling for control. The winds come in from over Lake Monona, arching up over the drumlin left by the last glacial action, and then surges inland as it whips and blows.

While the lake breeze makes it tough at times to read a newspaper when seated in the Adirondack chairs unless the paper is folded 'just so', it is also true that even on the hottest days of summer when there is grass to be mowed, there will be a breeze to make the work easier.

As a boy in winter I loved to get bundled up and head outdoors. "Run around the house a few times and get rid of your energy" seemed to be repeated request from Mom. Or was that an order? One of the greatest thrills on really wintry days was to venture around the house and head in a southwesterly direction, from where some of the best winter storms came. Gathering moisture over the panhandle region and mixing with the cold air moving down from Canada were the essential ingredients for a massive snow event that might make central Wisconsin look like the perfect picture postcard.

I can still see the sky colored a grayish-dark blue and the horizon blurred with a foggy whitish hue. The blowing snow came in sheets and the blasts that drove them would take my breath way as I made the turn around the family home. I would struggle to reposition my head and gasp for a breath, and then again face the onslaught of wind and walk into the snow piles that drifted in the same place where summer picnics would have occurred the previous July.

My Mom was not a fan of strong winds. One summer evening I still recall the wind whipping as I held onto the door handle of my Dad's light-green Buick parked in the driveway. I felt the first stings of sand from the driveway stir in the tumult and bite at my skin. "Get in the house!" was the only sound that was louder than the wind, as my Mom's order traveled down the driveway.

Living in the country she had to contend with the irresponsible farmers who did not use sound agricultural practices to prevent their topsoil from blowing away across the country. Many a warm day in the spring we could look off to the west and see the sky colored with grime as the dirt blew. My parents, along with many who live in the rural area, were never fond to see another large swath of trees be uprooted and removed for farming. Too many large operators had forgotten the common sense use of tree breaks to limit soil erosion. More importantly, trees left as a windbreak were signs that a farmer wanted to be a good neighbor.

'Brown-outs', though not the kind from overtaxing the electrical grid of the area, were not uncommon in the spring months. Traveling Highway 39 in the Plainfield area, with headlights on, and at speeds greatly reduced, traffic had to endure sights straight out of the Dust Bowl era. How this yearly display is accepted by the average citizen as part of the price for growing a crop is still a mystery to me.

Mom was not a fan. If anyone ever wanted to see blood pressure rise, and a serene personality turn very prickly, just mention to Mom that the winds were whipping up the sand. Mom was never fun to be around on days when her windowsills were getting covered in grit. She'd place a rolled up towel on the windowsills, and then in the mornings she would wipe the sills and screens so they were again clean. Following a bit of cleaning her bright disposition could return.

Since my Dad was not often around due to work during the height of winter storms my Mom felt all the pressures to keep 'the home fires burning', and while always fulfilling her responsibilities it did create stress. In the winter Mom would watch almost religiously so that the pilot light would not blow out of the heating stove when the high winds would whip around outside. Often a blast over the chimney would suck the oxygen out, taking the flame with it. If it was not the stove to worry about, the swaying and lifting of the canopy on the front of the house during winter's wrath would ensure my Mom would let all know she hated the wind.

On those nights when the winds and snow were most intense, and Mom was concerned about seemingly everything, she would leave the yard light on overnight. The light seemed to make her feel better. It did me too. I would open the drapes over the north windows of my bedroom, facing the light, and watch the flakes fall and bounce around in the storm as I drifted off to sleep.

My Dad had a different relationship with the wind. Often on a brutally hot summer day in the last decades of his life he could have been found in a lawn chair under a huge oak in the back yard. Facing the southwest, Dad would enjoy the wind rush by from the farm field on the other side of the road, over our land. He would say, "Feel that breeze!" Too often once the sun went down in the summer stillness would settle over the homestead, and the hot sticky darkness would take hold. My Dad was aware of that his whole life. He grew up only a few miles away. He relished the breezes when they offered themselves in the afternoons.

Only once did I sense with any discomfort that the winds of the Madison isthmus were too intense. I was seated outside reading when a strong low-pressure system moved over the area. There was no precipitation with the front, only winds that were gusting over forty miles per hour. The gusts would come and go until a mighty lash from Mother Nature split a thick branch from a tree on the other side of the street and lunged it out into the intersection in front of our home. It was not so much the limb coming off that bothered me. Rather, the amount of space the limb traveled before landing alerted me to the fact that it was time to take Mom's advice from years before: "Get in the house!" Her words, even in my mind, were louder than the force of the gale. (I also heard in my mind's ear Mom's follow-up comment when she would hear of my doing something like sitting out in a high wind where branches could land on my head: "I always have to worry about you." I am glad that she did.)

It was 2010 and James was outside with me as the thunder rumbled, and the clouds thickened, and lowered in the sky. Our friendly mailman, Joe, was wondering if his rounds would be completed before the rain started. I was doubtful, but gave him words of encouragement all the same. About fifteen minutes before the first raindrop landed, a huge wind bank thrust itself over Lake Monona and churned the water into whitecaps.

James and I ventured head-first into the gusty winds toward the B.B. Clarke Beach. No sooner had we made it down into the park than right in front of our eyes in very slow motion a huge tree was letting go of the shoreline. More troubling was the fact that there was a woman practicing Tai Chi only a short distance away. The tree tilted and leaned. The woman appeared not to notice. We shouted for her to get to safety. Running as quickly as we could toward the spot where she was so serenely meditating, we shouted for her to get out of the way. She did, and none too soon. The tree tilted and leaned a bit more until it landed on the ground. (I had never seen anything like it before, and certainly not in real-time. I don't know how things work in the forest when a tree falls, but in the city, they do produce a bit of noise.) Crack! The roots gave way from the earth holding them and stood on edge. I heard, even if only faintly, my Mom asking what in heaven's name I was doing out in the storm.

The roots of the tree had been exposed to the elements by

erosion. There was no way that the tree could have lasted many more seasons. I personally had predicted that it would fall in the dark of night, during a blizzard, or heavy rainfall, but never would have guessed that it would come down right in front of my eyes.

James and I ran to where the once tall tree then rested. We asked the Tai Chi practitioner if she were all right. She was visibly more serene than I would be if a huge tree had plopped down alongside me. Her meditation really worked, even if it had almost meant the death of her!

Needless to say throughout winter, the wind chills our home just a bit colder than it would if we were a block or so further inland. With only 'dead-space insulation' in our Victorian home (which was the norm at the time it was constructed) as a barrier to the outside means that comfortable sweaters are always stocked in the closet.

Our Madison home was built in 1892 of white pine, which rivals any of the more sought after hard woods as it dried. The house was made to last against any wind. Being a history buff I very much enjoy the 'real feel' of living here. Granted, central heating and cooling makes our home comfortable, and yet when the wind blows, and it comes in around the 'coffin door', I am reminded of what the first residents here experienced, and I smile. I think part of living in these homes is to experience them.

When I first moved to Madison whenever the first snowflakes fell there was always a phone call placed to my folks to alert them to the event. Dad really did enjoy knowing where it was snowing in the state, and always would add some back and forth about the weather in Hancock. For all the remaining years of my folks' lives, the calls came every fall when the first flakes fell.

With the passing of my parents, the season's news of the first snow at our home is now shared with a call placed to Aunt Evie who seems to delight in the weather too. It remains one of the special rituals of winter.

No matter how old I am there is still a thrill to waking up, looking out, and yelling to James, "It is snowing!" I have come to realize that this 'snow thing' is something that either one has in their DNA, or it is not. There is no way to force the love of snow, but when it has taken hold there is also no way to dislodge it.

My favorite place to view the winter storms now are from the large windows as I sit in one of our rockers. Only about twenty feet from the Adirondack chairs where we sit in summer, my wintertime perch is pretty posh. I know Mother Nature has sneaked up too fast with the change in seasons when I am inside all warm and cozy as the snow falls and I remark to James "Holy Cow, time to bring in the lawn chairs!"

When James and I moved into our home on the isthmus

a snow blower came with the house, and was stored in the basement. It had not been used much by the previous owner as the winters were not always intense, and in addition Henry was not much of an outdoors type of guy in the cold season. I think also he might have had some difficulties getting the blower in and out of the bulkhead door that leads into the basement. In fact, as we were to discover for the previous nine years the blower had sat untouched, and just did not operate.

We were forced to bring out the shovels, and we basically kept them out as we were responsible for snow removal from a record-setting Madison snowfall for the 2007-08 winters season. One hundred eight inches in total fell that winter. We were out there shoveling every other day.

Unlike those who have short driveways, and limited sidewalks to take care of, we have just the opposite. Our driveway is full length, and we also live on a corner, so that means we have 2,331 square feet of space to shovel. That comes out to about 1105 square feet of driveway, and 1226 square feet of sidewalk. I sometimes tell an unsuspecting person that the sidewalks are wider in winter than in summer, and it surprises me how there are a few who look puzzled. Somewhere on the next block as they walk away, I assume, it registers and a smile comes across their face.

I hold to the view that snowstorms and winter weather can and should be fun. When I was boy and reading every book I could about how weather events happened, and some of the science behind it, I was struck by a really grand idea. I will admit, however, that the look on my Mother's face when I told her what I had in mind was not what I had hoped.

With truly frigid weather gripping Hancock it was the time to get a mug of boiling water, and then go outside and lean away from the walking area and throw the water up into the air. My face erupted in a smile as the water turned to vapor and created a cloud of moisture. Here is what really happened: the water, as it is tossed in to the winter-chilled air breaks into tiny liquid water droplets, most of which will evaporate before they hit the ground. The rate of evaporation depends on the temperature difference between the water and the air. By dispersing the liquid water into a collection of liquid water droplets the surface area is increased. The combination of hot water, cold, dry air, and high surface area causes most of the tossed near-boiling water to evaporate before it hits the ground, and the tiny droplets that don't evaporate will freeze into ice crystals while still in the air. Science is exciting.

Feel that Breeze!

I know there any many who just truly hate snow and the cold temperatures. James claims not to be fond of such weather but I must say he is always willing to head out with me for the mandatory walks during winter storms. The ferocity of winter has lost its identity in Wisconsin, and that boy who once marveled at the snowfalls has lost some hair, and the rest is graying. What counts about winter weather and the snow is how it makes me feel on the inside.

I have always felt there are some rules that need to be followed when a snowstorm hits:

Get up.
Step outside.
Lift your head up.
Taste one snowflake.

Then think back to the first time you did this as a child. Too often we let our adult minds form how we think about the simple things in the world. Snowstorms make adults think about driving, shoveling, and snow on the roof. The adult mind just complicates everything. Slow down, take a few minutes of quiet time to think back to how you once saw snow, and then let it all happen again in your mind--at least for a few minutes. Then make the snow day count by steaming up the windows at home with a pot of soup, as my Mom always did. She was good at steaming up the windows. In fact, had there been close-ups of our home on those days there would have been, without doubt, no way to see through those then opaque panes of glass.

Why not get photos of your own house in winter. Don't let the scene be left out of your family album because of the apparent humdrum nature of the shot. Sometimes, the most ordinary of things make the best of art. If one had been able to take a picture from above our house a careful observer would have noticed foot tracks in the highest snow drifts--prints that would have been child-sized. Walking in the snow and storms is even better now as an adult since I have an amazing partner to enjoy it with me. We have lots of snapshots to prove it.

There is majesty to the quiet in the city when few dare venture out in a car during an all-out snowstorm. The quiet of the snow seems somehow more intense when it is dark outside. The winds howl and burst with energy around parked cars being covered in white layers, in between houses, and up the alleys making for what I consider a thrill ride taken on foot. My breath is taken away by the cold sharp burst of the unseen gust, and snow seeps down the inside of my coat. Who cares? Onwards! This is winter, and it is to be enjoyed! Weather is one of the joys free to be embraced. Weather is wild and unable to be tamed. It shapes us, and makes us conform to it. It proves what is powerful versus those who think they are powerful. It makes us the size we really are in the scope of things.

Before closing this chapter, I have a bit of a confession to make. The one thing I have noted, after having the issue brought to my attention, is how much mid-westerners are always talking about the weather. As proof, I point out that you, my reader, have, after all, graciously enjoyed a whole chapter devoted to it. I had never really noticed our proclivity for meteorological chatter until James, who grew up in Maine, pointed it out to me early in our relationship.

James was simply amazed at how truly serious conversations in my family, once they got testy or aimed to the heart of the matter being discussed would so abruptly get changed to how much rain had fallen that week, or when the latest cold snap would be over. Folks in Maine are not known to beat around the bush or couch dysfunctional behavior behind an argument over the latest low-pressure system. It seemed to James that, in my family, there was no issue that could unite everyone together better than the latest threat of rain, or the lack of it, or the number of days since it last fell.

After James made mention of this peculiarity common among so many in my family I started to take more careful note of it. I will be darned if James was not correct. There I would be in the middle of a phone call with my Dad where I wanted to talk about a real family matter that deserved attention, and Dad would suddenly start talking about the cloud cover over Hancock. I felt a surge of frustration.

Over time, when it became less possible to have a real conversation about things that mattered, I too would jump to the weather as a way to keep the dialogue moving. While Dad was embroidering the conversation with rain gauge results, James would be smiling at me with an 'I told you so grin'. As James looked at me, I would just point out the windows at some cloud formation and James would whisper softly, "Incredible. Just incredible." I don't think he was talking about the cumulus nimbus; James was commenting on the conversation that 'Ma Bell' was helping to facilitate.

> *"The purpose of life is not to be happy. It is to be useful, to be honorable, to be compassionate, to have it make some difference that you have lived and lived well."*
>
> —Ralph Waldo Emerson

Paying it Forward

James and I have many blessings in our lives. From having good parents and homes, to curious minds, and the means to explore those things that interest us, we find richness in the real sense of the word, even if not always in the material sense that so many use as a benchmark. While every life has hardships and turmoil, and ours is no different, we each have looked at life, even before finding each other, as something that we do not just for ourselves, but as a way to assist others when able. We believe in generosity.

Joy and a deep sense of fulfillment spread over me the first morning I walked to the Wisconsin Capitol as an employee. The grandeur of the building, the fact I had an office window and was able to participate in the legislative process, all of those things formed the basis for my very intense feelings of personal pride and self-confidence. Within weeks of starting my job I made a personal vow. Given how hard I worked to get there, I would make every effort to assist someone else who also had the desire to help shape public policy, and participate in a more direct way in our democracy.

I had no way of knowing when a young man entered our

office shortly after lunch one day that I was about to come good on my vow. Brad was looking for directions to a different office when he came through our door; as it turned out, he was the one I would in small ways lend a hand. Brad was seeking work in the legislature.

Initially, I directed Brad to the office he needed to find. When he came back to the office soon thereafter I offered him a Blue Book, a bi-annual publication that details state government and all sorts of data about Wisconsin. I also offered a little advice that I hoped might prove beneficial. There was no way to know then that Brad would not only in time gain employment in the Capitol based on his skills and character, but that he also would become my best friend.

I have been blessed with wonderful friends who have made my life richer with laughter and spirited conversation. Brad was the one who connected with me in ways that left me thinking of him as the brother I wished I had. Our conversations were easy and drifted from topic to topic as we commiserated about life, politics, hopes, secrets, and our fears. It all reinforced how close I felt to him. He was the type of person I needed to be around while growing up and know the qualities he demonstrated as a friend would have been beneficial over the course of my life. I was grateful finally to have found him.

When Brad talked about his brothers and how they bonded, kicking back at one family gathering around a lake as they all enjoyed celebratory cigars, it made me aware of how not having a brother in any meaningful way—other than by blood relation—was something I really had missed in my life. Brad was a twin and could relate countless stories that brought hearty laughter. He and his brothers were always getting in to some sort of hi-jinx together. I had no such stories to share. We set about creating stories of our own, though, and that felt marvelous.

Working at the capitol, payday came once a month, and with cash in our accounts two things were certain. The first was that Brad and I would go out and play darts, drink a couple beers, and grab some dinner. There was also a vow made each month that it was a new beginning for fiscal responsibility. We weren't very good at keeping that promise and somehow our oaths to be better monetary stewards became as much a line to smile over as it was a goal to reach. We each knew that the chance we might fail in our mission was rather high; we also knew in just another month's time we could start anew. Our 'conservative' friends, who lumped us in with the rest of the "tax and spend liberals" they seemed to fear so may have been on to something, but we would never admit to it.

There were so many times to smile with Brad, but the best

ones were the least expected.

After a night of fun, I would find myself at home and start emptying my pockets. I might discover that while leaning in to throw a dart that Brad had slipped a piece of cheese into a pocket of my slacks. The following morning his smile was priceless as I recounted my surprise at finding a slice of Wisconsin's finest!

One of the grandest moments we shared was in Memphis, Tennessee when we visited Graceland, or as James likes to call it, 'Mecca'. Brad's then-girlfriend now his wife Ayesha joined us. Over the years Brad had heard every Elvis story I could tell, and knew my intensity for 'The King' was most real. As we left Elvis' home aboard a shuttle bus winding its way down the driveway, Brad put his hand on my arm saying, "Now I am a believer."

What started out as a vow of mine to help someone else land a job at the statehouse turned out to have allowed me the joy of a truly wonderful friendship. Mom was always interested in knowing more about Brad as well. She knew Brad had come from Missouri; to her mind, that meant he had a good solid foundation. My having friends with character traits of which she approved was something that did not change just because I got older. Once a Mom, always a Mom. She was right about Brad.

Brad believes in being a friend in the good times and the bad. The day of my Mom's funeral Brad drove nearly three and a half hours from his home in St. Paul, Minnesota just to be with me. I will never forget it. He was so gracious and kind; I was a bit of a wreck. Brad sensed that I needed a shoulder to lean on that day, and provided it. He even offered to drive my car, with James and me as passengers, behind the slow-moving hearse which carried Mom past the family home on the route to the cemetery where she would be laid to rest. Mom had wanted to go home; this processional was the best we could do for her. Brad understood how painful it was for me to take that car ride, and he gave James some needed relief too in taking the wheel. Brad's compassion and continuing friendship has made my life richer.

Though it was never said in so many words around our home there was a lesson that came through in the actions that I witnessed over and over from my parents. That lesson: with blessings come obligations.

Dad helped more than one motorist to change a tire, or get free of a snowdrift. He helped others because he wanted to and would actually run from those who dared offer pay him for his generosity and time. "Just help someone else out when they need it," were the words that linger in my mind. In Dad's world, generosity was about the way things were supposed to work. Dad's system was pretty good, it seems to me.

With that as a starting point, it might then seem a most weighty question as how to repay the kindness of someone who writes a Will, and leaves you a home. That is what happened to James and me when we discovered that our friend Henry Dudek left his home, a condo in a Victorian duplex, to us upon his passing in 2007.

We were swept over by a flood of emotions when we learned of the news. James and I had been living on the West side of Madison, and while looking for a house had also not found anything that we liked in our price range. While we were content where we lived, we also wanted the freedom that comes with owning, along with the economic benefits that come with no longer paying rent. We had been to the credit union, approved for the search, but just never located a place we loved and felt comfortable enough with to want to call our own.

The morning after Henry's passing, we were asked to join several of his friends at Henry's home. We discovered that the place where Henry had called home for the previous fifteen years had been left to us in a bequest in his last Will. Quite literally overnight, we became the owners of a property only seventy steps from Lake Monona with an unobstructed view. There was a very deep sense of appreciation. Then there was the much larger question of how to say thanks.

Part of the journey in finding an answer about how to repay the kindness and extreme generosity was to consider how it had come to happen in the first place. About a year before Henry died, he called to ask us for some personal information. He said that he was updating his Will, a chore which he did every decade or so "whether it needed it or not". While we didn't fully know the extent of what he was planning, we gave him the information that he requested, and thanked him for including us in his plans. Before ending the conversation, though, Henry told us that he wanted to find a way "to reward our spirit of generosity". We didn't ask him what he meant at that time. We didn't want to seem craven since the discussion was focused on Henry's end-of-life planning. With that said, it doesn't mean that we did not spend time later trying to understand what he wanted us to glean from the conversation.

Henry first and foremost had a very engaging and generous spirit. He breathed classical music and had an astonishing, completely catalogued, collection of CDs. He also had two season tickets to the symphony--one for himself, and one so he could share the gift of music with others. In fact, Henry, an altar boy as a youth, long hoped that when he got to Heaven, Saint Peter would hand him a harp, not an accordion! James has been graced with that collection that numbers in the thousands.

Henry loved TV, films, entertaining, gardening, eating, and chocolate. His many friends, who enjoyed the ever-ready teapot and treats, treasured his wide-ranging observations on everything from language, and how he thought words should be more efficiently spelled, to flowers. Henry, a self-taught gardener with an eye for beautiful color combinations and an Olbrich Gardens aficionado, willingly gave of his plant material, enlivening the hearts and surroundings of many; he was generous to a fault.

Henry, in 2001 suffered a very serious heart attack, had decided to celebrate his friends and their compassion for him with these words in a Thanksgiving letter. *"I find myself grateful and even joy-filled as I awaken each morning and am gladdened by the new day... appreciate every moment of your life as truly the gift that it is. And never ever forget how important your mere presence can be for another person suffering physical and spiritual pain."*

Henry insisted that his home be an inviting place where raucous laughter and sparkling conversation shared among friends were the rule. It was in his Lake Monona home of so many smiles, merriment and spiritual tranquility that Henry passed away on May 11, 2007.

Though it was never put into writing we knew in our hearts the reason for the amazing act of generosity when it came time to include us in the Will was due to how we had acted over the years of our friendship with Henry. When it came to holidays or special events James and I always showed up with a small gift or a dessert for teatime. This was a stretch when finances were tight, and yet we always made an effort to be generous. That is just how James and I live, and Henry noticed.

Henry used to say to James and me that even in the lean times we never forgot friends on their birthdays or holidays. Henry use to laugh that James could make copper wire by pulling on pennies. Even when the cash would have been nice, it was not uncommon for James to give a language lesson for free, and to even throw in a quick lunch for a lonely student. Our apartment table was always a place where another plate could be set, and another face welcomed. James' Mom, Marion, was the same way.

Over the past few years it has become clear to me that saying 'thanks' is best done by continuing to live as good friends to those in our lives. Often I have found that I end letters or emails with the words 'the teapot is always on' and invite folks over to our home. It is just a natural reaction as it reflects how we really live life.

Our friend, Henry, truly admired generosity, and not just the material sort. Henry saw that we were also generous with our time, and worked to make a difference when it mattered. A few weeks prior to Henry's passing, he called requesting someone come down to his place just to talk; he was also asking for some assistance with a few routine tasks that he was too weak to handle given his health. We headed down to the isthmus to see what needed to be done. We would have gotten there earlier had we already been showered and James had his school bag packed for the night.

Never could we have imagined that upon Henry's death his home would be bequeathed to us. After all, that just never happens in the real world. We were friends, not relatives. And yet, as we joined Henry's friends that morning after he was found unresponsive, the home was ours. The question we needed to answer was how does one say thanks for such an enormous gift that has altered our lives, and profoundly impacted our way in the world?

Therefore, James and I both made a commitment, though not knowing exactly how it would unfold, to do something for someone else that really mattered. In the process we would come to learn more about generosity itself.

We have come to terms with those who are willing to give, and those who seemingly only ever take. We have seen time and time again that sometimes just giving is its own reward, and we are happy to have the time to be able to be as generous as we have been able to be. We recognize though that we could not have done it all without the generosity of others.

Henry wanted to "reward us for our spirit of generosity" by bequeathing us his home. By the time the gift was made, it was already too late to "say thanks" in the traditional sense. Without the home though, we would likely not have had the time to take on what was to be a project that truly made a difference for someone else, and assisted in continuing the human experience of 'paying it forward'.

When the nights get quiet and the neighbors' lights dim one by one, I often look out and wonder what others who stood at these same windows reflected on after the gas lights were turned off over a hundred years ago. After all, these homes are not just pine wood and blocks of stone. They are reservoirs of memories and stories. Real people lived, dreamed, loved, cried, and laughed here. New life came into the world within these homes. In other cases, like for Henry, some drew their final breath. In many ways though, we really feel that Henry's generosity wasn't in giving us the gift of his home. The real gift that Henry made to us was that of time. We've had time to reflect on our own lives, and that of the loved ones we have lost. We've enjoyed moments of peace and tranquility by the water's edge. But more importantly still, we've had time so we could help others, a much stronger gift indeed.

Albert Trull, Jr. was James' oldest Spanish language student in 2003. In Wisconsin, seniors have the opportunity to take classes at the technical colleges and universities for almost nothing more than a small administrative fee. Albert was taking full advantage of that program, and his presence in James' class would be not only the start of a friendship, but also the start of a long journey and a steep learning curve about one of the fastest growing diseases in terms of the numbers of Americans impacted.

James came home and told me that an elderly gentleman wanted to learn Spanish for the most unique of reasons. Albert wanted to learn Spanish so when he passed away, or "got to the other side" as he put it, he could communicate in the native language of his mother. Albert's mother was Pura Carrilles, a name that when translated means 'pure sounds of the bell', and she was originally from Cuba.

Albert was unique in all the ways that makes someone truly special; he soon became a friend who was invited for lunches at our home. He would join us too for political nights of convention watching or ballot counting. There were long chats on our lawn, one truly grand afternoon of bowling, and wonderful meals at restaurants. With the inclusion of other friends of Albert who lived at the Kennedy Manor on Madison's isthmus, James and I found ourselves laughing with a whole new group of people.

Albert was a most diversified conversationalist who could hold forth on the environment and the need for a green economy, which was his favorite topic, or the reasons the nation needed universal health care. He had a Ph.D. in Urban Planning and worked thirty-seven years at his private architectural practice in Tallahassee, Florida.

Albert was simply an amazing man given his scope of interests, and his relaxed southern style of living life. I never saw him mad at the world, but only at times frustrated with his own perceived lack of abilities. He was the consummate life-long learner.

A couple of years after meeting Albert things started to change as the disease that would become the last chapter of his life started to manifest itself more clearly. One day Albert asked James for help in setting up easier ways to do some simple everyday tasks. That morphed into arranging on-line payments for bills. In time James and I were seeking ways to make sure he was safe where he lived, and when that was no longer an option finding suitable housing for someone suffering with Alzheimer's.

Along the way we learned enough about the process of how to advocate for someone with Alzheimer's that we considered writing a book. The court granted guardianship of Albert to James, and the local Alzheimer's advocacy group suggested we might think about helping by advising others facing the same issues.

We had moments of drama when we tangled with those who we knew did not provide service for Albert as promised. But then we found angels who we praised as they understood that respect is something everyone deserves at all stages of life.

Never did we take our eyes off the goal, and that was following through on the promise we made to Albert at our kitchen table that we would look out for him right through the end. In his estimation, we did such a good job that he even referred to James and me as "Albert's Mafia". At times a number of staff members at the facility where Albert resided did seem a bit more attentive to Albert's needs when he used the term. More and more I am fearful that our nation is unprepared to handle the scope of this disease. We lack trained workers, solid and well-regulated facilities, and worst of all, we refuse to properly fund research to better understand the medical mystery that brings one of the most debilitating diseases to so many.

Watching a woolly caterpillar cross the sidewalk makes me very aware of the transitions that are all around us. Depending on what grandparent I recall listening to from my youth, the width of the black stripe either means a snowy winter, or a more moderate cold season. Either way, when we are in the last half of summer, with the school supplies piled high in stores, and kids starting to dread the return to classrooms, I am aware of the constant tug of time pulling us ever forward.

While I never 'wish time away' by hoping it was 'next Friday' or that special event down the calendar, I found a summer or two ago that I was trying to slow things down even more than usual. Albert, suffering from Alzheimer's, made me aware of the tick... tock...tick of the clock, and the importance of living life now; he made real the notion of living in the present.

For a number of years I had the ability to think of the more serious side effects of Albert's Alzheimer's disease as something that would happen off in the future. But when our friend who had authored an industry-standard book on educational planning could no longer write a check or tell time with an average dial I was aware that the progress of the disease had taken over my reluctance to accept all its side effects. While James and I served first as powers of attorney for our friend, and were making solid pragmatic decisions on the one hand, my emotional understanding of the situation had not kept pace. I was shocked at the idea of how a bright and inquisitive mind could be reduced to darkness.

Our friend bravely had fought and conquered cancer a decade prior to being diagnosed with Alzheimer's. With the latest medical technology he came through that harrowing medical experience only to find himself caught in the midst of a most hellish disease. The erosion of the mind, while knowing as time goes by that it is happening, is so cruel that it defies description. First Lady Nancy Reagan was far too kind when she termed it "the long good-bye".

I am one to laugh and joke, and so it was natural for me to comment, as I stood with Albert at the outside of a mutual friend's door one day after no one answered our knock, that she might be with her dark-haired Italian boyfriend out on the town. The blank look that crossed Albert's face hit me hard. The blank look was one of emptiness. No recognition that a lame joke had been told; there was no ability to put the pieces together. It took several seconds before there was a flicker of recognition, and I knew I had crossed a line that I would need to be more mindful of in the future. His ability to process even the most basic things had been severely impaired.

As we searched for a home where Albert could live in comfort and dignity, I was more aware than ever of the hardships that people with Alzheimer's face. Our friend had the resources to pay for his care, at least for a while, and would not be forced to ever see the inside of one of those dreadful nursing homes we all fear. Many are not so fortunate. Some will argue in dementia care that the patient will not be aware of their surroundings so the comfort is only for the family and friends who visit to make them feel good about where they put the one for whom they care so much. I disagree! I think it does matter. "There but for the grace of God go I" is the only way to proceed. I believe in the Golden Rule and I wasn't willing to abandon it.

Every now and then as I mow or weed or walk I wonder what prompted James and I to participate in Albert's emotional roller coaster. Much like seeing a kid in the street where a car is veering towards him or her, and we pull the kid back without thinking, this too has been on a much slower scale the same type of reaction. Not doing anything for our friend was never an option. We had the time, know-how and backgrounds to assist, and yet the process of acting is so segregated from the ability to reason the whys of this disease.

The indomitable spirit of our friend was truly amazing. During one phone conversation long after the disease had been diagnosed, Albert told me about wanting to continue to learn. His passion for knowing new things did not abate even though he had trouble processing what he read, and later had much difficulty at recalling it. He had found some tapes through The Learning Company on a topic that he wanted to buy. After a few minutes of conversation he told me he was having a really good day, and was truly happy. "I want all my days to be like this", he concluded as he ended our conversation.

Because of that call James and I did something we do not do very often, though I am not sure why. We drove to Michael's Frozen Custard and had malts. After all the tick...tock...tick...is something we all need to be mindful of, as the transitions of life do not slow for any of us.

When it came time for us to assist Albert in moving to a facility where he could receive better care than he was able to provide for himself, we devised a plan to make the transition as smooth as possible.

After an intense twelve-hour day James and I were exhausted in every sense of the word. Albert was moved to an assisted living facility in a fashion that was modeled after a White House move when a new president is inaugurated. That kind of transition was something I had often read about and it seemed like it would work well for Albert's needs, just as it would an incoming President. Everything was orchestrated from the one (Carmen) who would keep our friend active and away from all the 'action', to the workers who helped us make the transition by packing ('Gussie') and unpacking (Lori). From the letter that we prepared in advance for the staff at the new facility to read so to better understand the new resident that would appear among them, to top-notch guys from a moving company who went above and beyond the original plan, to the pictures we took of his bathroom and desk so to be able to re-create them, to the card we dropped in the mail so Albert would have something from the postman on the first full day at his home, we aimed to make Albert's transition a smooth move. Simply put there were many reasons to be thankful when all was completed. Nothing was left to chance, and every base was covered.

Prior to coming to a final conclusion in our own minds that it was indeed time for Albert to be relocated, we consulted with a specialist trained to help those of us caring for someone suffering with Alzheimer's disease. She was very helpful and kind. She advised us, after our inquiry into how best to prepare our friend for the move, that we should just take him out for an errand and wind up at the new home, presenting it to him with tender words. I was aghast. I held my tongue, but once in the car after the meeting James and I spoke of having different DNA in our makeup, making it impossible to deceive our friend. James was right there with me in agreement and said there was no way we could operate in such a fashion. After all the time being honest and forthright about matters, all of that good would disappear if we were to have acted in such a fashion. All trust with our friend would have been lost, and rightly so.

We chose a different path, and one that with some prayer and hope proved to be the perfect way. While we had talked about these matters at the time our friend put his wishes into legal documents many months prior, having that same discussion is much different when the mind is muddled by Alzheimer's. So we started introducing topics such as 'what items from your home would you want in the event that you were to move'? Albert was able to see the direction we were headed, and understood it was the path that needed to be taken. He asked us, "What sort of place do you think I need?" James replied, "I want you to go to a place where you can have the same level of care that Gregory gets at home." Albert smiled. I laughed. Albert knew I was pretty spoiled. We sat for a long time that Sunday afternoon discussing with Albert how we cared for him and had planned for an eventual move for many months. We asked him to trust us, as he had done all along. We told him that there was a place that we liked, and felt he would like too.

The next day Albert was moving ahead in his mind about 'a move' without knowing the specifics, all designed on our part to keep a level of unneeded anxiety from entering the picture. He wondered how the mail would be arranged, and how his friends would be alerted to the news. He was starting in small ways to claim ownership of the idea. With a gentle hand we had moved the plan ahead.

James and I arranged for a full day of friends and laugher when it came time for the move to take place. We engaged our friend Carmen to take Albert out for a day in the city. Meanwhile a truly special group of people assembled and started from scratch to move a large section of our friend's possessions to his new home. Later we would learn that he felt something like a move must be in the works as all the pieces from the previous days were falling into place in his mind. He also knew that once we said something would happen, it did!

With staff from other sections of the facility stopping in to see what was described to them as something 'very creative' being assembled, we were sure that the path we chose for our friend was indeed the correct one. From his unique wooden day bed to his drafting table from Italy, to his pictures on his wall, and large splashes of color in the room, it all became a true reflection of who was to live there.

When Carmen drove our friend up to the door of his new home he was thinking that perhaps this was the day of the move, but was not sure. When James ushered him into his room it was the look we had hoped for, one of surprise not so much at the fact he was in his new home, but the fact that in just hours so much of his world had moved and been arranged in the fashion he loved. He was genuinely moved and touched, sitting down and just not sure what to say. He gave hugs, and then gave more hugs. It was like Christmas morning as his delight was clear by the beaming smile, and then still more hugs.

I am sure there are many ways to deal with these matters at the time when a loved one needs more care than can be provided at someone's home. But I think it essential to allow the person most impacted to be a part of the process and claim ownership of the decision. I know the path we took allowed for a more productive time for our friend as he started that chapter of his life in a facility.

We told him as we left late that evening that he could have anything he wanted for breakfast, and his simple request was, "Do they know how to make grits?" We told him if they don't they will soon!

Several months later, we took our friend on a ride in our vehicle. That may not seem like news of any kind. It was, however, to be his last ride 'out and about' for fun. After that trip there would be less of an outside world to participate in, and instead more personalized care in a new home to match his growing medical needs.

Albert's agony during his later years made me wonder how this all fits into the bigger puzzle that we call life. This type of question has abounded since the start of time, and the answers are as elusive as they ever have been. That does not stop me from pondering "why", and for what purpose does all this happen?

Alzheimer's had robbed our friend of so many abilities that moving him about, as well as every other aspect of living, required skilled nursing care. There was no more carefree banter, or spontaneous laughter between us. The big stage light of a life was being narrowed bit by bit to a small glow. The Ph.D. could no longer even write his own name. In time, our friend journeyed to an even more specialized home at Badger Prairie Health Care Center.

In order to make the move possible there were a few legal hoops to jump through; since we weren't Albert's family, a judge needed to approve some of our decisions. James and I were in court to secure guardianship of our friend. It was not the first time that James and I felt the weight of the responsibility for our friend, after all we had done everything financially and legally as his representatives for several years by then. If we had to do it all over again, we would sign up as it remains the right thing to do.

There were times that James and I have shed some tears over being the ones that had to literally see his authority to make decisions erode as the powers that he signed over to us years prior forced our hands to insure his safety and well-being. While what we did met the praise of the court, social service agencies, Alzheimer's Association, and all the medical teams with whom we had interacted, there was no way to describe the taking away of ones' rights—for me, the worst was when the guardianship papers were signed and I realized that Albert had even lost the right to vote. I must admit there was some humor in the court room when it was stated (again) that our friend was not to be allowed to have a gun.

The journey that this disease had forced our friend to take was also one that has altered our lives and sharpened our focus on how to fight for what is right. From having his apartment fitted for safe-living, to finding alternate housing as the disease progressed, to fighting for better food and more activities in that facility, to then seeking more professional care as events warranted, there was always 'something' out there. We sat through a number of meetings that lasted up to two hours or more just to have contractual agreements fulfilled; we fought for fresh vegetables and more fruit at meal time, and assurances that medications made it to the pharmacy to be bubble-wrapped as was required by law. We worked to make sure no issues were dropped or ignored. We became pains in the butt to some, and friends to others, even if we never knew their last names.

When things did not go according to how we knew they should for the safety and happiness of our friend, Albert, we went to the state agencies that govern the facilities. We were not afraid of making a scene to insure the right things were done, especially when our solemn word was given years back to do the very best when things got tough.

Every assisted-living facility has a "Rosina".

The Rosina I knew was near ninety years of age, walked with a cane, and to be honest looked every bit her age. She was tall and thin, but I strongly suspect as a young woman was quite attractive. Over the months when we visited Albert, I chatted with her about once a week, and was able to make her laugh in my own quirky way.

As I walked down the hallway of the facility she opened her door and slowly came out. "Hey beautiful," I said. A broad smile spanned her face and she turned and looked back into the room and replied, "Who else do you see in there?" She was never short of a good response for anything I said.

And so our conversation started as I walked slowly alongside her down the hallway. She never walked far but she talked with every step. Her eyes were still expressive and when she told a bit of a fib, or something that she thought was slightly off-color, her eyes twinkled. I can say with candor that Rosina's eyes let others know she was younger on the inside than her wrinkled face suggested.

I could sense many things about the residents. Some doors were closed, and some while open never provided a glimpse of the person who then for one reason or another called that place home.

One man, Linus, sat in the same chair in his room every single day, looking out the same window onto the back road of the facility. I never failed to greet him, and during football season asked how his Dallas Cowboys were faring. He was watching his team the weekend when James and I moved Albert into the facility. For some reason he seemed like he needed a friendly "hello".

During one of our chats Linus told me he lived in "a prison". I could not argue with him, but did ask what I might do to make things easier. His simple request was to have another of the cookie packets that were kept in a drawer in the kitchen. After making sure he was not diabetic I grabbed cookies from the stash in the kitchen and dropped them off more often than not when I visited.

"It is against the rules", he told me. "I just made a new rule," I kept repeating. What could possibly happen at his age if he consumed a couple extra cookies? It certainly could not hamper his appetite any more than looking at the actual food they served in that place. (Truth is most of these facilities are the same when it comes to the list of complaints.) There is no way to truly describe the colorless, tasteless, and often odorless food that makes its way in front of each of these residents. Though James and I made the squeaky wheel sound, and at the edges created a difference both for Albert, and the others who lived in the facility, it was nowhere enough. We had meetings with the management of the place, and even got state agencies involved. In the end everyone willfully missed the obvious. Some old-fashioned cooking with real ingredients would do more to boost the spirits of these folks than any modern medicine. That fact can be taken to any bank.

Creating happiness is not difficult. Another of our new friends, Pat, who also lived at the facility told us they never had chocolate cake. "Everyone sure would love some," she mentioned as she sat in her wheelchair. James decided he would whip up a cake and take it with us on our next visit. The night when it was baking we decided to get an egg timer. The cake was baked! Burned would be another way to describe it. There was no way to take that one anywhere. We had to postpone our plan.

Shortly thereafter Pat was taken to hospice as her medical

situation turned very serious. I felt really guilty about not getting that cake request completed, and told James we had to still make one and take it to her. On a chilly Sunday afternoon in late winter we met her grandson and friends at the hospice facility. She smiled over the cake, but I am not sure she was ever able to enjoy any of it. She deserved better.

Pat wasn't alone. Rosina. Linus. Albert. Bette. They all deserved better.

One afternoon, as I was about to leave the assisted living facility I noticed a newspaper article. Taped on an office door was the face of Bette. The picture had been taken several years before I knew her. Her hair was thicker but still snow-white. I had always envisioned Bette having white hair early in life as a genetic hand-me-down, and not just from the effects of aging. Her smile in the picture was brighter than I ever knew it. Her cheeks were fuller. The words that cascaded below the picture were the ones that her family had penned for her obituary.

I had not known she had died.

I had spoken with Bette in the hallways of the facility and listened over the course of the spring and summer as she told me about surviving bouts of cancer. When she told me about the doctors suspecting she had lung cancer and the need to be tested all I could do was listen. At some point words are trite, and for a veteran of the cancer wars as she was, I knew I had nothing to offer. When the conversation could be turned gracefully I made attempts to produce some laughs and smiles. I found in that facility that laughter was more my strength.

Though my old-fashioned (some might say corny) humor has more of a chance with the men and women of Bette's age there is no way to keep the smile pasted on the faces of those who live in such places. In these types of facilities merriment is not easy to come by, and never lasts long. The reason is that many of these places where far too many older people live are really quite unprepared for much more than collecting the monthly payment. It's a harsh reality--but true. (There are some very nice facilities where the best of care is provided. The problem is that most people do not have the financial means to see their final years in such places.)

Bette would glide around in a mobility scooter that is often advertised on television. I thought when seeing her roll towards me that the ads were so unbelievably deceiving. The ads made it look like life was all one big bouncing moment where motorized rides would give a new lease on life. The latest such television ad has a frolicking moment as a woman spins in her new chair while family surrounds her.

Reality is of course far different. No one gets such a chair without more pain and woes than one should have to shoulder.

In addition, I suspect the television family never arrives with the chair. As with batteries, families are not included.

It was from the chair that Bette would tell me about how Albert was doing. After all, Albert was the main reason we stopped at this place. I relied on Bette and others to give me information about his good and bad moments. Bette always did so with razor-sharp clarity as her mind was as sharp as a new Bic shaver.

When the conversation would drift to other topics Bette would let me know the same thing I had heard from others I spoke with at this facility. There were hardly ever any fresh fruits or vegetables to eat. The food was from cans, over-cooked, and tasteless. "Eating had once been so fun," she told me one day. I can still hear her say, "I do not look forward to meals anymore." It was not because she was older, or sick. She was just tired of being so removed from what she once knew, and felt should be provided in this place she now had to live. After a lifetime and making it to old age there really should be more than mushy processed food from institutional sized cans. There really should be more for $3,400 dollars a month than to roam up and down gloomy hallways waiting to die.

As the baby boomers age, and live longer due to medical advances, more and more will find themselves in such places as the one Bette lived. At some point down the road, when it is too late, these boomers will recognize that they did not put enough muscle into affecting change in these facilities by making demands of lawmakers. At some point many will know full well, in their own lives, why Bette deserved better.

All of these tales about our friends from the assisted living facility leads me to where I am heading: life is too short not to make a difference for those around us. There are ample resources and groups in every community that can make a difference to some elderly and infirm people who live in assisted living facilities. It might be the Boy Scouts planting some fresh flowers along the drive, or in containers for the inside. It might be three to four voices from the local church with a pitch pipe that show up after dinner for a few songs. If might even be the local high school band getting a few kids with musical star power to play after school. Of course, a person from the neighborhood with good vocal chords to read aloud a short story some afternoon would also be a real tonic. Last, but not least, the demand for national health care must always be front and center in our discussions.

There is one thing of which I am sure. I know that wherever one reads this, or whatever activity it takes to get residents assembled, there will be a 'Rosina' in the crowd. She will be looking her age perhaps, but the twinkle in her eye will say it all. "Thanks for making me smile today".

On October 29, 2012 at 5:00 P.M., Albert passed away after having a rather typical day at the Badger Prairie Health Care Center, a truly exceptional and caring place with amazing staff. There was no pain, and it was very quick. As strange as it may sound given all that had happened, Albert's passing still seemed to me rather unexpected. It looked as if he just fell into a calm sleep. There is something sad, and yet comforting in the final image that I have of Albert. The body that had become a prison for Albert had released the soul.

We had kept our promise made to a very special friend.

Over the years while James and I had made a concerted effort to make sure that Albert had his needs met, and done so with respect by those who were charged with his care, we had suffered personal losses in our own families. Each of our Mom's would die from cancer, and my Dad from heart disease.

When it came to Albert's care there was a real sense that helping him allowed me to not only serve in a way that helped pay forward the blessings we had received, but also allowed me to place my energy in a cause when it was not possible to help with my own ailing father. While Dad was dealing with the problems that most experience as they get close to ninety years of age he was also dealing with an aneurysm that was inoperable, severe hearing loss, and most regrettably deep grief that was never addressed from the loss of Mom who had made the trains run on time in his world for almost sixty years.

There was never a way for me to address the needs my Dad faced, or for me to help make the concrete decisions that were needed to ensure that the best ones were being made for his care. I had worked in a legislative office, and knew how to cut through the red tape to get needed programs that could better assist Dad's problems. I had decades of life experiences outside of Hancock that allowed for the perspective needed to assist with Dad's multiple-layered issues that were both physical and emotional. By the time Dad was knee-deep in need of help James and myself already had for several years been dealing with Albert and his medical needs in such a way that a judge from the bench would address us with "If I ever need the type of care Albert is receiving I only hope I have two people like you to advocate for me."

As it became clear that there was no way to have any real input into the care of Dad I ramped up my energy and resolve to make sure that Albert had my full attention. My willingness to help and make a difference reminds me of water always finding a way to get through the cracks in the wall.

I knew that things for Dad were really terrible when I came home one weekend and found him sitting in his chair in the living room, his face lost to his memories. "I just can't keep the house as Genie had it," he said. I kneeled by him, and all I had to do was place my hand on his shoulder and he melted into vocal sobs and a deep cry. A couple years had elapsed since the death of his wife and he had not been provided with grief counseling or assistance with finding the avenues needed in how to vent his feelings over his loss.

I talked with him for a while that afternoon, and did what might be achieved in a short visit, but left knowing he needed my type of conversation every day, and that was not possible given the situation. Dad needed to know it was fine to talk about something other than the weather, and cry, shout, and scream. He needed to know that opening up and digging into the soul might hurt, but also was healing.

I had hoped that Dad might find comfort in his many friends in the community who gathered for a noon meal at the senior center. Healthy prepared food, but more important conversations and laughter with people he had known almost his entire life. I knew that this would be a tonic, even if he could not initially envision it. I knew that after a short time of eating there he would be getting up in the morning and looking forward to it as he was a very social person. But I was never able to convince Dad of that idea, and more importantly never gained other advocates to my cause.

Albert was not only a friend who I cared about but also a vessel in which I could place my skills and needed output of care and concern that I wanted to provide for Dad. Not being shy about getting counseling when I knew it would do me good, I questioned my therapist if I should feel guilty for 'using' Albert as a way to deal with not being able to assist Dad. "Everyone should have such guilt," was the therapist's response.

Over the years I have thought so many times about the gift that Henry made to us, and how that then allowed for us to provide time and energy to others who needed to be lifted up in their time of stress and turmoil. Henry had provided so much to charities over his life, and would have smiled knowing that his bequest of his condo continued the themes of his life through our hands.

I come from the old fashioned and perhaps politically toned notion that I am my brother's keeper. I deeply feel that if there is a way to help out someone then an effort should be made. In that way of thinking the term 'family' also takes on a larger connotation. We are all connected with each other even if we are not linked by blood. I know that Henry felt the same, and his actions by the use of his money prior to his passing, and the way his estate was divided after his passing only underscores his belief that family is much larger than the names in a genealogical chart.

Living life can be complicated, and it also can be quite simple. The lessons that are imprinted on us by our parents, and the inner compass that always directs shows the way. After that, it is up to each of us to take the next step.

James and I spent some time alone with Albert after he died. He was taken away under a Grandma-blue quilt. I followed a few steps to the door that was held open, the night had fallen heavy and Albert was pushed into the darkness. I looked up and the hazy full moon shined back. I stepped back from the door, and it shut. I turned to James and we hugged. It didn't seem all that complicated an idea to me. Paying it forward—being generous—all it really means is that we keep our promises made to very special friends. Sometimes, paying it forward is really just a way to keep a promise made to ourselves.

Saying 'thanks' for the gifts we are given in life might just be as easy as helping someone else get a job or dropping everything to go and spend time with an ailing friend. It might be about fetching an extra cookie, or baking a chocolate cake that makes all the difference. It just may be that when we are done here, they don't come to push us on a gurney out in to the darkness as it seemed they had for Albert. If we live life the way we are supposed to, they may just be pushing us in to a far brighter light.

> *"Show me your garden and I shall tell you what you are"*
>
> —*Alfred Austin*

A Shared Road

James and I reside in an old Victorian on a corner lot in the city of Madison. Seventy footsteps from the front stoop of our home my feet are on the shoreline of Lake Monona. The midway point to the lake from our home is Spaight Street. From there I gaze up the Madison isthmus to the magnificent State Capitol.

Every day in summer, we see walkers on their way to the bus stop, or out for an evening stroll. A biker's path along the lake affords us additional opportunities to converse with friends, and greet new faces. The corner lot where we live brings so many wonderful people our way. Robust conversations in our front yard create smiles. Living here is very fulfilling.

Strangers have provided insights into how to make this or that plant grow taller, where to get wild blackberries in Madison, or tales of graduate student studies in Africa. James and I have helped looked for lost cats and been invited to Karaoke.

James and I discovered in May 2007 that we were to inherit our home; the news came as a shock to us. Henry, a very good friend of ours had passed away and left us the condo in his will. That should have been the biggest surprise of the week. It was, except for a small incident which has lodged in my memory. While inheriting a condo may have been the biggest, it wasn't the only surprise. There are wonderful people in our neighborhood, and like everywhere there are those who stand out for being—well—unique. Let's be honest. People are funny, and to be more direct about it just plain 'peculiar'.

One of our first interactions with one of the neighbors involved a conversation that went something like this:

"I am so sorry about the loss of your friend."

"Thank you," we said. "This is all rather sudden and we are not sure of the next step we should be taking."

"Yes, it will certainly be a time of big changes for you. Heh? I suppose you will be dividing Henry's belongings soon. Would you mind if I had the shrubbery around the house?"

James and I must have looked like two of the most dumbstruck individuals on the block. Who makes such a request, and at a time like that? Who honestly gives away the landscaping to a home just because one of the owners has died?

"Well, no, thank you for asking." We responded. "Actually we thought we might use the shrubbery ourselves."

The neighbor was not finished.

"Well, how about that sunflower in the flower-pot? Can I dig that up and move it to our place?"

By now I was less than thrilled with the conversation, and declared that if the sunflower were left where it was, as the seed had been 'planted' by a bird or squirrel, everyone could enjoy it, including the neighbor and anyone else who might pass by our home.

Later in the summer, we did help Henry's Personal Representative to divide up the contents of Henry's home. We invited each of Henry's friends and former neighbors in to the house to say good bye to their friend and offered that they should take something from the table as a souvenir of their times spent together. Henry kept a drawer full of bobbles and do-dads on hand to give as parting gifts when he entertained. We had assembled all of those items and many of his pottery pieces and other personal possessions and suggested that people take something in remembrance of our friend.

Sitting outside on the lawn in our blue Adirondack chairs, I am constantly being reminded of both the good and the bad parts of being part of a neighborhood. Rarely will someone ask us for a clipping from one of our plants, or even if we wouldn't mind sharing a root when next we divide one of the hosta. We don't mind sharing in that way at all. In general, people are respectful and kind and seem to enjoy spending a few moments contemplating the view as they chat with us.

Some days are just more memorable than others. One afternoon a most pleasant sound wafted in on the warm lake air. A group of about ten women comprising a writers' group had gathered on the back patio area of a neighbors' place. They were there to talk about their creative efforts, and gain feedback from each other. A neighbor was sending out her first children's book to publishers at the time. The light-hearted banter and gentle laughter mingled with the tingling of glasses of ice tea. I was transplanting flowers, and doing some watering in our yard adjacent to theirs. The conviviality of the group was a most welcomed sound. It was the sound of friendship and sharing. Magnificent.

If I had to put all of this another way, I would have to say that socializing with others comes easily to me. Our neighborhood is a safe environment where James and I can live our lives openly. I have always needed that sense of safety that comes from knowing that I can be me unabashedly.

When I first started to school, kindergarten was a little rough. I was intensely shy and I felt a real need for personal security. For the first couple weeks, I insisted that I be allowed to keep my coat on and I simply refused to relinquish it. Hot or cold, I was not giving that jacket up to the teacher. For one, I saw no reason to since I "wasn't staying" anyhow. For another, that coat served in some fashion as a personal protection device. Linus, of Charles Shultz's *Peanuts*, had his little blue blanket and I had my coat. What could be more normal, right? As I grew more comfortable with my surroundings, and fought back my initial shyness, the teacher, Mrs. Dee, expressed much relief with regards to my progress in socialization. She reported to my parents that it was OK to remove the coat at long last.

Once I had that matter of personal safety and well-being resolved, I started to talk, and talk. I haven't stopped since. My gift for gab is an inherited trait. I come from a family that likes to talk. My Mom's family can start a conversation, and if there is coffee and a comfortable place to sit they will still be at it hours later. I am very much the same. Some of the best times for such talks were on Sundays when I went back home and Mom and I would chat about almost everything. After dinner Dad would go to the living room to watch *60 Minutes* but Mom and I would stay seated at the table and continue talking with a fresh cup of coffee.

You can imagine the dismay of my elementary school teachers though. There are still reminders of those childhood days in my office space at home. Perched up on one of the shelves of my bookcase there is one of the round badges on manila paper that my first-grade teacher made for me to wear in class. The badge's message is quite clear: 'Silence Is Golden'. Apparently, my teacher wanted me to reward her munificently in peace and quiet; I suspect she felt quite impoverished in that regard all year long.

When the golden silence that my manila badge promised to deliver failed to materialize, my first grade teacher came up with a different approach. Her novel idea: she instructed me one Friday afternoon to go home and talk all weekend long. I was not to stop talking even for a moment so that on Monday morning I would be all talked out. I would simply have talked so much that I would have nothing more to say when I returned to class the following week. Ideas like that must have looked good to her when proposed in the margins of her lesson planning book, but they failed to be taken seriously. More importantly, I am not sure what my parents thought about that teacher and her concocted plan over the weekend in question but I can assure everyone that the desired goal was not achieved. I was right back in class on Monday telling everyone around me what I had talked about all weekend.

Chatting it up was not only something that came down the DNA line from my Mom, but also from my Dad. The best example of his ability to strike up a conversation with someone he did not know came on Saturdays when my family went shopping. Many of my boyhood Saturdays were spent in Stevens Point. My folks drove there to buy groceries, clothes, shoes, and just about anything else we needed. My Grandma Schwarz called the medium-sized city simply the 'Points'. No matter what the place was called, Stevens Point offered the nearest real shopping experience to where I grew up.

I recall how we bustled around, and left our Hancock home at about ten o'clock so that we could spend the better part of Saturday in the city. My Mom looked forward to 'getting out of the house' and into the stores to browse. As a boy that concept was totally lost on me. How could anyone be amused by looking at bolts of fabric? But by the time my mid teenage years hit, I had changed my tune and fully understood the tug of browsing. I found myself wandering around music stores, and book stores. I was delighted to get out a bit too.

At times Dad and I would find ourselves sitting in the car in a parking lot in downtown Stevens Point. We'd either be located not far from the JC Penney store, or on a side street a block from the Montgomery Ward (which had hard wood floors that allowed for every customer's footsteps to be heard). In my mind I can still see the parking spaces where Dad would parallel park (not a skill that I profess to have) as it was shady during the summer, and would make the wait more relaxing. Dad was never a 'browser' but instead would read the newspaper or the mail that he needed to get caught up on while we waited patiently in the car for Mom.

Dad wasn't alone. There were plenty of other men waiting in nearby cars who seemed to have the same Saturday occupation as Dad did. On the days when I accompanied Mom to the shops, she and I would come back to the car to find Dad conversing and laughing with someone he had just met. Dad and his new friend might talk about cars, weather, or the latest headlines.

When I was old enough to start wandering on my own, Main Street in Stevens Point was full of wonders. It was alive, vibrant, and exciting. It was so different from my small hometown where a limited number of stores existed, and an even smaller number of people would be out at any given time. Saturdays in Stevens Point consisted of large store windows, honking car horns, interesting people to watch, and all those items that I could dream about owning someday. (My parents thought it a bit too exciting at the far end of Main Street where a bevy of bars were located. I was instructed to stay away from that area. Like they were going to serve a teenager!)

Main Street businesses in Stevens Point were not gleeful when the mall concept soon was all the rage. A shopping mall's appeal seemed to be tied up in the fact that all the shopping could take place 'out of the elements'. I much preferred darting raindrops or seeing the sun as I went from store to store. At holiday time, many of the older stores pumped music out into the streets, and Main Street was just like an old-fashioned Christmas card with snow packed crunching sounds underfoot, and crisp cold air.

Saturdays today are not so different for James and me. We go to Farmer's Market at the Capitol. I think about life while I am there and how fun it can be to just do nothing but talk with others. This is what my Dad enjoyed so much in life, especially on those long Saturday afternoons in the car. Dad was never able to sit on our lawn, and enjoy that part of our Madison life. He was never to see the view out onto the lake. Yet, there are times when there is a certain something in the way the breeze blows, or the way the sky looks, that makes me think perhaps he is seeing it after all. If he is listening in on the conversations from our lawn I know for certain he is thinking, "That's my boy!"

I grew up in the country. My neighbors consisted of my grandparents, and two sets of aunts and uncles. It made for a safe and nurturing environment, and was a good life for a kid, but there were many times when I desperately wanted more excitement. Watching a long row of bean-picking machines rumble down our country road was just not enough for me. I knew from reading newspapers and books that I wanted to feel the excitement of a city up close.

When I landed in Madison I found some nice apartments, and even some great friends who lived in them. For the most part the experience was limited in that I did not feel like I was a part of any community. I started out living in a small apartment downtown. While being independent and living on my own was exciting and rewarding, I did not have that sense of neighbors and inclusion at the time. I also was working hard at of the office and more focused on my career than on local issues in my neighborhood. While I saw some of the same faces in the building each week there was never an opportunity to talk and form any deeper sense of community. It was as if everyone were a satellite orbiting in individual paths. Otherwise said, I lived in the city but did not feel intertwined in the fabric of the place. Big apartment buildings breed isolation, not only within the actual residence, but also as a frame of reference. I recall that a pollster asked me in 1988 if I felt more a member of a neighborhood, our nation, or the world community. Clearly at that time in my life I did not feel a part of a neighborhood. I forget what my final answer to the pollster was.

Many of my friends at the time were experiencing what I still wanted from the places I lived. They resided in a neighborhood setting in Madison, and seemed to blend so easily. Many had grown up in other cities where blocks were dotted with homes and friends. I envied that sense of belonging, and wondered how one made it happen. The answer to my question was I just needed to give things more time. Life moves us in unique ways, if we are open to the changes.

James and I have both always sought out the sense of security that comes with knowing where we live is safe. We also wanted comfort in our surroundings. Over the years, before moving into our current home we had talked about what we would do if ever winning the lottery. One of the first things we both agreed at once in doing was buying a house, and having it paid for so that regardless of everything else we would have a home to live in, and call our own. We also wanted a place where we could live in harmony with others and ourselves. If one cannot feel at peace in one's own home than nothing else in life is going to be successful.

Needless to say, it was a big day when James and I became homeowners. At our kitchen table on September 15, 2007 where we share our meals every day, the legal documents authorizing the transfer of property were signed. (The day had an additional special side to it; it was also the fortieth wedding anniversary for James' parents.)

Becoming a homeowner evokes all sorts of imagery about the American Dream. We snapped photos of the signing, and know that it was a real milestone. Unlike lots of others who sign such papers there is a bit of old-fashioned rationale that goes into our thinking.

I know that there were those who harbored resentment that James and I were the new owners of our home. I had always heard my parents talk about how at the time of someone's death all sorts of very strange and unseemly behavior can take place, but I could never understand how that could happen. When it became known to a few how Henry had willed his condo it was not always pleasant, and that was a real wake-up to me about the ugliness that surrounds jealousy.

One such disgruntled person stated to everyone who would listen that James and I would not know how to decorate tastefully our new home. The person left the strong impression with others that we lived in a dorm-room style of mismatched furniture and cast-me-offs. Nothing could be further from the truth. We decorated our home with fine wooden furniture, a baby grand piano, and attractive matted and framed art pieces. The notion that we were in any sense not of the caliber to move into one of the historic districts of Madison because of a lack of design sense, of course, was absurd. The Probate court is not the arbiter of good taste after all; it rather has bigger fish to fry.

Too often we read and hear that the American dream of owning a home has lost some of its luster. This may be based on the reasons for which some buy, and own homes in the first place. As we all know falling home prices and foreclosures made for an economic nightmare. As a result many had come to think that home ownership was no longer a safe investment, but instead was more of an economic trap.

A safe investment! That whole notion runs counter to everything I have experienced in my life, and what James knows to be true as well. While I would never suggest anyone enter into a home purchase without the ability to pay the mortgage, I also would not steer anyone away from home ownership because it might not be a 'good investment'. In fact, I would argue that the investment view of home ownership is part of the problem we have had in this nation. Too many opted to make money with the purchase of a house. Buy big, and sell bigger was a theme that too many espoused. Greed and more greed were somehow thought of as good things.

I grew up with parents who became homeowners after World War II. The home they bought was not new, in fact, it was nearly one hundred years old, and needed lots of work. Over the years many projects were completed, including one that allowed for my brother and later me to have a new bedroom off on the side of the house. I have often joked that my parents were even smart enough to time our births so there was never a question my brother and I would have to share that room. He moved out on his own just as I needed to enlarge my living space.

For all the years I was growing up in the family home there was never, *not once*, any word spoken about what this improvement, or that addition, would do for the value of the house. The value of any improvement was the day-to-day pleasures and conveniences it made for the family. It was nothing more, and nothing less. The family home where I grew up was not so different from all those in my community. Inside were the favorite places to tuck away to read, the family kitchen where everyone gathered no matter how many people there were or how small the room might be, and the favorite window to watch the snow pile up or the rain fall. The home was a place to live and relax. It was a place to 'be'.

For many in our nation instead of thinking of a home as a place for treasured memories to be made and stored, houses have become a mere stepping stone to a larger house. The home became a simple house, nothing more than an investment. A warm place was reduced to a cold financial transaction. That, to me, is sad.

A house is cement, wood, walls, and a roof. A home is what is contained within the structure; some that can be seen, but more importantly sometimes home can only be felt. When I came back from a three-day camping trip in the sixth grade sponsored by the public school I entered the house at the back door made of wood. Mom greeted me with a huge hug as she had missed me; that alone made it so good to be home. That is the difference between house and home that too many with eyes only glued to money making ventures seem to forget, or never learn.

When James and I were making a series of improvements before we moved into our Victorian home, which included painting every wall in warm and bright colors, we were asked by lots of folks, "What about the resale value?" After all there is no beige or sea-foam green so how on earth can we ever think about making money on the house? We both had a stock response: "The next time we make a move we hope we are the ones that will be going in a box" (as in being planted in one). "Others will have to think about what colors *they* like; we plan to live in this house for a long time."

Long before I met James, and still longer before we moved into our home I was in the process of working out my own questions about where I wanted my life to head. Finding our way in the world, a place where we belong, and fit in is not easy. It seems all my life I have tried to think things out, and reflect about where I am, and where I want to head next. Trying to gain inner perspective is not always easy, but it is something for which I have continually strived. I know that it has allowed me to become a stronger person, and clearly a much happier one.

Starting the next chapter of life for anyone is never easy, or self-evident. I learned that in order to move forward an honest and careful review of the past needed to be undertaken. I like to be in touch with my emotions, and work to take steps at self-improvement, though slow and stodgy at times that process may be. I was eager in many ways to discover my path forward after leaving the office at the State Capitol. My very identity, it seemed, had been housed for many years at the statehouse. I needed to rethink my future self.

Over the course of my adult years I had always held to the idea that at those times when I felt lost and confused and wondered if things could ever be better was when I needed to go somewhere deep within, and hold to the faith that better days were ahead. I had always allowed myself the opportunity to confront and feel everything that I was being dealt, regardless of whether it was fair or not. By knowing that all my emotions and feelings were mine, and I owned them and they were a part of me allowed for a real examination of them. After that, I could try to find a more happy and productive way to move ahead with life.

This huge examination of my 'self' started in earnest in the summer of 1994. The events that would unfold over the next two years would in time lead me to a new set of priorities for my life.

It did not happen all at once. It never does.

My lessons in introspection began in the early fall that year while sitting on a bench at the Wisconsin State Capitol. I had pulled my car into a parking space on the Square. The fall elections were underway and open parking spaces were not hard to find. The legislators were back in their districts pumping the hands of voters for support.

On the front seat of my car was *The Hunt for Red October* by Tom Clancy. Though I always read a lot, it was the first fiction book I had picked up since graduating high school. The last fiction book I had read prior to moving to Madison was *The Fifth Horseman* by Larry Collins and Dominique LaPierre. It was a riveting drama about a terrorist threat from Libyan leader Gaddafi as New York City is held hostage with the threat of a hidden nuclear bomb. With such a long stretch between reading tense dramas I walked to a bench alongside the square that fall afternoon with the first of the *Jack Ryan* series, and sat down to read for a few minutes.

As I looked about I saw guys in suits, professionally dressed women, lobbyists, members of the press all proceeding along with the duties of the day. There is no place like the statehouse for excitement, and I just sat and watched the various players move about in their unrelenting missions. At a real level I missed being a part of the process I saw playing out in front me, working with those who made the headlines that would get printed in the next morning's newspaper. As I watched I also knew there was something missing in my life. Some deeper contentment that I could not put my finger on was absent from my life. I just felt something else 'was out there', and available to me if I could only tap into it.

It wasn't as if my life was unhappy during the years at the Capitol. In fact, it was much the opposite. I had a nice salary, dated, went out at night, and had friends who shared good times. As I sat there that afternoon looking at the statehouse, I knew I wanted something different, something more meaningful. When I smiled I wanted it to be more authentic. I wanted to be more content, and in a way that I was not even sure how to identify, or put my finger on. I just knew I wanted it.

There is a saying that 'the universe provides'; the universe gives us the lessons we are to learn. The question is then, do we learn from these lessons as they are presented to us? Even when the lessons are brought to us in the form of sadness and grief, if we take the time to ponder what is happening, something useful can be attained.

Events occurred that moved me from thinking about that day on the bench into taking actions to make my life different, and moving in the direction that my internal guidance system wanted me to head--even if my brain and everything I thought I knew was not clear as to what it was.

In January 1995, my Mom called early one morning before the sun started cracking over the horizon. I had fallen asleep that night to a movie and was on the sofa downstairs as I reached for the phone. I was not yet awake so the words seemed blurred when she informed me that one of my nephews had been in an accident. I asked, "Is he OK?" One word came back, and it was not the word as much as the tone and choked response of "No" that settled like a boulder on my chest. Trevor Dean had been killed in a highway traffic accident. Trevor was, needless to say, very special to me. His being gone in an instant at such an early age, just after getting his first job that he was so proud of caused for much reflecting, and long nights with a glass of whiskey and water as I sat by myself in the weeks after his funeral trying to make sense of it all.

I was not questioning the existence of God, as I have always had faith that there are reasons for everything. The tragedy was such that it required me to ask for some answers as to why. I started to look at the fragility of life in ways I had not done before. My best friend, Todd, had committed suicide following high school and his act was based on the action and decisions he took. I also knew the back story to his inner turmoil and I could somehow logically process it. Even though Todd's death was horribly sad, I could place that event into some context. Trevor's passing left me no way to come to a reasonable explanation. I had to find some other way to deal with his passing.

The second major lesson that came my way was one of those personal calamities that scar the soul in ways that are hard to define. A needless fire had been set by a careless second-floor wooden-balcony griller. The fire, caused by placing hot embers and coals in to a paper bag on a wooden balcony, ravaged my apartment complex in 1996. I lost my loft apartment, and many of my belongings. More importantly I had lost a sense of personal security; I had lost my home.

The fire was devastating but I came in time to recognize the power of being resilient. The human spirit wants to move forward, and though I slept for months with lights on in every room until I had moved beyond the images of charred walls and possessions in my mind, I was learning something very important.

I came to realize that of my belongings the things that brought me the greatest pleasure and delight were also the cheapest. There is no way to minimize the traumatic aspect to a fire, but that event made me aware of what really mattered when it came to personal possessions.

When it came time to retrieve those things that did not burn I was struck how some items that Mom had given me to start my life in Madison meant to me. The flower vase that came from home, my favorite coffee mug at the time, and some dishtowels that collectively would not have cost twenty dollars all of a sudden were treasured.

Between the tragic and sudden loss of Trevor Dean and the fire which robbed me of my belongings and sense of security, I started to put a different price structure on the important things in my life.

But the biggest lesson was yet to come.

It was not until I woke up at St. Mary's hospital following a medical procedure to see if a growth in my chest was malignant that I really started on a new path. Weeks earlier during a physical my doctor became concerned about some issues that had progressed to the point that a biopsy was required.

The day of the procedure I drove myself to the hospital in the early morning, carrying with me Ted Koppel's *Nightline*. A very sweet and warm-hearted female representative of the clergy talked with me for a while as nurses prepped me, and stuck tubes that dripped all sorts of things in to my body. By the time I was back in recovery my parents had arrived, and I was so groggy that later I had to ask what had happened. The lump was benign. The clergy who had spoken with me before the procedure was again at my bed, and she held my hand and smiled.

In the following weeks and months I worked to clarify how my life could have meaning separate from what I did for work. I struggled to define how my existence had meaning apart from how

I spent my free time even. If life were this fragile, and indeed it is, then I wanted to experience more fully those things that made me smile inwardly as much as outwardly. Wild summer thunder storms. That first cup of coffee. A good book. That is what I wanted to embrace. I suddenly could give a darn about meaningless bric-a-bracs or added lines on a resume.

There are no easy ways to attain the lessons needed for working at living a contented life. If I had the answer to life's all-consuming question I would be famous and wealthy! Indeed, it would be so much easier if we came with a user's manual at birth, along with instinctive qualities that the young have in the animal kingdom. Instead, we go through life picking up knowledge along the way, and hopefully learning from it, and then acting wisely. I certainly have not amassed all the answers, but I have cut through lots of the clutter and feel much inner peace about where I am today.

Even after working through many of my personal feelings there was one more large part of life I wanted addressed: I wanted to meet my life partner. I really do think we are meant to be matched with that one special person who when placed into the complexity of our life fits like a puzzle piece. In the midst of all the angles, twists, turns, unanswered questions, and confusion I felt there was one person 'out there' for me, and I wanted to meet him.

Over the years I had searched for the other half to my life. Somewhere in the 1980s I had seen the necklace of a half-heart where the partner or spouse wore the other portion. That symbol struck me because it was so simple, and yet filled with so much meaning. It portrayed a simple truth that seemed to match with the long running marriage of my parents, and that of most of my relatives.

Some friends told me I was picky and too strict with my 'must have list' when it came to dating or finding closeness with someone else. While I had some very charming and personable dates, and we had good times there was always something missing that I felt essential for a long-term relationship. Often it was just a feeling that no one else could understand, but over the years I came to know I had not met the person who was to own the 'half-heart' in my life

Over the years my close buddies and I would go out to a movie, play darts, or go for a long walk, and at the end of the evening they would head home to be with their wife, girlfriend, or partner. The friend I hated to drop off more than any other was married, and owned a house. When in his driveway, the lights of their home would always be on; glowing with a warm invitation. He got out and went into domestic tranquility while I drove home to be alone.

I hated that feeling.

Over time I jelled to the idea that perhaps it would take longer for me to find my life partner. I was not bored with my life, in fact I was much pleased with the free time to explore my curiosities, and do what I enjoyed. But I also wanted someone to wear that other half of the necklace in my life.

It was after many years of waiting that one of life's truths made itself known. Some of the best things happen when we least expect them. That is of course what our parents always told us, and it did turn out to be true.

James

I went to Borders Books and Music one Saturday afternoon following a rainy Dane County Farmers' Market. That was May 2000. I had found a seat in the café and browsed a couple travel books about Wyoming at my small table. I carried with me too the newspaper that I was reading. Off to my side, a voice inquired, "Anything good in the news's today?"

I had just met James.

James had come to Madison from Maine at the New Year. He was tired of an untenable teaching assignment in Virginia. His close, married friends, also Middlebury College graduates, encouraged his trip to Wisconsin. They invited him to stay for several months, if that was what he needed. As James searched for a teaching position, he took a job at Borders. That store, with its wide selection of books and music, had become over the years my hangout—the place I could grab a cup of coffee, search for books, read the paper, and do a crossword puzzle. I had never been a drinker, hated bars and loathed the smell of smokers. I opted instead for the world of books and java as my place to relax.

James at times worked the front desk of the store. He patiently and cordially processed people's purchases and made them feel welcome to return any time they felt the inclination. When I entered the store and he was on duty, I would notice him and we would nod, and smile.

That particular Saturday afternoon, James was on one of his mandated breaks, eating a cinnamon roll in the café area. We spoke for a few minutes. He is eleven years my younger, roughly the same age as my eldest nephew. James had an energy and conversational style that I instantly found attractive. I knew he needed to get back to work so I asked if he was free that evening. I learned that his shift ended at eight o'clock. I asked him out for dinner.

When James said yes I was very pleased, and also a bit nervous. I wanted to make a good impression and so prior to picking him up went through every shirt and pants combo I owned. When I had made the decision about what to wear, it looked as though my bed were a having a tiny garage sale. Clothing lay scattered everywhere. The place looked a disaster, but I was looking fine.

Choosing an outfit to wear on a first date shouldn't have been such a complicated task. It was. I admit it. When I was settled with that first crucial decision, I picked James up from the back parking lot of the store where he had agreed to meet me and we headed downtown.

That evening, we first had tea at the Café Royale coffee shop. We swapped stories about our day and conversation about what brought each of us in turn to Madison. We then enjoyed dinner at Husnus, a Turkish restaurant on State Street. The evening was a non-stop conversation. I have always taken that as a good sign, regardless of whether I am in the company of one person or a group. James and I haven't stopped talking and sharing since.

At the end of the evening, I drove James in my white Dodge Duster back to the apartment he was sharing with his friends, and gave him my phone number. Sometime after we had known each other, he confided in me that the first thing he did upon entering was to call the number. He wanted to see if I had given a real number. I had to ask myself if I somehow had not registered enough sincerity. In the end we all have our insecurities and James just needed to be assured that where he stood was indeed on a solid foundation. I liked that.

Our next date was perhaps the most 'eventful' of any I had ever been on in my entire life, and now in retrospect remains one about which I smile. The spring when James and I met was one of the wettest Madison had experienced in many years. It rained not only often, but also in amounts that just saturated the soil. James had invited me over to the place where he was staying. When I arrived, he was busy creating the first of what would become countless meals that simply make the mouth water from the time they are being prepared through the last bite. He had learned his cooking skills in the old-fashioned way. James' Mother Marion had one of those kitchens where saying 'I love you' comes not from a can but through the art of cooking genuinely. No one ever went hungry at Marion's table; once when I visited, I asked for a small second helping of mashed potatoes. Ph-lump! A mountain of locally grown Maine spuds landed on my plate and Marion tells me, "That'll put some meat on your bones!" (When I mean local, I mean Marion's elderly Mother and Step-father had raised them not a half mile away from where we were having dinner. You can't get any more local than that!)

James' grandmothers had also helped teach him how to cook over the course of one summer of his youth. Then as a college student living in France, he only refined his skills. A friend asked me after being at our home for dinner once, "Do you know how lucky you are?" Well, yeah! Of course, others have been saddened that they don't have a James at their home to cook. Our attorney friend, Jennifer, inquired after lunch one day, "Do you guys always eat like this?" She had just had one of James blended leek and vegetable soups followed by a toasted salmon sandwich with micro-greens, avocado and rémoulade sauce. "No," I replied, "we usually have this for dinner." Jennifer did not find that comforting; my response seemed only to reinforce her point. People just don't get to live like this usually.

On the night of our second date, the table was dressed with a nice table cloth and fresh cut flowers filled a ceramic water pitcher that James' friends had been given as a wedding gift. Cloth napkins were laid gently across the two place settings and music from the motion picture soundtrack *The Mission* played from the other room.

James had started the evening with a chilled shrimp cocktail served over a fresh tomato salad with lemon vinaigrette, lavender, shallots and flat-leafed parsley. From there, we enjoyed Normand white fish in a Calvados (apple brandy)-infused béchamel sauce over court-bouillon scented rice, baked in the oven. (This most wonderful fish and rice dish still is one of my favorites.)

We knew it was raining, and the sound of it coming down hard upon the window panes of the small apartment where he was staying was really quite wonderful. I thought the whole scene quite romantic, but that is where things looked to be starting to go awry. James got up from the table to clear the salad plates and to serve the fish when he happened to look out the kitchen window. Holding firmly the bottle of sauvignon blanc he had just then uncorked and was poised to pour in to crystal-footed glasses, he calmly suggested I may need to move the car.

"Why would I need to do that?" I asked.

"Because the water is rising in the parking lot!"

I quickly grabbed an umbrella and started outside where in just a few steps the wind inverted my rain shield, rendering it perfectly useless. I was soaked before I was off the landing. By the time I made it to the car, the door when opened skimmed the top of the surging water. You hear about these things, but never think it can happen so close to home. With the quickest of movements I stepped in to the car, ignited the engine, and realized that I had no idea where to head. James' apartment was already perched on the top of one of Madison's highest plains. Where in heck might uphill be located when one is already at the summit? The not well-drained parking area suffered from poor engineering in light of the Midwestern storm which filled the sky. I moved the car alongside some others that seemed on higher ground, and far enough away from the torrents, all the while rationalizing that should the waters flood even where I was parked there was not much to be done.

I waded my way back to the apartment, and was met at the door. James had a kind and understanding look on his face. He regretted not having keys to his friends' car so that we could move it as well. The water flowed through the steering wheel of that one, and nothing could be done to save it. In short, neither of us had ever been on a date quite like this one; perhaps we knew there would be a way to laugh about this in time. After securing safety for my Duster, we went back to dinner. When we regale others with this story, though, James' version goes something like this: "So there he stood soaking wet, and I told him he needed to get into dry clothes. He was most reluctant to take his shirt off, but he was out of his pants in no time flat!" I do not recall it quite that way, but it always makes for a laugh. The sumptuous evening meal, capped off with a fruit sorbet, was superb, and later the waters in the yard receded slightly. I was eventually able to return to my own place, grateful for the night I had spent, and even more pleased that I still had a vehicle to drive me there.

Had things not turned out as they had, meaning if my car had been lost to the flood waters at Eagle Heights, I am certain that I would have read the event as a bad omen and James and I may not have forged a relationship together at all. I feel today that I must have been under the watchful eye of a guardian angel who read my heart filled with longing, and who knew how to part the waters like one of his saintly friends must have taught him. My Dodge Duster was safe, and my life forever transformed.

Two weeks after we met, James returned to Middlebury College for six weeks of summer school. I was not sure where we were headed, but thought such a long separation was surely a most awkward and problematic development. His time away, however, proved to be a very powerful way to bring us closer and allowed me to become surer of what I wanted from our relationship.

Every single night while he was away, James and I talked on the phone for about an hour. Since we were not talking in person, the conversations seemed more focused and meaningful. We told each other our life stories, hopes, fears, and how we got to the point where our meeting was such a joyous connection. We did not know where things were heading, but it was clear that if I could help make it happen, when he returned to Madison we wanted to continue to see each other.

I helped locate an apartment for James when he moved back to Madison at the end of the summer. It was situated downtown on, as coincidence would have it, Wilson Street so he could be close to a part-time job he had secured at the State Capitol as a tour guide.

James was at home on Wilson Street on 9/11. Sixteen months had passed since we had met. Using some apples he had picked from a tree just down the block from his place, a tree standing along a desolate parking lot, James was baking a cake when the towers were hit. I was at my apartment, and called him with the news. He struggled to stir cake batter and hold the phone to his ear while I recounted the breaking news.

No one alive at that time will forget the day the Twin Towers of New York fell, or when the plane destined for the US Capitol crashed in to the field in Pennsylvania while another struck the Pentagon. Chaos. Whatever mundane things we were doing that morning are etched on our memories. Given the gravity of the events, and the years which followed, we as a nation will never forget them.

I was at my apartment, and had turned the television on as I came downstairs for coffee. The first plane had struck one of the towers, and the smoke could be seen pouring out, but the general consensus, such as it was, hoped that an accident of some kind had taken place. Then the second plane struck, and by now I was holding my cup and wondering what in hell was happening. Though none of us knew precisely what was taking place, it was clear that some type of national attack was underway.

I called James at once. He had worked as a teacher in New Jersey, and had friends living in New York. His first classroom had a view of the Towers from the other side of the Lincoln Tunnel. He used to spend time gathering his thoughts between classes, contemplating their massive size. (We would learn later that he, like so many others, lost college chums who worked in the Towers.)

As I mentioned earlier, James was in the midst of making an apple cake, and was finding he had more batter than pan. Since we spent a lot of time together, he had his apartment fitted out for basic living but somehow had not found it necessary to have a television. I couldn't just tell him to turn his set on and watch. Over the phone, then, I was telling him to get his radio dial turned to WBBM-AM 780, the all-news station from Chicago that had been my station to turn to for instant information since being a teenager. I knew that James was not a fan of AM radio, often mimicking the sometimes static sound with a cupped hand over his mouth while trying to impress on our friends that I am more unique then they had any idea about when it came to what I listened to on the radio. Not skilled in fine tuning radio dials as I, James struggled to get the station set and listen along. I think that on the morning of 9/11, James altered his feelings a bit about radio as he listened to the news. (Though I did question if his conversion were complete.)

In those first minutes of the national tragedy, we made plans for me to pick him up later in the morning. By then, we might know a bit more about what was happening on the east coast, and James' cake would have been successfully removed from the oven and cooling on the stovetop.

I next called Mom, and knew instantly she was truly upset. She did not want to think about what was going on in New York. Dad had taken the car out for something to be fixed that morning, and so Mom was hearing all the news by herself. She was scared, and alone.

Shortly afterwards news reports made known that the Pentagon too had been hit. I called an older friend, Kaye, and asked, "What is happening to my country?" Kaye had worked for years in our Capitol office as a 'floating secretary', a member of a pool of assistants loaned out to the various legislators. We had become good friends.

Over the years Kaye and I had traded phones calls about every sort of news event as we both loved politics and history, but this one was so god-awful that I recall crying while talking on the phone and watching the events play out on television. She was nervous, and yet more contained. She had, after all, lived through World War II. My generation, however, had never witnessed anything like this. (Our friendship would sadly dissolve after I took a firm and outspoken stand against the Iraq War in 2002, and marched for my beliefs. My involvement in the protests was something Kaye very much disproved of, and she let me know of her feelings in brusque terms.)

When the Towers fell, it was the most gut-wrenching moment ever to fill the television screen. I bolted to the shower and just wanted to get together with James. There was something about the events that played out that day which demanded connection to others. On the way downtown, I stopped for more coffee at Borders and will always remember that one of the nicest guys who worked there was arriving as I was entering the store. We had talked many times in the past, but that morning we looked at each other and both just shook our heads, and walked in silence through the store door.

James' cake was cooling by the time I arrived at his apartment and we started that running conversation that would last all day and into the night, and in time would include more people along the way. Since James lived on the isthmus we walked just a couple blocks to the Capitol Square and were struck by how quiet it was. People were out and yet the loudness of the city was calmed by the horror that had struck the nation. No one was yelling, or screaming across the street. It was a serene sadness. Signs were going up on banks and stores; each of the signs had been individually created. Each shared the same purpose: alert customers that their place of business was closing at a certain early hour in light of the news from New York. No two signs were alike, and yet each conveyed the same sadness and the same shock that we both felt.

We took the cake to the home where eventually James and I would come to live during the fall of 2007. We dropped the cake off with Henry, and made plans to come back and meet all the others for dessert and tea. We were part of the grouping that made up Henry's 'salons'. Over the years, politics, books, and movies were the topics of grand discussions at Henry's place.

James and I had lunch that afternoon at a small Chinese restaurant on Regent and Mills Streets. The *Capital Times* had printed their afternoon edition, and it had landed in the news boxes where I bought two copies. On the front page a searing image of one of the towers on fire dominated any print about the story. Inside the restaurant, the mood was somber. All were watching *CNN*, and eating slowly. There are big windows that face out onto Mills Street and young college students were huddled but lacking the usual energetic movements that accompany such a gathering.

Later that day back at Henry's, his usual group gathered in the living room, and watched hour after hour as the coverage continued. The only bright spot was the apple cake with whipped cream topping and the tea selection that always made Henry's home a perfect place to weather a storm.

That single day changed our politics, international affairs, how we fly, and the way we think, and unfortunately how we view others. As a nation, everything changed. In the weeks following the incident, heightened security measures were in place even at the Wisconsin statehouse where James worked. On a personal level, while we still have many of those same people over for tea and dinner and conversations I am hopeful that we never again meet in this nearly one hundred twenty-five year-old house for a day like the one when we joined in friendship to deal with 9/11.

Our journey to living in this home took us down roads with twists and turns. For me the trip really started in 1986 when I moved to my first apartment in Madison, also on the isthmus. My first apartment was on of all places--Hancock Street!

I always knew growing up that I wanted to live in a city, and experience the bustle and energy of urban life. I wanted to live in a city large enough so as to partake in all the possibilities, but not one so large that I could not find my way around (I am directionally challenged, as James tells it), or get lost in the urban jostling. While I love Chicago, with its rich history, the countless wonders awaiting a walk down her streets, and the awesome sky line, I feel far more at home in Madison where 'the big little feel' of all that a city should contain exists. Madison is just the right size, not limiting in the humanity and warmth that I desire.

Moving to Madison was one of the best decisions I ever made. I have never doubted that the isthmus is still the most vibrant, dynamic, and yet at the same time most serene of all the places to be found in the city. There are the bustling farmers' markets and dynamic political power plays but there are also the warm summer nights when the moon lights up the lakes and soft laugher can be heard from down the block.

Two years to the day of our meeting James and I picked up our keys for a new apartment we decided to move in to on the West Side. It was a large upper story apartment with a nice balcony that overlooked a wooded city preserve. The area was dark at night, and comforting as it felt in small ways like what we had known as boys in our respective country homes.

I had not lived with anyone since leaving home as teenager. I had waited and made sure that James was the person I wanted to spend the rest of my life with before making the decision to start domestic life together. It did not take much time to prove that I was well suited for such an arrangement, as my concerns about how the toothpaste tube was squeezed or which direction the tea pot handle would sit on the stove proved all to be rather ridiculous. In fact, I learned new quirks to add to my collection. James desires that all the shirts hanging in the closet be arranged according to the color spectrum. With all the hangers facing the same direction, in case as he says there is ever a fire and we need to get the lot of them out of the closet in a hurry, all of the shirts line up one by one: red, orange, yellow, green, blue, indigo and violet. It is a non-negotiable. (I have mentioned earlier that James had gotten rid of my gray outfits, so poorly suited to good mental health. There would be no need for those on the rainbow in our closet!)

We lived for five years in that west-side apartment, and were very content with our surroundings, along with the ability to add plants and small shrubs around our home. Even though we did not own we wanted our place to reflect who we were, and strove to make a difference. Clearly we were homeowners in the making.

We had no way of knowing how soon that process would start, or how.

Henry, our friend and 'benefactor' was born in 1941, and grew to a brilliant man, schooled in the classics (Latin and Greek) at Duquesne University, and the University of Michigan, Ann Arbor. He soon found that his many talents and skills were just as useful in the classrooms of New Wilmington, Pennsylvania, and academic counseling offices of Madison, where he began his career, as they were in Wisconsin Governor Thompson's budget office.

I first met Henry on the job while working at the Capitol, and reconnected with him through James after his arrival in the city. Henry, throughout his life, offered his friends colorful and insightful morsels of cultural or social critique, kvetch, current events, garden tips, recipes, a bit of philosophy and a whole lot of humor. Anyone who knew him can attest to his always funny, and opinionated intelligence.

Henry always had chocolate and tea for anyone stopping by for a visit. In our quest to continue the big-hearted nature of his life in this home we always tell people that the 'tea pot is always on', and we mean it. Our table has often had another plate set, and a meal shared with warm and hearty conversation as that is the way we first came to know of this home.

When I told my Mom that we would be moving into this house she wondered where it was located, and if it was a safe neighborhood. She had nothing about which to worry. Whenever we moved to a new location we called the police to find out the type of calls that were made for their service. When calling about our isthmus home we were told that the biggest concern included calls late at night about skinny dippers at the beach. We felt we could live with that.

If I were to sum up in a brief fashion the neighborhood where James and I live it could best be done with an event that happened shortly after we moved into our home. A police car had pulled up to our residence after I had called about finding a full set of keys in the area. I ran the keys out to the officer and chatted for a minute. As the officer drove off I started walking back to the stoop when a young woman who lives several blocks down walked by and asked "Is everything OK, you need anything?" I think that speaks volumes about a neighborhood community where people are connected to each other, and care.

Mom in fact would love our home, and my Dad would find the old house comforting. Our old Victorian house was built in 1892, and is located across the street from the B.B. Clarke Beach, designed by the city architects to give the public access to a swimming hole in the city on its "third lake". The B.B. Clarke was first known as Monona Park when it was established in 1902, then

Spaight Street Park. The park was renamed in 1929 for Bascom B. Clarke, a Madison businessman who earned a fortune in Indiana by manufacturing threshing machines before he moved to Madison in 1890. From 1898 to his death in 1929, Clarke published the *American Thresherman*, an influential international journal specializing in the development and use of farm machinery. His home at 1148 Spaight Street, designed by Claude and Stark Architects, was designated as a historic landmark by the Madison Landmarks Commission in 1981.

 We have a wonderful old photo taken from up the street prior to the construction of our home. There are so few buildings to impede the sight line that the columns on the Capitol can be seen. In this particular photo, where our home now stands is a grassy area with some type of livestock grazing. It remains one of my favorite pictures.

 When digging around further in the history of the home, we learned that our house shares a common link with the one located next door. That residence was built in 1885 for Mrs. Johanna Bartsch, widow of the late Captain August Bartsch, who was injured in the Civil War, and would die in 1873 from a war-related affliction.

 In 1885 Johanna built a house for herself adjacent to where our home is now located, and for a while Walter Bartsch, a painter and probably her son, lived there, too. In 1892 she built another house on the family property, which is where we live today. She wanted more entertaining space and so moved into this house. The house was built out of white pine and fashioned with square nails.

 A succession of residents in the neighboring house makes it appear that she used it as rental property though this has not been confirmed by tax research. It should be noted that according to the 1919 Madison city directory a Catherine O'Keefe, a nurse, was a resident next door. Of course, Georgia O'Keefe, the famous artist, is not listed because high school students usually are not, but it seems probable that she stayed there at some point while she worked on her schooling at Edgewood High School on the other side of town.

 The history of this part of the city is most interesting. I often sit late at night and wonder what the others experienced as they lived within these rooms. They had the joys and lighter moments of life for sure. They also had moments of darkness and death, too.

 This old Victorian has a 'coffin door', and no doubt at some point loved ones had been brought out through it in a slender coffin. That was the time period when funeral homes were not used as they are now, and families held the wake in the front parlor. Since living here James and I have suffered the loss of family and close relatives and from time to time think what the white pine wood that frames the funeral door would say about the feelings of loss that others experienced here.

    I wonder late at night if others also sat up and looked out the window into the night while gazing at the stars and the blackness of the water. Or perhaps they sat in rather amused silence when the moon was out, and the lake was a glassy shimmering reflection of beauty.

    Living here has also made James and me want to add items that look like the period of the home. I love old things that speak of another era, but also have a practical use today. My love of history, and the curiosity about who else owned and used old items never ceases to amuse me. The look of old steamer trunks has always caught my eye, and my imagination leads me to believe they all must have been used for some adventuresome voyage. From the Westerns on television where the trunks were strapped to the top of the stagecoach, to the immigrants who traveled to our shores with few belongings, the trunks carry an epic type image with them.

    The first two such trunks that we purchased sit in our entryway, and hold our shoes that are not in season and therefore not worn day-to-day. They match the historic nature of everything else. One of them needed a little restoration, and so we painted it a nice blue color. We thought the trunks matched the feel of the tall ships and ocean in the lithograph we had hung in that space, while also serving a purpose. Our shoes were not what we wanted people to see when they came to our entryway.

    When we spotted a curved-top steamer trunk at a sale my heart thumped. In the time that we were looking at it, and considering if we should make the purchase, another man came up and wanted to lift the lid and look inside. I blurted out, "Don't touch, that one is sold!" It was at that point we decided the trunk was coming home with us. The pressed metal is detailed on the top and sides, and is quite remarkable.

    It's my understanding that the curved top ones were more desirable to travel with way back in the days when they were used on journeys, because they always ended up at the top of the stacks in a ship's hold. Others that were flat might have been stacked at the bottom of the pile, and I suspect more likely to be damaged as a result. The curved type could only be placed on the top of a pile. Inside are the old wooden trays and closures that was another reason for the thumping of my heart. After it was all cleaned up James placed table linens and accent pieces into the trunk. Now when friends stop by I tell them the stagecoach leaves at ten, and the trunk is ready!

    It is easy to see why I think about who put their dress or pants into the trunk. Were they headed for a new start, or a dreaded trip that they wished would never need to start? Was there an ocean to cross or maybe just the state of Texas? The biggest question is how did a family let go of such a memory as a trunk?

James and I recall our familial traditions as we add new ones to the mix. All my life the care for the lawn back in Hancock was taken quite seriously. Cutting the grass, and making sure it looked nice is something that was important to my parents. Many a summer night Dad mowed the lawn while Mom trimmed, spruced, watered and transplanted flowers. It is not strange then that once James and I announced we were moving into our home that Mom and Dad started thinking about our new lawn, and how it needed to be tended.

In the summer of 2007 Mom told us to stop by, and pick up the push lawn mower, and take it to Madison. Since we have a small yard she had been telling us for weeks that it would be perfect for the up keep and maintenance of the grass. "No reason to buy a mower for a small lawn," she told me, "when you can use the push mower".

That mower with the old-fashioned spinning blades had been stored in the grainery, and then the new barn all my life. As a boy I recall thinking the mower to be so out-of-date given that modern mowers were so much easier to use, especially considering my parents had a huge lawn out in the country.

In addition, my Dad always warned everyone that the blades were sharp and they could cut fingers 'off like that', which was the point in the sentence where his verbal admonitions were always followed with a snap of his own fingers for the perfect effect. The day we picked the mower up the same dire warnings were offered about the fate of my fingers. But this time my Dad also added that James needed to keep his fingers out of the blades too. The concerns for such matters never ended in my family, they just included more people in the circle. I never asked if there were a high number of fingerless people as a result of mowing in the 1940s, or if my Dad just felt I had a higher propensity for such an accident. In either case, it seemed best not to know.

The mower was bought in 1948, a full fourteen years before I even formed eyelids. My father's uncle Hiram said that the mower from the stores never came with sharp enough blades, so my Dad tells the story of how Hiram sharpened them soon after the purchase. I had to smile at the job Hiram did as we mowed our lawn for the first time. Dad says they were never sharpened after that first time since the mower was not used once the motorized ones came along. The mover buzzed along in August 2007 as fast as we pushed it, and did the job nicely. As we mowed a lady walked by, greeted us, and then said at once that the mower was perfect, as it made no noise.

All was perfect for the first couple years, with each spring a time to take the mover to Ace Hardware to have the blades sharpened. But one spring it rained every other day, and the grass grew like gangbusters. I had also started our own lawn care program of adding seed and nitrogen so as to make for a fuller greener lawn. The mini jungle of grass was getting harder to mow and maintain with the push mower. If it were not cut every three days, with the rate it was growing the job of slogging through it was nearly impossible. It was time to concede that the push mower, for all the sentimental attachment I had for it was too much work for the lawn. I had hoped when first starting with the mower to use it for decades. I will always be comforted with the knowledge, however, that my folks desired me to have it, and gave it to me in a time of upheaval as my Mom was sick. The gift of the lawn mower showed me that in the face of adversity it is important to have a sense of continuity.

For James the best holiday of the year is Groundhog's Day. The almost forgotten holiday was a time for James and his Mom to enjoy lighthearted moments when at times other pressures of life were weighting down. With warm sentimentality James reflects on and celebrates this holiday each year that for him is tied as much to family as the weather.

Groundhog's Day is steeped in Maine's seasonal wisdom. Any good farmer knows that by the time February rolls around there needs to be 'half the wood and half the hay' remaining out in the barn just to make it through the rest of winter. Having less meant deprivation or worse in the old days.

James also recites this classic poem which he learned in grade school every year in February:

> *Little groundhog down below,*
> *Underneath the wintry snow*
> *Come out and tell us true:*
> *Is Spring Coming?*
> *Is Winter through?*

James waits attentively to learn the prognostication of the American marmot. He likes to know with precision when spring will arrive; he doesn't fully trust the old *Farmer's Almanac* like I do. Armed with all the information we can gather from both sources, James and I tend to start moving things forward with spring when the temperature gets to forty degrees. I know it sounds funny to hear that so much should be made of a thermometer reading that is only eight degrees above freezing, but some years it seems that winter drags on a little too long. Even if we do not always get lots of snow there is always the cold frigid air. I swear that sometimes I have even heard a bird in our front yard lament the fact that it was so cold he had to put his bird seed into a crock pot before eating!

It is not uncommon to see James and me work with the stronger rays of the sun so as to better work magic on our front lawn. A little shoveling here, and some raking of the snow there, this way and then back, and soon there was nothing but grass. The look of spring takes some work, but it is good for the psyche.

The ritual of spring is the same every year. Turn over the old mulch, and get some fresh mulch to spread, place a new coat of varnish on this chair, or that one, and ponder where my latest whims about flowers I deem essential should be planted. We get excited about the half-inch snow-blossom flowers that sprout in the sun near our home, and again listen to the song of happy birds in the tall trees. I get excited at the first robin the in the yard, and the first blooms of the daffodils.

I love to go for walks when there is a 'March wind' blowing. It can be mighty cold, but the smell in the air is not the type associated with winter, but instead the impending arrival of spring. On these types of walks I love to encounter Sam, our eldest neighbor. The nonagenarian World War II veteran always stops to talk. He is always out walking his black lab Rahal (named for the race car driver) and seems to be the first to hear the seasonal return of the geese. There is something so promising about the noise from a flock as they make their passage back to the North. I once told Sam after spotting robins early in the season that we had an old saying in the country: it must snow on the back of a robin three times before spring arrives. He had never heard that adage before, and chuckled as he told us guys to let him know how that goes.

I really do love winter, and bemoan those years when there is little snow. Those years when there is more brown lawn than white reminds me of a cartoon from the newspaper of a young boy pulling a sled up to the door of the Bureau of Missing Persons. The man sticking his head out of the door informs the lad "We'll need a better description than 'ole man winter'".

If spring is the focal point of the start of the year, it is the holidays at the end of the calendar year that make for the broadest smile on James' face. Christmas is a time of wonderment here. When James is done, this home is decked out in the most festive feel that it has probably ever experienced.

I know that every year the holiday season is going to commence a bit sooner than in most homes, and know without a doubt that very few are talking about holiday decorating plans in the heat of summer. Come Thanksgiving time, it is hard to know precisely what trips the accelerator in his mind that all systems are 'a go' for decorating, but once the green light flashes it is full speed ahead. He will tell me he is going downstairs to get an item, and minutes later the house is filling with boxes that contain holiday magic.

I very much love the holidays too, but used to think waiting until the day after Thanksgiving was the 'proper' time to ramp up the Christmas music (vinyl favorites from over the years) and to get the boxes out of storage in the basement for the all-out decorating blitz. I concede that I may have been wrong about that; there is something warm, cozy, inviting, and charming when this old Victorian is decked out, the trees up and decorated (you read that correctly, treeS, four of them of different sizes to be precise) and the albums of Christmas music spinning.

In 2012 after having had two Holiday Seasons consumed by family suffering and grief, James and I agreed that we needed to 'go big' for Christmas. We were not talking about spending lots of cash. Rather we were thinking 'Victorian', and making the holiday old-fashioned, while creating the over-stuffed look, and feel that which the pictures from that era seem so well to capture. Since moving into our home, and having far more space than we were accustomed to, the holiday decorations are always aimed at producing a folksy and warm environment. That tradition comes from the way we were raised, and are an extension of how we live our lives the rest of the year.

James' Mom in Maine loved Christmas, and there is no way not to feel her warm embrace now with how things look and are arranged in our home. My Mom loved the holiday music, and though she decorated with a more simple touch there was always seasonal warmth to the parents' home in Hancock. James and I both had Dads who were lucky to have found someone with a touch for making a house feel like a home. If I have a pinch of talent for decorating, James has a handful.

Over the years we have amassed many–and I mean tons–of

ornaments. There are probably no more than a dozen out of the 1,500 ornaments that come without a memory. We bought special ornaments together over the years we have been together, others were gifts, some were from our childhood homes, and others are household items from our past.

One of our holiday traditions is over a decade old. We invite a couple friends over, and mostly they have no idea what is about to happen as we sit at the table with tea and sweets. Then we open a box that contains solid colored ordinary Christmas ornaments that can be bought at any store, thirty small pots of acrylic paints, and some newspapers to stop a mess in its tracks. With a smile we explain our mission. We take a few plain Christmas bulbs and transform them into something seasonal. Using acrylic paint the object of the activity is to make the ornament unique. With my lack of artistic skills 'unique' is the kindest one can say about the result. As our friends prove, there is a lot of talent when there is patience with a small paintbrush. When the painting and laughing is done, and the ornaments dried with the hair blower, they are placed on the tree.

Every year thereafter when decorating the trees James and I remark on this or that ornament, who made it, and recall the memories along the way. Out of all the ornaments we hang each season, there are about fifty created with the love and smiles of friends.

Aside from traditional ornaments are additions to the tree such as a small coin purse that was used by James' Mom, and was once owned by his Great-Grandmother. It still holds a small coin and a wooden die (the plural would be dice). I have several of Mom's wooden clothespins that she used all her life. We have items (from Henry's family) such as a piece of garland made during the Depression by workers in an aluminum company in Pennsylvania. The men stamped out the pieces of heavy tin-foil type material, and then ladies at home stitched them together. After Henry's passing his family gave us a piece of the garland that we place each year on the tree.

James and I have long saved the gift tags with the handwriting of loved ones from over the many years. We have laminated them. They now are all hung on one tree. There is a small red star made by my nephew, Trevor, which always gets near to the top of a tree, and copper measuring spoons that James's Grandmother gave to his Mom in 1967 when she and Robert were married. In other words, our Christmas trees are memory trees while being festive.

We celebrate Christ's birth, and do so with the knowledge that life goes on even when the road seems uphill. With faith there is always a place to stop, rest, and find joy. That place for us is home: from our childhoods which still seems so near despite the years and changes, to the present when we go for a walk and come back home to the glow of the trees from inside our home. Blending the life James and I now live, with the memories of the past is like walking hand in hand with your best friend. There is no doubt that James and I are a team. We love each other, and love life. We have been blessed in so many ways from the families we grew up in, the way we were raised, the values we possess, and the perspectives we have about life. We are also glad to be living so closely with our memories from the past.

One winter day not so long ago James sent me a quote from Alfred Austin. It was short and direct, "Show me your garden and I shall tell you what you are". I pondered that for a bit and then concluded what it meant for me, and as an extension for our life and home.

When someone asks me how I handle stress I point to one of our flowerbeds. Digging out sod and making holes for new plantings is perhaps one of the best days of the warm months in Madison. It means that weeks of planning, looking, and thinking about the project will have allowed for colorful expectations to be created. Thumbing through seed catalogs during the winter months and thinking about plants is akin to the way I lingered over Christmas catalogs as a boy. There is just no end to the possibilities.

The love of flower gardening with the desired end result is a joy that James and I share. More than one person who has stopped along our sidewalks in the warm months has said that if one of us is digging a hole another must be in back getting the mulch. If one is mowing, the other must be trimming. If one is staking up a leaning flower, the other must be getting ready to water the plants. There is a harmony not only of color in the gardens, but equally important of our personalities. I could not imagine gardening with anyone other than James.

The flower gardens, and the work that goes into them serve a real purpose. Over the years we have come to comprehend what is important in life, and about life. Both as individuals, and as a couple we are reinforced with the ever-constant knowledge of what is truly important, and what is just noise. To put it another way we know what constitutes a bloom, and what is merely a weed that needs to be pulled. That is an important lesson to learn, but a difficult one to practice.

When the winter months force us indoors, the chairs where

we sat and read in summer among the flowers put away for the season, the rose cones in place, and the ground bare of color there is only one thing left--that is hope.

There is always a spring day just ahead when you have a flower garden. There is always the promise of a morning when you pull open the blinds and the first tulip of the season beckons, or the first splash of yellow from a daffodil catches the eye. There is always a summer evening when if you are still the hummingbirds rush in and sample the red flowers. There is always the knowledge that one day not so far down the calendar the scent of fresh-cut grass will bring a broad smile.

Upon reflecting on the quote from Alfred Austin I have some words for those who look at our flower gardens and ponder who we are based on them: James and I are survivors, companions, dreamers, and lovers of life. Our lives are complete in the way we want them to be.

"The most authentic thing about us is our capacity to create, to overcome, to endure, to transform, to love and to be greater than our suffering."

—Ben Okri

Epilogue

With the passing of daylight in the winter months, the halogen lamps of the living room are lit. Dinner is over, and we return to reading. James relaxes on the sofa while I sit nearby in the rocker where I love to turn the pages. As it gets to be 10:30 P.M., James mentions that it is time for this or that show. We both wave it off and continue reading. A few blocks away the sound of the train whistle carries its message to our home. The deep rumble of the cars are not only heard but sensed. They seem full as they lumber along on the rails. We are in our own way like the Native Americans placing their ears to the ground out in the prairie so long ago to hear the 'iron horse'. At times I look up at and smile while scanning the living room. I ask myself if we are getting old as we both sit curled up reading a book. Perhaps not 'old' but 'content'.

The last song I played on WDOR at the end of 'another broadcasting day' shortly before Christmas 1986 was "My Way" by Elvis, a perfect summation of that time in my life. Not only did I shut the station down that winter night, but Elvis helped me close out my time on the air.

Elvis had always meant more to me than just an essential component in America's musical development. Whereas Sam Phillips, the first person who took note of Elvis' abilities and signed him to a record contract was delighted because he had found a "white man who had the Negro sound', I had a more personal reason for connecting to the music icon.

When I was searching for a way to get through my teenage

years the stories of how Elvis would wear pink shirts and comb his hair back and up when others his age had closely clipped hair and wore sedate colors made me more aware that being oneself could be achieved successfully. Elvis broke rules that had no right to be respected, and I liked that. Even though Elvis started his rebellious acts almost a decade before I was born he still resonated for me when I was a teenager.

As I look back on the first fifty years of my life, I claim far more smiles and laughter than tears and heartache. On that basis alone I say that my life has been good. I have learned a lot over the years, but perhaps the best way to sum up the most important lesson is to quote the legendary Southern Gospel artist, Vestal Goodman. She stated the most important of those truths in a matter-of-fact fashion often when on stage. She knew how to live happily, and summed it up this way: "If people like you—great; if not, tough".

In my earlier years I was too concerned about what others thought, and at times adjusted my life to meet the expectations and needs of others. I have a rather easy-going disposition, and I suspect at times some considered me an easy mark. Too often I plain just allowed some to take advantage of me. As I grow older, am more experienced with life, wiser, and more confident; I walk my own path and hold my head high.

The vastness of change that divides me from the man I was in my youth is astonishing to me. The lost, confused, and at times lonely man has developed into someone that I am mighty proud of today. I am a more sure-footed and secure person and it is in part because I set myself on a path to reach this end.

There is also another reason. James. James is the man who stands by my side. The last thirteen years has taken us through a series of events that no one could have predicted. Some of them were grand, others profoundly sad. Each moment however, was shared together as a team. Smiles or tears, we clasped together our hands and faced life as one.

If there is anyone who wants to know what a true partner and companion looks like, they only need to take a look at James. If anyone wants to know the definition of a family in America, they need only to sit at our dining table. James has been the anchor of my life, and the wind that lifts the sail of my heart. I love him so very much.

I close this memoir then with a bit of Jimmy Rodriguez's poetry that I find myself humming from time to time.

> *I realize now after all those hard times*
> *And Lord knows we've had us a few*
> *Together, forever, wherever we are*

I couldn't be me without you

I couldn't be me without you
I couldn't be me without you
Together, forever, wherever we are
I couldn't be me without you

Take my hand James, and let's get walking...we have lots more of this shared road of ours to walk.

Appendix

Here's a sample of what DXing provided on the radio dial when I was a boy. Stations other than the ones in Illinois are easier to find and hear in the winter, and late at night.

WBZ	Boston, MA	1030AM
WRVA	Richmond, VA	1140AM
WIND	Chicago, IL	560AM
WBBM	Chicago, IL	780AM
WGN	Chicago, IL	720AM
WLS	Chicago, IL	890AM
WSM	Nashville, TN	650AM
WHO	Des Moines, IA	1040AM
KOA	Denver, CO	850AM
KDKA	Pittsburgh, PA	1020AM
KAAY	Little Rock, AR	1090AM
KMOX	St. Louis, MO	1120AM

Menu

Entrees:

Boiled Dinner

Lasagna

Barbecues

Sides:

Summer Squash Casserole

Potato Salad

Heavenly Orange Fluff

Condiments:

Bread and Butter Pickles

Pickle Salad

Fresh Sliced Tomatoes

Desserts:

Dark Raisin Cake

Pumpkin Pie Desert Squares

Angel Cookies

Appendix: Dinner with Mom

Recipes

Entrees:

Boiled Dinner
Freshly dug potatoes
Cabbage
Carrots
Parsnips
Beets
(Any other root vegetable you like)
Beef

Placed the washed and prepared vegetables in a large pot on the stove with a nice sized piece of beef. Slow simmer all afternoon, until the dinner fills the home with a fantastic aroma, and perhaps there is a light covering of steam on the lower portion of each kitchen window pane. Serve hot.

Lasagna
1 lb. hamburger
1 large onion
1 clove garlic or 1 tsp. garlic salt

Brown and cook until done. Add:

1 quart tomatoes
1 small can tomato paste
1 small can tomato sauce
1 tsp. pepper
½ tsp oregano
2 tsp salt (less if you have used garlic salt)

Simmer slowly for 30 minutes.

Cook noodles and drain. Cool noodles in cold water. Arrange noodles in stripes in bottom of pan. Cover with meat and paste. Top with cheese slices. Repeat for about three layers. Bake 375 degrees for 30 min. Let stand 15-20 minutes before cutting.

Barbecues
1 tablespoon shortening (melted in pan to keep beef from sticking)
1 pound ground beef.
Cook and drain off fat.

Chopped celery
Chili powder
Salt and pepper to taste
1 can Campbell's tomato soup

Simmer ingredients together. Serve over toasted buns split long way.

Sides:

Summer Squash Casserole
Take two or three medium sized yellow (crook-necked) summer squash and cut them into large chunks (one half inch thick, about). Sauté for a few minutes to partially cook off some of the water that comes from them. In a different skillet, take about a half a package of bacon, chopped into pieces like French lardoons, and cook--not crispy, but tender. Drain off the extra fat. In a casserole dish, put a can of Campbell's Cream of Chicken soup, a couple of tablespoons of milk to loosen it a bit, and the chunks of squash and bacon. Stir and bake until done. Let cool a minute or two to set it up. Season to taste and serve.

Potato Salad
Boil half the 5 pound bag of potatoes in water with a bit of salt. Cool.
4 hard boiled eggs
Onion
1/3 quart of mayo
Teaspoon of yellow mustard
Teaspoon of sugar
1/3 can of evaporated milk

Mix gently until ingredients are well coated. Keep refrigerated.

Heavenly Orange Fluff
Make the day before serving in a large glass cake pan:

2 (3 oz.) pkg. orange gelatin
2 cups boiling water
1 small can of frozen orange juice (thawed)
2 (6 oz.) cans of mandarin oranges (drained)
1 large can crushed pineapple (not drained)

Dissolve gelatin in boiling water and add frozen juice, undiluted. Add orange sections and pineapple and stir well. When set, cover with lemon topping:

1 cup milk
1 pkg. instant lemon pudding
1 cup (half pint) whipping cream

Add milk to the pudding and beat until thick.
Whip cream and fold in to pudding.
Put on top of set Jell-O mixture.

Condiments:

Bread and Butter Pickles
18 cups or 8 slicing cucumbers
1/3 cup salt
4 onions—sliced
1 green and 1 red pepper
2 ½ cups vinegar
3 cups sugar
1 tsp. turmeric
1 tsp celery seed
1 Tblsp. White mustard seed

Slice cukes. Sprinkle salt over and let stand over nite or several hours. (Several hours are sufficient.) Drain very well. Do not peel the cukes. Slice onions. Chop the peppers. Mix all together and bring to a boil. Do not over cook. Pack in jars and seal.

A few suggestions for the perfect pickle:
Use distilled white vinegar to ensure clarity of vegetable color.
Do not use copper, brass, galvanized or iron utensils.
Make small batches. Never double a recipe.

Pickle Salad

In the summer, as the garden began to ripen off, Geneva would make a "pickle salad". To make her salad, which is one of my favorites, all that you have to do is peel and slice the fresh cucumbers (one or two medium sized) into rounds and put them in a bowl with salt. Coat them well and let stand for a couple of hours to draw some of the water out of the cucumber slices. Rinse well and drain. In a bowl mix about a quarter of a cup of mayonnaise and some milk to make a somewhat thick and creamy sauce. To this sauce add a couple of table spoons of sugar to taste. Stir in gently the wilted cucumbers and chill. This is a great summer salad that goes well with most everything, especially some fresh vine-ripened tomatoes.

Fresh Sliced Tomatoes

Select from the garden four or five large tomatoes, ripe to the touch. When picked they are not hard, but with just the most gentle of squeezes one can feel the juices through the thin skins. Pick gently. Wash them. Carefully peel the tomatoes like Mom, who was a not a fan of the skin used to do. Remove the stem. Slice horizontally (against the grain) and place in a large white bowl to serve on the table. (Dad was not a tomato eater, but loved to grow them and show off his gardening skills.) Salt and pepper the slabs of tasty delight to taste. Enjoy with any meal throughout the summer season.

Desserts:

Dark Raisin Cake (originally printed in the Schwarz Cookbook)
2 cups sugar
2 tsp. salt
2 cups hot water
2 tsp. cinnamon
4 Tbsp. lard
2 tsp. cloves
1/2 lb. Raisins

Boil 5 minutes – cool.
Add 2 tsp. soda in small amount of lukewarm water and dissolve. Add 3 cups flour and mix. Bake 1 ½ hours in slow oven. (Always a family favorite anytime of the year!)

Pumpkin Pie Desert Squares
1 package yellow cake mix
1/2 cup butter or margarine, melted
1 egg
Filling:
3 cups (1 Ib. -14 oz. can) pumpkin pie mix
2 eggs
2/3 cup milk

Topping:
1 cup reserved dry cake mix
1/4 cup sugar
1 tsp. cinnamon
1/4 cup butter or margarine

Grease bottom only of 9 X 13 pan.
Reserve 1 cup of cake mix for topping.
Combine remaining cake mix, butter and egg. Press into pan.
Prepare filling by combining all ingredients. Pour over crust.
For topping, combine all ingredients. Sprinkle over filling.
Bake at 350 degrees, 45 - 50 minutes, until knife, inserted near center, comes out clean. Serve with Cool Whip or cream.

A big hit with family anytime it is baked, especially during winter. A rich dessert!

Angel Cookies
1 cup brown sugar
1 cup white sugar
2 cups shortening
2 eggs
1/2 tsp. salt
1 tsp. vanilla
2 tsp. cream of tarter
2 tsp. baking soda
4 cups flour

Mix sugar and shortening. Add eggs and beat. Add flavoring. Add dry ingredients. Allow dough to rest and chill in the refrigerator for 20 minutes before baking. Shape into balls the size of a walnut and roll in colored sugars. (As the years went along my Mom at times left this out, and it did not detract from the yummy-ness. I also recall that as a boy Mom placed the sugars on the cookies midway through the baking process.) Place 2 inches apart on a greased baking sheet. (That is to say that these cookies do not

Appendix: Dinner with Mom **273**

turn out well on a non-stick cookie sheet, but rather on a traditional pan that has been greased instead.) Bake at 350 degrees for 20 minutes. As Mom's recipe notes, "Makes a pretty Christmas cookie."

Appendix: Anti-Bullying, Suicide Prevention and LGBT Youth Resources

It Gets Better Project
http://www.itgetsbetter.org/
> The It Gets Better Project's mission is to communicate to lesbian, gay, bisexual and transgender youth around the world that it gets better, and to create and inspire the changes needed to make it better for them.

The Trevor Project "Preventing Suicide among LGBTQ Youth"
http://www.thetrevorproject.org/
> Lifeline: (866) 488-7386
> The Trevor Project is the leading national organization providing crisis intervention and suicide prevention services to lesbian, gay, bisexual, transgender, and questioning youth.

GLSEN—Gay, Lesbian, Straight Education Network
http://www.glsen.org/
> GLSEN fights so that every student, in every school feels valued and treated with respect, regardless of their sexual orientation, gender identity or gender expression. GLSEN believes that all students deserve a safe and affirming school environment where they can learn and grow.

GSA Network—Gay Straight Alliance Network
http://www.gsanetwork.org/
> Gay-Straight Alliance Network is a national youth leadership organization that connects school-based Gay-Straight Alliances (GSAs) to each other and community resources through peer support, leadership development, and training.

Lambda Legal
http://www.lambdalegal.org/
> Lambda Legal is a national organization committed to achieving full recognition of the civil rights of lesbians, gay men, bisexuals, transgender people and those with HIV through impact litigation, education and public policy work.

Jamie Nabozny
http://www.jamienabozny.com/
> Jamie writes, "Throughout my Middle School and High School years I was verbally and physically bullied for being gay. With the help of Lambda Legal Defense and Education Fund I fought back. I won a landmark federal lawsuit against my school administrators for failing to stop the harassment. I now speak out for the millions of kids bullied

Appendix: Anti-Bullying, Suicide Prevention and LGBT Youth Resources

in our schools every day. I share my story and consult with schools to make sure what happened to me is never repeated."

Matthew Shepard Foundation
http://www.matthewshepard.org/
The Matthew Shepard Foundation Speakers Bureau visits schools, universities, colleges, companies, and community groups around the nation to talk about supporting teens and young adults with sexual orientation and gender related issues; providing schools with the tools they need to create safe learning environments for all.

PFLAG—Parents and Friends of Lesbians and Gays
http://community.pflag.org
PFLAG promotes the health and well-being of lesbian, gay, bisexual and transgender persons, their families and friends through: support, to cope with an adverse society; education, to enlighten an ill-informed public; and advocacy, to end discrimination and to secure equal civil rights. Parents, Families and Friends of Lesbians and Gays provides opportunity for dialogue about sexual orientation and gender identity, and acts to create a society that is healthy and respectful of human diversity.

Appendix: Hancock Public Library

State Representative Lary Swoboda and I shared a love of books, and the libraries which store and make them available to everyone.

My Dad, Royce, always made sure I had a ride to the one in my hometown. I would have claimed the Hancock Public Library as my second home if Mrs. Carlton would have let me move a bed in when I was a child.

If you feel the same way that I do about books and book lovers, and wanted to make a book or monetary donation in their memory, please consider doing so at the *Hancock Public Library* of my hometown. It is an active resource for the community, and is continually updating and growing its collection of both print and archival materials.

Donations may be made to:

Hancock Public Library
114 South Main Street
Hancock, Wisconsin 54943

Some Pursue Happiness

Life was made
Under a cascade of lights,
Of sparkling music.
O smiling love!
The monument to their desolation torn away,
They bend to caress invisible flowers…
Two souls together
Drinking cups near a well
Not believing themselves worthy of the revelation,
They finally see the far sides of the clouds.
What a luminous construction!
The solitude which was their daily bread
Troubles their sleep no more.
They cry softly today a deeply buried happiness
And they accompany the sun.
The euphoria of afternoon swims
Intoxicate the grasses with the sea foam of life.
They give of the omnipotence of their hearts.
Only the shared road knows the secret
To becoming what we will be tomorrow
      (I need you so!)

Lebensgefährte[1]

Redness seeps from the day,
night arranges herself around us.
Gentle breezes sweep the field, and we sit,
counting stars through the holes in the blanket.

                        Listen carefully at my chest.
                      Hush, whispers the grasses;
               Be still, counsels the susurrant trees.
                  Hear the story going on and on...

Imagine finding a man to take you,
to take you to places you don't dare go alone;
Imagine what's never been.
The story, our memories, our unified voice.

                       Your heart fell in love with mine;
              we're on that shared road counting stars.
                         Oh! my Lebensgefährte.

---

[1] The one who travels life's road with you

A Shared Road

Your voice in me awakens
an insatiable desire
To open myself up to the world
Know other realities

Your beauty in me provokes
an internal battle
Command your words
Be controlled by them

I want that you seduce me
Infinite possibilities of creation
I pray that you challenge me
To take advantage of the differences;
laud the similarities

Word, Verb, Lover, Friend

I beg that you teach me
Liberty, peace, honor and happiness
I desire that you see in my future
A shared road; falling into caring arms

Your sweetness in me strengthens
my reason for being
Enjoy life
Give my other every pleasure

Your essence in me inspires
divine celebrations
Exist by your side
Or take away a part of me

Index

$50,000 Club 170
9/11 245
60 Minutes 231
93.9 FM. *See* WDOR Sturgeon Bay, Wisconsin
910 AM. *See* WDOR Sturgeon Bay, Wisconsin

A

Abrahamson, Shirley 168
Ace Records 12
Acuff, Roy 26
Adams County 194
Air Castle Of The South. *See* WSM Nashville, TN
Albert's Mafia 216
Alden, Ginger 1
Algoma Record Herald 145
Algoma, Wisconsin 37, 172
Allen, Eddy Jr. 10
Allen, Ed Sr. 37
Allen, Lorene 54, 61
Allen, Paige 61
Alzheimer's Disease 216
AM 650. *See* WSM Nashville, TN
American Thresherman 250
Angel Cookies 70, 267, 272
Annen, Jennifer 243
Avon's Wild Country 88

B

Badger Prairie Health Care Center 225
Barbecues 267, 269
Bartsch, Captain August 250
Bartsch, Johanna 250
Bartsch, Walter 250
Baum, Dave 28
B.B. Clarke Beach 203, 249
Beggs, Bob 190
Beggs, Evie 143, 190, 204
Bell, Jadin 93
Bernstein, Carl 76
Bette 223
Bible 64
Big Brothers of Dane County 116
Big Little Books 196
Bill Monroe and his Bluegrass Boys. *See* Monroe, Bill

Blackwood Brothers 11
Blessed Assurance 64
Bob 112
Boiled Dinner 267, 268
Borders Books and Music 241
Bread and Butter Pickles 267, 270
Brezhnev, Leonid 20, 168
Bricknell, Michael VI, XIII
Brinkley, David 168
Brussels' Hill 8
Buick 185
Bush, First Lady Barbara 160, 161
Bush, President George Herbert Walker 160, 171
Buttercup Avenue 194
Buz Sawyer 76

C

Café Royale 242
Caffeinated Politics 25, 178. See http://dekerivers.wordpress.com/
Cameron, Prime Minister David 168
Cape Canaveral 21
Capital Times 146
Carlton, Winifred 50
Carmichael, Hoagy. See Ole Buttermilk Sky
Carrilles, Pura 215
Carter, First Lady Rosalynn 110
Carter, President Jimmy 109, 141, 172
Cathedrals 11
Chancellor, John 167
Chicago Ed. See Schwartz, Eddie
Chicago Tribune 60
chocolate fudge 70
Chris 116
Christmas 255
Clancy, Tom 237
Clarke, Bascom B. 250
Claude and Stark Architects 250
Clinton, President Bill 140, 160, 166, 176
coffin door 250
Collins, Larry 237
Coloma Chicken Chew 47
Coloma, Wisconsin 67
communal living 85
Cooper, Wilma Lee 26
Costello, Elvis 13

Country Kitchen   147
County KK   81, 184
County Road G   194
Crane, Roy. *See* Buz Sawyer
Cronkite, Walter   61, 77, 143
Crystal, Billy. *See* Soap
culverts   192
cycle of life   83

D

Dane County Farmers' Market   241
Dark Raisin Cake   267, 271
D-Day. *See* June 6, 1944
Dickens, Little Jimmy   26
Dillon, Matt, Marshal. *See* Gunsmoke
Dole, Senator Bob   164
Donald, David Herbert   140
Door County Advocate   145, 178
Dudek, Henry X.   74, 87, 212, 229, 235, 247, 249, 256
Dukakis, Governor Michael   160, 170
Duquesne University   249
Dust Bowl era   202
DXing   19, 266

E

Earl, Governor Tony   147, 149
Egg Harbor Reporter   8
Eisenhower, President Dwight D.   180
Eliot, T.S.   41
Elizabeth Inn   86. *See* Plover, Wisconsin
Emerson, Ralph Waldo   209

F

Ferraro, Geraldine   31
fiftieth wedding anniversary   65
Fleming, Ian VI. *See* James Bond
Flowers for Dad's coffin   86
Ford, First Lady Betty   172
Ford, President Gerald   42, 172
Frank, Jeffrey   180
Fresh Sliced Tomatoes   46, 267, 271

G

Gaddafi   237

Gay Lynette 41
Gay Straight Alliances 107
George 114
Ghandi, Indira 20
Golden Rule 102, 107
Goodman, Howard 12
Goodman, Vestal 11, 12
Goo Goo Clusters 24
Gore, Vice-President Al 166
grainery 53, 252
Grand Ole Opry 23, 26
Grandpa Jones 26
Graves, Denyce 148
Groundhog's Day 253
Gussie 218

H

Haggen, Festus 41
Hancock, Wisconsin 26, 293
Happy Goodman Family 11
Harvey, Paul 29
Harwell, Ernie. *See* Detroit Tigers
Heavenly Orange Fluff 267, 270
Hermening, Kevin 143
Homecoming Friends 12
How Great Thou Art 64
Hume, Brit 32
Humphrey, Cora Van Buskirk 67
Humphrey, Geneva Schwarz 10, 15, 23, 25, 29, 36, 41, 42, 47, 48, 53, 143, 156, 164, 184, 193, 201, 226, 231, 238, 249, 252
Humphrey, Gregory 23, 145, 219, 293
Humphrey, Hiram 68, 252
Humphrey, Royce R. 6, 15, 23, 25, 29, 43, 47, 48, 55, 66, 82, 164, 172, 184, 190, 202, 204, 225, 252, 276
Humphrey, Trevor Dean 5, 91, 238, 239
Humphrey, Vernon 67
Husnus 242

I

Iran-Contra 158
It Gets Better 108
Ivan 114

J

Jack Ryan 237
Jackson, Alan 24
Jackson, Jesse 160, 165
James, Sonny 5
James, Trevor 145
JC Penney 17, 232
Jim 156
Johnson, President Lyndon 17
Judith L Sullivan 188

K

Kaye 246
Kelly, Brad 169, 173, 210
Kennedy, Senator Ted 167
Kewaunee, Wisconsin 37
King, Steve 28, 38
Kjentvit, Roger 43
Koppel, Ted 239

L

lady who made pastry 9, 10
Lake Monona 58, 203, 213
LaPierre, Dominique 237
LaRoccas 199
Lasagna 267, 268
Lincoln, President Abraham 171
Linus 222
Little Raccoon 75
Loftus, Tom 142
Los Angeles Times 77
Louvin, Charlie 13, 26
Louvin, Ira 14
Lucey, Governor Patrick 169
Lynch, Father Dennis 64

M

Madison Landmarks Commission 250
Madison's Tea Room. *See* Ivan
Main Street, Hancock 49
Mao 168
Martha White Flour 24
Marv. *See* Barber
McCullough, David 162
Memphis, Tennessee 211
Merrill, WI 31

Middlebury College 187, 241
Miller, Bruce 18, 112
Milwaukee Journal Sentinel 81
Minnie Pearl 26
Mister Bob's 114
Mogan David Wine 113
Mondale, Walter 31
Montgomery, Melba 14
Montgomery Ward 17, 232
Mormon Tabernacle Choir 10
Mosgaller, Bill 146
Mosgaller, Dorothy 146
Mr. Fowler 52
Mudd, Roger 167
Music City. *See* Nashville, Tennessee
Muskie, Edmund S. 158

N

National Life and Accident Insurance Company. *See* Grand Ole Opry
National Public Radio 27
National Storm Center 190
New Wilmington, Pennsylvania 249
New York Times 60, 77
Nichopoulos, George. *See* Baptist Memorial Hospital
Nightfall, Carmen 218, 219
Nightingale, Earl. *See* Our Changing World
Nightline 239
Nixon, President Richard XV, 6, 17, 57, 76, 78, 139, 171, 180
NPR. *See* National Public Radio
Nudie suit. *See* Wagoner, Porter

O

Oak Ridge Boys 11
Obey, Congressman Dave 144
O'Keefe, Georgia 250
old barn 71, 72
Old Farmer's Almanac 187, 254
O'Neill, Former Speaker Tip 168
Oshkosh (large plow) 185
Oshkosh, Wisconsin 33
our driveway 205
Ozone, Arkansas 162

P

Parton, Dolly 8
party lines 56
Pat 222
Pelosi, Former Speaker Nancy 168
per diem 174
Peterson, Fred 147
Phelps, Michael 187
Phillips, Wally 27
Pickle Salad 47, 267, 271
Pinkie 72
Plains, Georgia 172
Plover, Wisconsin 161, 163
Points. *See* Stevens Point
Potato Salad 267, 269
Presley, Elvis 1, 13, 156, 211, 261. *See* The King
Priestly, J.B. 183
Proust, Marcel 58
Pumpkin Pie Desert Squares 267, 272
Putin, Russian President Vladimir 168
Putnam, Johnnie 28, 38

R

Rather, Dan 3
Reagan, First Lady Nancy 21
Reagan, President Ronald 2, 21, 32, 33, 158, 160
Reeves, Del 42
Rest of the Story. *See* Harvey, Paul
Reynolds, Frank 168. *See* World News Tonight
Roberts, Lori 218
rocks 81
Rodriguez, Jimmy 262
Rogers, Kenny 8
Roosevelt, President Franklin D. 155, 167
Roosevelt, President Theodore 109
Rosina 221, 224
Rowe, Marion Guppy 256
ROY G BIV 248

S

Sajak, Pat 29
Sam 254
Schulz, Charles. *See* Charlie Brown
Schwartz, Eddie 27, 109

Schwarz, Annabelle 47, 60, 72, 143, 196
Schwarz, Bertha Kline 60, 61
Schwarz, Herman 67, 162
Schwarz, Jacob 60
Scowcroft, Brent 158
Sears, Dan. *See* WMPS
September 15, 2007 234
Shaw, Bernie 170
Shea, George Beverley 10
Sherr, Lynn 32
Shippy Shoes 101
Shultz, Charles 231
Silence Is Golden 231
Simon, Senator Paul 164
small green suitcase 195
Smokey Bear 81
Southern gospel music 9
Space Shuttle Challenger 20, 21
Speer Family 11
Stamps Quartet 11
Statlers 11
Stauffaucher 37
Stevens Point 232
Stevens Point Journal 6, 53, 75
Strope, Arnie 30
Stubbs, Eddie 25
Sturgeon Bay, Wisconsin 47, 64
Sugrue, Dan 38
suicide 106
Summer Squash Casserole 47, 267, 269
Swaggart, Jimmy 10, 13
Swoboda, Lary 139, 142, 153, 170, 175, 178, 276

T

Thatcher, Prime Minister Margaret 168
the barn 72
The Fifth Horseman 237
The Hunt for Red October 237
The Mother Church of Country Music. *See* Ryman Auditorium
The Throne of Saturn. *See* Drury, Allen
Thompson, Tommy 149, 152, 171, 176, 249
Thompson, Uncle Jimmy. *See* WSM Barn Dance
Todd 238. *See* best friend; *See* best friend
Tower Report 158
Town Supervisor 191
Trainor, Mary 110

Trans American School of Broadcasting 111
trash talk 22
Trevor James 5, 30
Trevor Project 102
Tribune Tower. *See* WGN Chicago, Il
Tri-County School 183
Trull, Albert 215, 223, 225, 226
Truman, President Harry 17, 162, 167
Turner, Grant 24
Twenty-third Psalm 64
Twilight Zone 113
Twin Towers 245

U

University of Michigan, Ann Arbor 249
Utopia 147

V

Victory At Sea 171
Village of Hancock 49

W

Wagoner, Porter 24
wailing tree 79
Walker, Charles 45
Walker House. *See* Bed and Breakfast
walking up the ramp 7
washing stick 54
Washington, D.C. 156
Washington Post 76, 77
Watergate 76. *See* Nixon, President Richard
Waushara County 162, 185, 194
WBBM Chicago, Illinois 245
WBZ Boston, Massachusetts 19
WCHY Madison, WI 20
WDOR Sturgeon Bay, Wisconsin 1, 2, 4, 5, 10, 11, 12, 15, 19, 20, 22, 29, 31, 35, 113, 145, 152, 173, 261
WDUX Waupaca, WI 29
Weber, Clark 28
Weekly Reader 77
Wells, Kitty 25
Wetmore, Johnnie the electrician 196
Wetmore, Leslie 173
WFHR Wisconsin Rapids, Wisconsin 16, 27, 30
WGN Chicago, Il 38

WGN Chicago, Illinois 27, 37
White, Teddy 140
Wild Rose Hospital 84, 105
Wild Rose, Wisconsin 42
Wilson, James R. XIII, 7, 42, 47, 48, 57, 63, 65, 70, 73, 82, 90, 187, 193, 198, 200, 203, 206, 219, 229, 234, 236, 241, 245, 253, 261, 293
Wilson, Marion Sweet 47, 187, 213, 242, 253, 255
Wilson, Robert 88, 188
WIND Chicago, Il 27
Wisconsin Broadcasters Hall of Fame 30
Wisconsin Dells, Wisconsin 13, 26
Wisconsin Public Radio 27
Wisconsin State Historical Society 158
WMAD Madison, WI 20
WOLX Madison, WI 20
Woods, Rosemary 139
Woodward, Bob 76
woolly bear caterpillar 186, 216
workbench 72
World Series 189
WSM. *See* Grand Ole Opry
WSM Nashville, Tennessee 27, 151
WSPT Stevens Point, Wisconsin 16
WTMB Tomah, Wisconsin 17

X

Xi, General Secretary 168

Colophon

    This book has been typeset in Bookman Old Style and formatted in the contemporary mass-market size of five inches by eight inches.

    Bookman or Bookman Old Style is a serif typeface derived from Old Style Antique designed by Alexander Phemister in 1858 for Miller and Richard foundry. Several American foundries copied the design, including the Bruce Type Foundry, and issued it under various names. In 1901, Bruce refitted their design, made a few other improvements, and rechristened it Bartlett Oldstyle. When Bruce was taken over by ATF shortly thereafter, they changed the name to Bookman Oldstyle.

    In addition to the printed version, a digital format has also been created. This text may then be read with the aide of any of the digital book readers or pdf-supported computers.

About the Author
(The Short Version)

Gregory A. Humphrey wrote *Walking up the Ramp* based on the experiences gained from the first fifty years of his life. Growing up in Hancock, Wisconsin, and working first in radio broadcasting, Gregory was later employed in the political and policy environments of the Wisconsin State Capitol. He also has experience with non-profits. All of this has allowed for colorful insight into a wide range of interests and curiosities.

Gregory lives with his life-partner of thirteen years, James R. Wilson, a long-time professor of modern languages, in an old Victorian on Madison's isthmus.

Made in the USA
Lexington, KY
04 September 2013